Soviet cinema has always been closely connected with national political reality challenging the conventions of bourgeois society and educating the people. Substantial scholarship has been devoted to the Soviet cinema of the 1920s and of the Khrushchev "thaw," but the last two decades have been largely neglected. In this pioneering study, Anna Lawton examines the fascinating world of Soviet cinema under glasnost and perestroika. She shows how the reforms that shook the foundations of the Bolshevik state and profoundly affected economic and social structures have been reflected by changes that revolutionized the film industry and in the films the industry produced.

Professor Lawton discusses the restructuring of the main institutions governing the industry; the abolition of censorship; the emergence of independent production and distribution systems; the problems connected with the dismantling of the old bureaucratic structure and the implementation of new initiatives. She also surveys the films that remained unscreened for decades for political reasons, films of the new wave that look at the past to search out the truth, and those that record current social ills or conjure up a disquieting image of the future. Together they portray a society in search of its roots and of new directions.

Kinoglasnost: Soviet cinema in our time is based on primary sources, interviews with filmmakers and critics, and the viewing of more than three hundred films. Anna Lawton not only presents a comprehensive picture of the contemporary Soviet film industry, she also analyzes the historical development of the Soviet Union. This book will be widely read by students and specialists of Soviet history, culture and society, and media studies as well as by anyone with an interest in Soviet films and the current transformations of Soviet society.

Anna Lawton is a Professorial Lecturer at Georgetown University. She is a specialist in Russian literature and film and her publications include *From futurism to imaginism* and, as editor, *The red screen: politics, society, art in Soviet cinema*.

Kinoglasnost: Soviet cinema in our time

Cambridge Soviet Paperbacks: 9

Cambridge Soviet Paperbacks is a completely new initiative in publishing on the Soviet Union. The series will focus on the economics, international relations, politics, sociology, and history of the Soviet and Revolutionary periods.
The idea behind the series is the identification of gaps for upper-level surveys or studies falling between the traditional university press monograph and most student textbooks. The main readership will be students and specialists, but some "overview" studies in the series will have broader appeal.

Publication will in every case be simultaneously in hardcover and paperback.

Cambridge Soviet Paperbacks

Kinoglasnost: Soviet cinema in our time

ANNA LAWTON
Professorial Lecturer, Department of History,
Georgetown University

CAMBRIDGE
UNIVERSITY PRESS

To Auguste and Louis,
and many others . . .

Published by the Press Syndicate of the University of Cambridge
The Pitt Building, Trumpington Street, Cambridge CB2 1RP
40 West 20th Street, New York, NY 10011–4211, USA
10 Stamford Road, Oakleigh, Victoria 3166, Australia

© Cambridge University Press 1992

First published 1992

Printed in Great Britain at the University Press, Cambridge

A catalogue record for this book is available from the British Library

Library of Congress cataloguing in publication data
Lawton, Anna (Anna M.)
Kinoglasnost: Soviet cinema in our time / by Anna Lawton.
    p.   cm. – (Cambridge Soviet Paperbacks: 9)
Includes bibliographical references and index.
ISBN 0 521 38117 7. – ISBN 0 521 38814 7 (pbk.)
1. Motion pictures – Soviet Union.   2. Motion picture industry –
Soviet Union.   I. Title.   II. Series.
PN1993.5.R9L36   1992
791.43′0947 – dc20   91–43582   CIP

ISBN 0 521 38117 7 hardback
ISBN 0 521 38814 7 paperback

wv

Contents

Illustrations

Preface and acknowledgments

The scope of this book comprises the period between 1976 and 1990, including the waning of the Brezhnev era, but focusing mainly on the years of perestroika and glasnost. I chose 1976 as a starting point because that year can be seen as the beginning of the decline of the Brezhnev administration, and the consolidation of the "period of stagnation." The first nine years are treated rather cursorily and condensed in one chapter, while the next five years occupy the other seven chapters. This imbalance is deliberate. My main goal in presenting the cinema of stagnation was to provide a background against which to measure the radical changes that took place later, under the Gorbachev administration.

In Part I (chapters 2 to 4), I have discussed the restructuring of the main institutions governing the film industry, according to the new policy; the abolition of censorship; the emergence of independent production and distribution systems; and the problems connected with the dismantling of the old bureaucratic structure and the implementation of new initiatives. In Part II (chapters 5 to 8), I have discussed the films that reflect the spirit and the politics of the first five years of glasnost. These are the films that lay in limbo for decades because of censorship and were finally released; the films of the new wave that look at the past and probe into history in order to restore the truth; those that record and espouse current social ills; and those that conjure up a disquieting image of the future. Together they present a reliable portrait of a society in search of roots and new directions.

Nevertheless, I am very well aware of the many gaps that could not be filled. For example, I chose not to discuss the cinema of the Soviet republics in a systematic way, given the space limitations. My selection is largely of Russian films, with other national films discussed whenever warranted by special circumstances, politics, or outstanding artistic values. While my choice was motivated by practical reasons, it is justified statistically. The Russian republic accounts for two-thirds of the global feature films production. Just as I avoided geographical and ethnic classifications, I also avoided headings based on famous directors, movie stars, and studios. I preferred to take a historical approach, and to organize the materials chronologically and by topics of sociopolitical relevance. This method proved more valuable in painting a broad canvas of a country at the turn of two eras.

My interest in Soviet cinema dates back to the early years of my scholarly career, when I was studying the avant-garde in literature and related arts. In those days, I approached cinema from a theoretical standpoint, focusing on narrative structures and the semiotics of montage. A growing dissatisfaction with an approach that tends to disassociate art from life, however, prompted me to broaden the scope of my research and to study cinema as a cultural object shaped by politics as well as the reality of the industry and the market. This was not a total rejection of aesthetics. On the contrary, I consider the fundamentals of film language to be an essential tool for the interpretation of a cinematic text, and for a close reading of its political implications and potential impact on the mass audience. I therefore combined these two approaches whenever possible. This book stands in between the academic works which offer detailed analyses of world renowned masterpieces, and historical surveys that, until very recently, treated culture without insight and interpretation. Now a new area of scholarship is emerging among American historians, which focuses on various aspects of Soviet culture, with the realization that while the traditional approach provides useful information, it is the human factor inherent in culture that leads to a deeper understanding of the Soviet nation and its people. This book on cinema will complement those which have already appeared on popular novels, music, art, television, leisure, and entertainment.[1]

While substantial scholarship, both in the West and in the USSR, has been devoted to the classical period of Soviet cinema (1920s), and to a lesser degree to the cinema of the Khrushchev "thaw" (1950s and 1960s), there were no major works dedicated to the cinema of the past two decades when I began this project. The bulk of the printed materials available to me were magazine articles, scholarly papers, encyclopedia entries, newspaper reportage, pamphlets of film organizations, and conference proceedings – in a number of languages, but mostly in Russian. Other essential sources of information were interviews with Soviet filmmakers, critics and scholars, and the films themselves which I viewed over the past fifteen years. The main concentration of viewing occurred in the period of glasnost, when I had the opportunity to take several trips to Moscow on the invitation of various film institutions and organizations. My preliminary research resulted in a long essay in *Post New Wave Cinema in the Soviet Union and Eastern Europe* ed. Daniel J. Goulding (Bloomington, IN: Indiana University Press, 1989), on which I based the first chapter of this book. I wish to thank Indiana University Press for kindly allowing me to use that material. Another product of my involvement with film is the collection *The Red Screen: Politics, Society, Art in Soviet Cinema* (London: Routledge, 1992), which I edited, and which includes the papers presented at the Kennan Institute Conference on Soviet Cinema (1986) – the first international scholarly conference on the subject in the USA. In the course of my research, I published several articles, parts of which have been incorporated in the present book, in a modified version. I used part of the materials that previously appeared in *Jahrbücher für Geschichte Osteuropas, Soviet Observer, Wide Angle,* and *World and I,* and I wish to express my appreciation to these journals for their support.

This project would not have been completed without the cooperation of numerous individuals and institutions. I received generous financial support from the Woodrow Wilson Center, the Kennan Institute, the International Research and Exchange Board (IREX), the American Council of Learned Societies (ACLS), and the Hoover Institution. The following institutions have been most receptive to hosting and sponsoring Soviet film programs, symposia, and lectures: the National Gallery of Art, the Smithsonian Institution, the Library of Congress, the American Film Institute, the American Committee on US–Soviet Relations, The School of International Affairs at George Washington University, and the Washington FilmFest. Thanks to them, in the past five years Washington became a most active forum for exhibition and discussion of Soviet cinema, and the ideal place for seeing films and meeting with specialists, outside of Moscow. The Department of History and the Russian Area Studies Program at Georgetown University deserve a big thank-you for having introduced a specialized course on the history of Soviet cinema in their curriculum, which I am privileged to teach.

I also want to extend my deeply felt thanks to the Moscow-based organizations that helped me in this research: the All-Union Scientific Research Institute of Film Art (VNIIK), Goskino, the Filmmakers Union, the House of Cinema, the Moscow Film Festival, and the Association of Soviet Film Initiatives (ASK), which most generously provided me with hospitality, guidance, and facilities, and gave me access to screening rooms and libraries.

Most of all I want to thank all the colleagues and friends who supported me along the way, sharing their knowledge, time, and kindness. Special thanks to Ben Lawton, with whom I took the first steps into the realm of the moving image with the unbounded enthusiasm and curiosity of youth. My deep appreciation to Vasily Aksyonov, Harley Balzer, James Billington, David Goldfrank, Daniel Goulding, Andy Horton, Annette Michelson, Peggy Parson, Ludmila Pruner, Frederick Starr, Marianna Tax Choldin, Helen Yakobson, who in different ways equipped me with intellectual, material, and moral strength. Denise Youngblood deserves to be commended for coordinating Soviet cinema research through the Working Group on Cinema and Television. She has shared with me her vast knowledge of Soviet film and has sustained me as a dear and close friend. Vivian Sobchack, Robert Rosen, and Vance Kepley, Jr. – my co-members on the ACLS Commission on Film and Video Studies – have worked intensely to develop and implement joint projects with Soviet counterparts. Wesley Fisher, of IREX, administered the Commission's work and generously funded exchanges and symposia. Without their contributions my work would have been much more difficult, if not impossible. I also benefitted greatly from the insightful and thorough research of my students who spent endless hours scanning the Soviet press. I want to thank them all collectively, and to mention in particular Rebecca Morrison, Moira Ratchford, and Valerie Sperling, whose papers are cited in this book. Eric Johnson has also been invaluable, as a student and as my computer teacher.

On the other side of the ocean, I want to remember my colleague and friend of many years, Gianni Buttafava, who recently passed away. I am indebted to Lino Miccichè, one of the few experts in the cinema of the Soviet republics, and to Marc Ferro, for enlightening me on poorly known aspects of Soviet film history. Richard Taylor and Ian Christie have engaged me in lively interaction at several conferences, and have widened my knowledge and my perspectives. Soviet colleagues, including film critics, scholars, directors, screenwriters, and administrative staff, have helped me more than they can imagine. Heartfelt thanks to Liudmila Budyak, Daniil Dondurei, Viktor Dyomin, Valery Fomin, Raisa Fomina, Leonid Gurevich, Rustam Ibragimbekov, Elena Kartseva, Igor Kokorev, Savva Kulish, Mark Levin, Elga Lyndina, Yuri Mamin, Andrey Nuikin, Paul Pozner, Kirill Razlogov, Andrey Razumovsky, Olga Reizen, Yuri

Salnikov, Galina Strashnenko, Valentin Tolstykh, Maya Turovskaya, Mark Zak, and many others.

Richard Stites' contribution to this book cannot be measured in words. I am deeply thankful for his presence, encouragement, and intellectual input; for his close reading of the manuscript; and for his ability to turn serious endeavors, and life itself, into sheer fun. Finally, I am grateful to my parents, who first introduced me to the performing arts through their profession, and have been an inspiration to my work ever since.

For the transliteration of Russian names I used the generally accepted English spelling in the text and in the notes. I used the scientific Library of Congress system in the bibliography and in bibliographical references appearing in the notes. The filmography includes Soviet films only; films of other countries occasionally mentioned in the text are not listed. Soviet film titles are given in translation in the text, but in the filmography they are listed both in English and in Russian for the reader's convenience. Abbreviations of journal titles are provided on the following page.

At the time of writing the Soviet Union was still a country, Gorbachev was still in power, and the August *putsch*, which precipitated the fall of the empire, was only a fantasy of some filmmakers. The facts covered in this book, and the opinions expressed, reflect the historical reality up to the end of the year 1990. Some of the chapters have a journalistic flavor, due to the recording of the events as they unfolded. Some of the commentary needs revisions in light of the latest developments. Nevertheless, this remains as a testimony of a fateful moment that has changed the course of history.

Abbreviations

CSM	*Christian Science Monitor*
CDSP	*Current Digest of the Soviet Press*
EG	*Ekonomicheskaia gazeta*
HJFRT	*Historical Journal of Film, Radio and Television*
IB	*Informatsionnyi biulleten'*
IK	*Iskusstvo kino*
KZ	*Kinovedcheskie zapiski*
KIARS	*Kennan Institute Reports*
KP	*Komsomol'skaia pravda*
LAT	*Los Angeles Times*
LG	*Literaturnaia gazeta*
NF	*Novye fil'my*
NOR	*New Orleans Review*
NYT	*New York Times*
RLRR	*Radio Liberty Research Report*
SE	*Sovetskii ekran*
SF (E)	*Soviet Film*
SF (R)	*Sovetskii fil'm*
SK	*Sovetskaia kul'tura*
SO	*Soviet Observer*
SR	*Sovetskaia Rossiia*
WP	*Washington Post*

Introduction

Soviet cinema from its inception has been strictly connected with the national political reality. It could not have been otherwise. Born with the revolution, it started as a revolutionary art. One of its functions in those early years was to lay the aesthetic foundation of a new social order through a bold, dynamic cinematic language that challenged the conventions of the bourgeois melodrama.

Equally important was its educational function. Lenin's famous statement that "the cinema is for us the most important of all the arts" reflected the government's perception of the new medium as an effective propaganda tool. Most filmmakers, on their part, felt they had a moral commitment to enlighten the masses. As cinema spread to reach the lower urban social strata, and the provincial and rural population, so did the idea that a movie had more to offer than mere entertainment.

The masters of the 1920s – Eisenstein, Dovzhenko, Kuleshov, Pudovkin, Vertov – while sharing the revolutionary ideals, devoted themselves to cinema as an art form. Consequently, their films were both positive political statements and great artistic achievements. Cinema put the Soviet Union on the international cultural map. Those films, however, were not popular with the masses at home because of their innovative style and "difficult" language. Audiences preferred comedies and dramas, dealing with issues of everyday life, made by directors who deserve to be better known abroad – Barnet, Eggert, Ermler, Kozintsev and Trauberg, Protazanov, Room. Other favorites were the imported films, especially those that came from Hollywood.[1]

During the 1930s, because of the onset of stricter centralized control and the institutionalization of "Socialist Realism" – the doctrine stipulating that all aspects of Soviet culture should optimistically reflect the ideal socialist society – creativity was suppressed and cinema gradually turned into sleek political propaganda. Cinema was a popular form of entertainment in those years. Because of the grim reality of the day the people appreciated the escapism of the movies, which offered a promise of an oncoming utopia. While plots were generally weak, several films achieved a technical level of sophistication and were graced by superb performances. Such were the musical comedies of Grigory Alexandrov, featuring the acting-singing-dancing star Lyubov Orlova. Some art films were also made or planned in that decade, but many of them did not see the light of day. Eisenstein's *Bezhin Meadow* (1935) is a case in point, as is *A Stern Youth* (1936) by Room.

This trend was reinforced after World War II, throughout the 1940s and early 1950s. During this period, Soviet cinema was characterized by stereotyped images of patriotism, civic valor, and military heroism, most often converging into the figure of Stalin. The "cult of personality" took its toll on the cinema as well as on all other aspects of public life. However, even in those years there were some exceptions – the most notable being Eisenstein's last film *Ivan the Terrible* (Part I, 1944; Part II, 1946, released only in 1968; Part III is believed to have been destroyed). After World War II, and in the Cold War years, the Soviet produced a number of anti-American films, which were amply reciprocated on the American side. This trend was accompanied by a political campaign against "cosmopolitanism," which resulted in the ostracism of many excellent directors. The irony is that in Hollywood a similar witch-hunt against alleged communists took place at about the same time.

Soviet cinema experienced an artistic renaissance at the time of Khrushchev's cultural "thaw." In the late 1950s and early 1960s, the change in the political leadership and the emergence of a new generation of talent brought fresh energies into film production. Creativity was allowed a freer hand and new themes and styles, inspired by a general concern for the individual and his inner world, made their way to the screen. In addition, there was a revival of formalistic experimentation, most notable in the "poetic" style of several directors from the southern republics, and in the works of Andrei Tarkovsky. The trend of the 1960s reflected to a great extent filmmakers' aesthetic and moral concerns, as well as the public demand for engaging subjects and emotional appeal. After two decades of make-believe, audiences yearned for a measure of truth. How large that measure could be, no one knew for sure. Notwithstanding the relaxation in cultural policies, Party directives could not be ignored. Filmmakers had to test their limits and operate within the realm of the permissible. The revival of film art in those years brought Soviet cinema to the attention of international audiences and critics and, as in the 1920s, it scored high marks. Soviet cinema underwent such a radical renewal that the conservative aftermath of the "thaw" could not erase what was gained, much less turn the clock back to the forms of the Stalinist years.

In the 1970s – a period of stagnation in every area of Soviet life – there was a new trend in the motion picture industry, due primarily to socioeconomic factors. In that decade, commercial considerations gained more and more weight. The increasing availability of television required cinema to become competitive. To fill the movie theaters and fulfill the yearly financial quota established by the government, film producers, distributors, and exhibitors had to cater to public taste. The genre repertoire widened considerably, and the commercial film directors became more and more skillful at presenting ideology as entertainment. Public expectations of the previous decade for *engagé* films were dulled by the prevailing consumerist atmosphere, which was reflected in light genres and simplistic morals. There were few troubling discoveries; rather, self-complacency and benign irony created a comfortable psychological setup. Selected foreign films appeared on the Soviet screen and fared well with the masses, even if they were largely third-rate films from India and the Third World. The mass audience liked to feel that they were somehow part of the international community. Within this general trend, however, there were isolated achievements. A few talented directors were able to rise above the level of greyish mediocrity and stand up for humanistic values and artistic integrity. Most of them belonged to the generation that emerged in the 1960s as an innovative force, others were equally talented newcomers. Unfortunately, a number of remarkable films made in the 1970s were either shelved or at best had limited circulation. Only in the time of perestroika, as a result of the change that reshaped the Soviet film industry, were those films released.

Following a brief period of transition, the 1980s marked the end of an era and the beginning of a new phase in the history of the Soviet Union. There are some parallels with Khrushchev's "thaw," but the differences outnumber the similarities. While in the 1960s the upsurge of creativity happened as the by-product of a general policy of liberalization, and was soon contained, this more recent artistic renaissance has been planned and sustained by the Party, under the leadership of Gorbachev. Furthermore, the new regime has created the conditions for a radical restructuring of the cinema industry, which will make it difficult if not impossible to reverse the process of decentralization. This is not to underestimate the role of the film-makers. In fact, a creative ferment had been building for more than a decade, and the glasnost and perestroika policies provided a much needed outlet not only for the filmmakers' creative talent, but also for their participation in the political process.

Part I

The melting of the ice

1 The waning of the Brezhnev era

The least stagnating art

The year 1976 was the middle point in the Brezhnev administration and marked the beginning of its decline. The Ninth Five-Year Plan (1971–1975) had produced rather disappointing results. Designed as the first plan to provide for a fast growth in the consumer sector, it projected a dramatic rise in the standard of living through a combination of scientific and technological innovations, greater managerial efficiency, and increased labor productivity.

Several factors intervened to thwart those optimistic goals. The automation of factories and industries depended to a great extent on the steady input of new technology and expertise from the West. However, there were already signs that *détente* would not last forever. Even more damaging to the process of modernization was internal opposition from conservative economists and Party ideologues. Unable to come to terms with revisions of the Marxist–Leninist doctrine, they defeated the Kosygin reforms of 1965, and subsequently fought against any deviations from Communist orthodoxy. They denounced such innovations as systems analysis, economic forecasting, and decentralized decision-making, and opposed the Plan's assignment of priority to the consumer sector. A passive and corrupt managerial class was eager to defer to the conservative view in order to avoid responsibilities and unnecessary stress.

To worsen the situation, the country suffered two major crop failures, the first in 1972 and the second in 1975. Grain imports alone could not make up for the food shortages, and the standard of living which had been slowly improving in the early seventies took a turn for the worse. Even before the latest crop disaster the average family spent 40 to 50 percent of its income on food. After it, prices rose and the state had to intervene with massive subsidies in order to stifle public discontent. However, the revenues from energy exports temporarily compensated for the mismanagement of the nation's economy. The negative results of two decades of government passivity became painfully obvious in the early 1980s and inflicted an unseen but mortal blow on the Party and state gerontocracy. But, for the time being, the old guard still held firmly to their key positions.

The XXV Congress of the CPSU, held in February 1976, did not offer any new perspectives. On that occasion Brezhnev criticized some failures in the economy, but found many achievements to praise and restated the same goals for the next Five-Year Plan, with an even more optimistic forecast. He stressed the need for an immediate restructuring of the economy and exhorted scientific and technical personnel at all levels to improve efficiency and quality. But the guidelines he issued did not translate into action.

Younger leaders of the new generation were needed to carry out the plan. They were slowly rising through the ranks and impatiently awaiting their day. Meanwhile, more of Brezhnev's cronies were appointed to the Central Committee and the Politburo. The consequences were disastrous for the political, economic, and cultural life of the nation. As the ailing leadership clung stubbornly to their chairs and to each other, refusing to relinquish power and demanding order and stability, the granting of privileges to an extended family became a common practice and corruption was rampant. During his last years, a direct ratio can be observed between Brezhnev's failing health and his accumulation of honors and titles. This was apparently an attempt to sustain the leader's prestige which was rapidly fading both nationally and internationally.[1]

After the honeymoon with the Nixon and Ford administrations which allowed the Soviet Union to improve modestly its standard of living and to rise to an international position of strength, Brezhnev clashed with Carter over Soviet policies in Afghanistan and Poland. Ratification of the SALT II treaty by the US Senate was suspended, the American athletes boycotted the Moscow Olympic Games, and the Soviet Union closed the doors to Jewish emigration. The era of *détente* came to an end and was replaced by a renewed Cold War syndrome that plunged to severely low temperatures with the incoming Reagan administration. The deterioration of international relations was paralleled by a domestic atmosphere of cultural reaction and rapid economic decline.

The general political trend of the period was reflected in the administrative structure of the cinema industry as well as in film production and distribution. From the time cinema was nationalized, in 1919, by a Lenin decree, film production and distribution had been regulated by a government institution, the State Committee for Cinematography (Goskino),[2] which gradually gained complete control over the film industry. In the 1970s, Goskino suffered from the widespread national epidemic of bureaucratic growth. Its inflated cadres, securely entrenched behind their desks, ran the film industry as a state chancery. They dealt with the artistic sector as they would with an unfortunate nuisance. The newly appointed head of Goskino, Filipp Ermash (1972–1986), came from the Central Committee's Department of Culture and enjoyed high connections in the Politburo as a relative of Andrei Kirilenko, one of Brezhnev's closest personal and political associates.

Brezhnev's foreign and domestic policies had brought about a measure of material comfort, especially perceptible toward the middle of the decade. Mounting corruption in the higher echelons and an increasing preoccupation with material goods trickled down to the middle and working classes.[3] The prevailing atmosphere favored the breeding of a consumer mentality. The public taste in entertainment turned "bourgeois." Goskino was quick to exploit this conjuncture. Under Ermash's leadership, the Soviet film industry moved decidedly in the direction of commercial films which met the public demand and increased profits for the Soviet government. The educational function of cinema, however, could not be neglected. Conveniently, the commercial genres were labeled "popular." Unlike the "elite" films that indulge in aestheticism, popular films were supposed to sustain orthodox ideology and socialist values. This combination found its most successful expression in the film that crowned the decade, *Moscow Does Not Believe in Tears* (1980), and which was hailed in equal measure by Party ideologues, Soviet audiences, and, ironically, the Hollywood Oscar prizegivers. But most of the time commercial considerations worked against not only artistic endeavors but also ideology. Toward the end of his tenure, Ermash was despised by the film artists and disapproved of by the ideologues.

Cinema in the Soviet Union had been for decades the main filler of leisure time. As television became available to a larger number of the population, movie theater attendance registered a sharp decline. While in the late 1960s ticket sales were close to 5 billion a year, in 1977 they had dropped to 4.2 billion, representing an average attendance per capita of 16.4.[4] Very revealing of public taste is the breakdown of attendance figures per film, which show that a mere fifteen percent of all Soviet feature films released in a given year (the yearly output was approximately 150 films) account for eighty percent of all ticket sales. A comparison of the already mentioned *Moscow Does Not Believe in Tears*, which drew 75 million viewers over the first twelve months of its circulation, to Andrei Tarkovsky's philosophical parable *Stalker*, which was seen by a mere 3 million over the same period, shows where the people's preferences lay. True, *Stalker* did not enjoy the support of Goskino and had a very limited circulation. Nevertheless, there are indications that it would not have fared very well in any case. Research conducted at the All-Union State Institute of Cinema (VGIK) ranked some common film features in the order they appealed to the masses:

1 contemporary theme
2 Russian production (as opposed to other republics)
3 adaptation of a popular book
4 fast tempo
5 continuity (no flashbacks)
6 simplicity
7 spectacular (special effects, crowd scenes, and costumes)
8 active and attractive leading characters
9 appealing title[5]

By adding sex and violence and substituting "American" for "Russian" in point no. 2 this list could be used to characterize most of US box-office successes of the past decades. In fact, Ermash was known to be an admirer of the Hollywood motion picture industry.

Thus, Goskino promoted the production of films that suited the public taste. In order to do so it needed the cooperation of the film workers. This meant the Filmmakers Union, which supposedly represented the interests of the workers in the field. However, the Union supported its members only nominally. In effect, throughout the 1970s and up to 1986, the Union was burdened by a very conservative and passive leadership, which did not stand up for creative freedom and decentralized decision-making.

Lack of support from the Union was reflected in the studios where the actual creative process took place. Of all the studios of the fifteen republics, Mosfilm was, and still is, by far the largest and most prestigious, followed by Lenfilm (in Leningrad), Gorky Studio in Moscow, and at a considerable distance, the Georgian, Ukrainian, Armenian, and Kirgizian studios. The production of the Baltic republics was negligible.[6] In the 1970s, both the head of Mosfilm, Nikolay Sizov, and his deputy in charge of screenwriting, Leonid

Nekhoroshev, were well regarded by the filmmakers as rather sensitive intellectuals, authors of several books. They were also well connected politically. Sizov had been a Party functionary and was currently a member of the Moscow City Council and a deputy chairman of Goskino. Nekhoroshev was a graduate of the Social Science Academy of the Central Committee. Both were seasoned politicians not devoid of intellectual sophistication. Mosfilm therefore managed to satisfy the requirements of Goskino while giving elbow room to the creative directors. In fact, besides the bulk of commercial films, known as "greyish" films from an aesthetic as well as a political point of view, Mosfilm produced a good number of stimulating pictures. However, the best pictures were not always released, and if they were, only in a few prints.

The tendency toward the mass genres enlarged the traditional repertoire with a considerable number of melodramas, comedies, detective stories, science-fiction films, and musicals. Because of their poor quality, however, the majority of these films was not well attended. The audiences demanded light genres, but they had reached an average level of sophistication (at least in the major urban areas) and would not put up with facile plots and sloppy techniques. Often, but not always, the films that rose above mediocrity were also the most successful with the public.

Slice-of-life genres, historical dramas, literary classics

One trend revived from the repertoire of the late 1920s and early 1930s became predominant: the *bytovoy* film. The term can be approximately translated as "slice-of-life" film. These are stories about contemporary society, individual lives and relations, current problems, and human values. The *bytovoy* film could be anything from comedy to "problematic melodrama."[7]

The preoccupation with economic growth and reforms was reflected in a long series of films concerned with factory problems – the "production movies." The prototype of the trend, many times imitated but hardly ever matched, was *The Bonus* (1975), by Sergei Mikaelian.[8] It marked a new approach to the worker and the workplace. This film does not follow the traditional Socialist Realist model where enthusiastic shock-brigades overcome the challenges of saboteurs, fight against all odds with superhuman strength and moral stamina, overfulfill the plan, and are decorated as heros of socialist labor. In *The Bonus* there are no farfetched dramatic situations, no heroics. Most of the action unfolds in one room during a meeting of a construction enterprise's Party committee. The only dramatic device that gives the screenplay the tension necessary to sustain the action is the conflict which arises between workers and management when a construction team refuses to accept its yearly bonus.

The situation is odd in a society accustomed to accepting benefits from above. What is the workers' motivation? The screenwriter, Alexander Gelman, has a solid reputation in the theater as a writer of psychological plays with popular appeal. In *The Bonus* the reasons behind the workers' behavior turn out to be complex and engaging in their apparent simplicity. The construction team refuses the bonus because it feels cheated. The workers think that bad management and poor work organization were responsible for low productivity and personal financial losses which were not adequately compensated by the bonus. However, the workers' motivations are not totally materialistic. The token bonus becomes a symbol of the hypocrisy and concealment which surround the country's problems, hinder economic growth, and thwart the possibility of healthy social development. The film does not provide a solution to the problem, but it raises the viewer's awareness of a life based on complacency and devoid of spiritual values. It also suggests that it is the people's responsibility to denounce the current situation both in their own interest and in the interest of the nation.

The confrontation takes place between the brigade leader, Potapov, and three executives of the construction enterprise, while the Party representatives preside over the meeting. It is clear from the outset who is the villain and who is the hero. The attribution of roles, however, was bound to generate uneasiness. This perhaps explains why the film's authors, although breaking important ground in this direction, stopped short of carrying the denunciation of management to the very top. The main villains are the senior engineer, a weak, servile man with an unctuous smile, and the assistant director, a ruthless careerist whose main pleasure in life is to carry out the director's orders. However, the director himself is not devoid of redeeming qualities. A pragmatist versed in the art of compromise, he comes to the meeting with the self-assurance of an experienced negotiator convinced of an easy victory. But Potapov's tough stance and unshakable convictions make it difficult for the director to score with his usual ease. Actually, the values of youth, which had been dulled by the requirements of a managerial career, are reawakened, and allow him to make a moral choice.

On the other side, fighting for truth and justice, stands the brigade leader Potapov. No knight in white armor, he is a stocky middle-aged man, slightly overweight, with a round, good-natured face and a bald pate. The role was performed, brilliantly, by Evgeny Leonov, better known to the audiences for his numerous comic characterizations. But already in the film *Belorussia Station* (1972) there were signs of his change toward serious, engaged roles. Nevertheless, when director Mikaelian cast him as Potapov the choice made more than one eyebrow rise among the members of the production team, including the screenwriter. In fact, the script called for "a young Communist," assertive, principled, with high morals – in other words, a traditional "positive hero." Leonov does not fit the exterior model, but the inner qualities he gradually displays are worthy of his role. The hero Potapov, at first awkward, somewhat bashful and ineffective, looks like an easy match to his opponents and a disappointing champion to the audience. But in the course of the meeting it becomes abundantly clear that Potapov's modest appearance conceals a lively mind, sound common sense, and the courage to stand up for his co-workers' rights and for basic truths. Because of these qualities Potapov turns out to be stronger than his more powerful and sophisticated adversaries, a true folk hero who strikes a deep sentimental chord in the viewer's heart. How does the transformation take place? Mikaelian explains: "In the shooting of *The Bonus* everything was subordinated to the actors. Therefore, down with cinemascope, no music with eternal 'accents,' no contrast of colors. It was not necessary to vary the place of the action (oh, how they insisted on that!). Let the camera follow the actors, let it come closer to the actor in the course of the film, closer and closer . . . In this film an old truth triumphed: the depth and strength of a person's character are revealed by the totality of the smallest features."[9]

Another variant of the *bytovoy* film is the light comedy involving a love story, humorous situations, and vignettes of social and private life. One of the most successful directors of this genre is Eldar Ryazanov, who since the middle of the 1950s has worked both in cinema and the theater. He co-wrote a large number of stage plays together with Emil Braginsky, as well as many scripts for his own films. The first movie comedy that brought them fame and popularity was *Beware of Automobiles* (1965), starring the actor known abroad as the Russian Hamlet, Innokenty Smoktunovsky. One of their hits of the mid 1970s was *Irony of Fate, or Have a Good Sauna* (1975), originally made for television and based on a play which itself was staged in more than one hundred theaters all over the country. This film has been called a "comic-musical-psychological-fantastic tale."[10] Its appeal comes from the use of a classical comedy-of-errors plot device set in a modern urban context. On New Year's Eve, a man, after a drink too many, goes home to what seems to be his apartment only to discover that he is in another city and in the apartment of an unknown woman. The residential outskirts of the big cities, and the lives of their dwellers, have become so uniform and depersonalized that this sort of mix-up is conceivable, with a little stretch of the imagination. It is even conceivable to use the key to one's own Moscow apartment to open someone else's door in Leningrad. But the encounter of two strangers, after a first moment of fear and hostility, leads to the discovery of love and brings magic back into everyday routine. *Irony of Fate* won the popularity contest held every year by the journal *Soviet Screen* among its readers, by a wide margin, and has since been shown on TV as an annual New Year's film.

A few years later, another comedy by the same authors, *An Office Romance* (1978), became a box-office success and scored the highest mark in the *Soviet Screen* contest. In many ways this film resembles its predecessor. In an ordinary environment (a statistical bureau) and among ordinary people (middle-aged clerks whose zest for life has been dulled by years of office routine) a "miracle" suddenly takes place. The bureau director, a stern, colorless woman, falls in love with one of her subordinates and, as if by magic, she is transformed into a sensitive, elegant, young-looking beauty (an easy feat for the make-up artist, since the role was played by the indeed beautiful Alisa Freindlikh). Similarly, the initially frightened petty clerk turns into a self-assured, attractive man. What is more, the love that radiates from the happy couple gives a rosy coloration to the office and its drab occupants.

Some Western feminist critics have read the transformation process as a male affirmation of traditional sex roles.[11] This is a possible reading, given the general social context of male chauvinism in the USSR. Nevertheless, it seems that in these films transformation works primarily as a traditional fairy-tale element. Ryazanov and Braginsky have snobbishly been criticized for creating contemporary urban fairy tales meant to "reassure" the viewer, to which Ryazanov

1   *Garage* (1980) directed by Eldar Riazanov

answered: "First of all, to reassure, to encourage the viewer, in order to make it easier for him, to cheer him up, to help him believe in himself – it's not such a sin in my opinion. And secondly, when I work with Braginsky on our stories we do not force a happy ending on them. Perhaps, we are so disposed that it's more interesting to us to talk about what unites people, rather than what separates them."[12]

Perhaps, but are Ryazanov's "fairy tales" as innocent as they seem? From the very beginning, satirical elements were interspersed in the text, although offset by the general tone of good-natured humor. In their next film, *Garage* (1980), good-natured humor decisively turned into biting satire and the film's overall effect was quite unsettling. This was a departure not only from Ryazanov's and Braginsky's dominant style but from common practice. Satire was virtually effaced in Soviet cinema by the non-conflict theory of Socialist Realism. One of the characters in *Garage*, having learned that the woman he is talking to is a scholar doing research in satire, says: "You have an odd profession. You are studying a subject which does not exist."[13]

In *Garage* conflict and contrast, both on the narrative and the stylistic levels, are the main structural elements. A group of citizens, the staff of the Research Institute for the Protection of the Animals Against the Environment, has entered as a cooperative into a contract with the state to build a number of garages (a commodity in very short supply) under the supervision of a Committee. Halfway toward completion of the work, the state changes the plan, and four garages now have to be scratched from the project. The Committee chairman calls a meeting to decide which staff members will lose their garages. The film starts at this point. The action is static, developing in one place at one time, and the subject is ostensibly banal. The meeting takes place in the Research Institute's exhibition hall, which hosts an array of stuffed animals in danger of becoming extinct. Through a clever *mise-en-scène* and skillful camera work, the Institute staff blends with that fauna and in the viewer's eyes becomes an endangered species itself – and one that needs "protection against the environment." In fact, under a veneer of democracy mixed with self-congratulatory pomposity, the Committee chooses as victims the four most harmless and helpless of the "animals." The decision is supported by the collective which, although aware of the injustice being perpetrated, turns against its kind in order to ensure the members' own survival (or, more appropriately, the survival of their garages). Ryazanov himself plays the role of Sleepy, one of the four victims who sleeps throughout the entire meeting. Another victim, Mute, is the only one who is ready to protest the decision but unfortunately has no voice because he is suffering from laryngitis. And so, the meeting is adjourned.

What follows is a turning point which, according to conventional plot rules, should radically affect the outcome of the story. As the participants are about to leave, it turns out that the door is locked and the key is lost. They are totally cut off from the rest of the world, entrapped in a grotesque menagerie of mummified mammals. What is worse, in a desperate act of protest Mute has swallowed all the documents relative to the garage project, which means that the organization no longer exists since, within a bureaucratic structure, identity depends on papers. Having lost their official status, the members of the group gradually reacquire some human characteristics. They go through a night of *mea culpa* speeches, confessions of wrongdoing, stories of corruption, hypocrisy, and callousness. Finally, the Committee is disbanded and the cooperative members resolve to decide their destinies by drawing lots instead of relying on arbitrary decisions. All seems to be fair and good: repentance and catharsis. With the light of a new day the door opens and, as the tired

2 *Moscow Does Not Believe In Tears* (1980) directed by Vladimir Menshov

protagonists leave the building, the viewer is confronted with an open ending. Is this the beginning of a new life based on moral principles? Or, is this a return to routine law and order, and the usual *mores* after the night's carnival? The sustained grotesque that runs throughout the film heavily tips the scales in favor of the second option by undercutting all the conventions of the Socialist Realist model structure, including a moralizing happy ending.

Ryazanov had to pay a price (however small) for depriving the viewer of fairy-tale psychological comfort. Although held in great esteem by the educated public and the liberal critics, and in general well attended, *Garage* turned up in the ninth position in the popularity contest, whose first place that year was taken by the great favorite *Moscow Does Not Believe In Tears*.

Moscow, by Vladimir Menshov, had all the features of a blockbuster. Attractive characters and sets, linear narrative, sleek technical qualities, contemporary everyday life, a retro glimpse of "the way we were," and a Cinderella theme. The film recounts the story of three girlfriends over a period of twenty years, and offers an indirect commentary on the social conditions and the political mood under the Khrushchev and the Brezhnev administrations. The story follows the lives of the protagonists from 1957 to 1977 – a period depicted as a positive progression from the childish, foolish years of the cultural thaw to the consolidation of economic goals and an affluent and mature society. The three friends are believable characters, with whom the viewer can empathize, rejoice, or grieve. But they are also three social types (the "worker," the "peasant," and the "parasite") with their destiny sealed in from the very beginning by the logic of narrative stereotypes and of the Marxist–Leninist ideology (with a Brezhnevan consumeristic twist).

Ludmila, who picks light jobs in the service sector and is interested in celebrities' glamour, ends up with an alcoholic husband and ultimately a divorce and a lonely unfulfilling life. Tonya, the ideal wife and mother, lives in the country and is satisfied with her traditional role of the nurturing, caring woman. Tonya has no ambitions, and, although a positive character, she is only second best. Katya, on the other hand, is the carrier of the socialist flag. Her life in the factory spells progress and historical development, from simple worker to general manager.[14] Being human, Katya made some mistakes in her early years, which resulted in an unwanted pregnancy and the challenge of single parenthood. But she compensates for the errors of youth with a life of hard labor and sacrifice, and having turned forty she finds herself rewarded with a beautiful daughter, a prestigious position, a good apartment, stylish clothes, and even a car. The viewers are mercifully spared the pain of Katya's difficult years, they only see the results, after a twenty-year jump cut. To top it all, Prince Charming comes along in the person of a handsome worker – Goga – who, although modest in social status, is able to quote Diocletian and to engage in high-level scientific debates. Goga, however, is uneasy with Katya's superior position and salary, and before making a commitment he sets the condition that he will be playing the "man's" role in the family, and will be the only authority – to which Katya is eager to surrender, driven by her natural feminine inclinations and by the desire to live happily ever after. Vera Alentova and Andrei Batalov, who played the leads, became synonymous with happiness in the viewers' consciousness.

The film touches upon the "woman problem" – the conflict between work and happiness, duty and love, loneliness and marriage – and offers a syrupy solution. Equally simplistic are other hints at controversial social issues – alcoholism, juvenile hooliganism, trivialization of culture in television, and a spineless intellectual class. These are no more than vignettes, at times comical, in the portrait of an otherwise healthy socialist paradise. Not only the urban environment is idealized. The depiction of the countryside borders on the legendary image of a land of plenty in the films of Stalinist make. The apotheosis of the country's achievements under Brezhnev is contrasted with the juvenile mood of the earlier period. Life under Khrushchev was like an ongoing youth festival, an irresponsible fairground of attractions that promised disaster for the country's future. Yet, some episodes are highlighted which are sure to trigger a nostalgic note in the forty-year-old viewer – such as Andrei Voznessensky reciting his verses in Mayakovsky Square to an ecstatic crowd, or the still unknown Innokenty Smoktunovsky attending the first French Film Festival as a simple spectator.

By portraying a conventional literary plot in a classical cinematic form (in the sense of "Hollywood classical"), the film reiterates traditional values as the foundation of society, while effacing the disturbing problems connected with the disappearance of those values. In other words, in this film the hero is a hero and the heroine is a heroine; success and happiness await them at the end of the road because they are dedicated to work, moral rectitude, and human compassion. Obviously, average viewers (and not only in the USSR) are willing to suspend their disbelief in order to identify themselves with the "winners" – successful, respected, loved – rather than with Ryazanov's pathetic specimens of an endangered species. Paradoxically, notwithstanding its celebration of the socialist system, *Moscow* may be easily classified as a "bourgeois" film according to Western theories of Marxist criticism, insofar as it sustains the *status quo* by reaffirming that everything is for the best in the best of all possible worlds, while *Garage* falls into the category of "revolutionary" films, which are meant to disturb the established ideology and challenge the viewers' self-satisfied perception of themselves.

The year 1980 saw the appearance of still another remarkable film, *Autumn Marathon* by Georgi Danelia, closer to *Garage* in spirit and style than to *Moscow*. Danelia made his debut in the 1960s with the delightful film *A Summer to Remember* (1960), co-directed with Igor Talankin. He then proceeded alone with a steady flow of good movies, among them *Afonia* (1975) and *Mimino* (1977). *Autumn Marathon* is a sympathetic but ironic portrait of a gentle university

3   *Autumn Marathon* (1980) directed by Georgi Danelia

professor in his mid-forties, entering the "autumnal" phase of his life. Incapable of turning down anyone's requests, professor Andrei Buzykin (interpreted with extreme sensibility by Oleg Basilashvili) has spread himself so thin that he can no longer cope with the increasing demands of his professional and private life. Although meaning well and trying to please everyone, he ends up causing great unhappiness to both his wife and his mistress and disappointing his greedy colleagues as well as his concerned friends and neighbors. At one point Andrei seems to have found a way out of the impasse. But it is only a brief delusion; life then returns to the normal routine. He is trapped in a vicious circle which he has helped to create. In fact, his positive qualities – intelligence, sensitivity, kindness of soul – are offset by one dominant trait: total passivity. He does not act in life: he simply reacts to people and events as best he can, without any protest and with a resigned smile. This is what he does every morning when his foreign colleague, a Danish professor and a physical fitness devotee, rings his doorbell and drags him out to go jogging.

The structure of the film is circular. It starts and ends with a jogging session in the dark morning hours. In the northern city of Leningrad, where the action takes place, darkness is a sign of autumn and the oncoming winter. The visual metaphor does not suggest the possibility of a new spring in Andrei's life. In the final sequence the jogging path is punctuated by a row of street lamps leading to infinity. This comedy of manners – whose elegiac tone is enlivened by a measured sense of humor – seems to find its inspiration in the cultural tradition of the past century by proposing an updated version of a literary figure, the "superfluous man." Certainly, it is not by accident that Danelia chose to set the story in Leningrad, the city that since Pushkin's time has bred a vast fictional progeny of gifted and inept anti-heros.

Although a Mosfilm production, *Autumn Marathon* shares many features of the "Leningrad school," which emerged in the middle of the 1970s. This group includes directors such as Alexei German, Gleb Panfilov, Ilya Averbakh, Vitaly Melnikov, and Dinara Asanova, whose films are characterized by stylistic restraint in treating the "eternal questions" of the human predicament. And yet, they probe deeply into the complexity and ambiguity of everyday life. While most of these filmmakers are little known abroad, Gleb Panfilov was noted from his first films, and Alexei German came to the attention of foreign audiences and critics in the late 1980s with the release of films previously censored. However, the sensationalism attached to the films' belated release is less important than their intrinsic value.

Panfilov started his career with the film *No Ford in the Fire* (1968), followed shortly by *Debut* (1970). In both films, as in those which followed, his wife Inna Churikova played the leading role. A gifted actress, Churikova has been called a Soviet Giulietta Masina because of "her touching and comical facial expressions, and awkward movements."[15] But to Panfilov she has "a face, a personality, marked by God."[16] She very aptly embodies the central theme of these two movies: the idea that the divine gift of artistic inspiration resides in an unsophisticated and sensitive soul. In the first film a young peasant woman turns out to be a naif painter of great talent, and in the second a simple worker is chosen to play the role of Joan of Arc in a movie and reveals the same spiritual stamina of the French heroine. Panfilov's next film, *May I Have the Floor* (1977) continues to develop that theme, although the heroine here has superficially changed. She is now the mayor of a provincial town and, therefore, a middle-class lady, with a middle-class family and a mid-level education. But her purity of soul, inner strength, and creative potential remain those of the simple women of the previous films. It is to Panfilov's credit that he succeeded in presenting true heroines while denying the heroic genre through both stylistic and narrative devices.[17]

After this film, and some disagreement with the local authorities, Panfilov moved to Moscow to work at Mosfilm where he obtained approval for his next picture *Theme* (1979). Upon completion, however, *Theme* was shelved for seven years. It is once more the problem of artistic creativity which constitutes the main "theme" of this film, and it is once more Churikova who represents the source of spirituality. She is contrasted with the figure of a renowned and solidly established playwright whose artistic vein is drying up, played by the seasoned and talented Mikhail Ulyanov. The central character, by the ironical name of Kim Esenin,[18] has reached a creative impasse. Accompanied by a colleague – a hack writer more interested in the comforts of life than in the pangs of creation – Esenin takes a trip to the ancient town of Suzdal to find inspiration for the historical theme of his new play. There, immersed in the atmosphere of old Russia, in touch with the land and the people, he rediscovers the traditional values which he had lost, and realizes that his highly acclaimed works and his very life are a sham. What precipitates Esenin's spiritual crisis is the encounter with the local museum guide, Sasha Nikolaeva, who is the quintessential expression of the Russian soul and the custodian of the national cultural heritage.

An interesting counterpoint to Esenin is provided by the character of Borodaty (the Bearded One), with whom Sasha is in love. Borodaty is a disaffected Jewish writer who, having suffered some injustice, seeks to emigrate. The issue of emigration is discussed in a dramatic confrontation between Sasha and Borodaty – he maintaining that he must leave in order to seek creative freedom, she maintaining that he would no longer be able to create in a foreign land after having severed his cultural roots. In the end, Esenin's crisis, as well as the other characters' destinies, remain unresolved, as the film focuses on the human drama and avoids easy solutions. The camera work underlines the human turmoil by contrasting expressive close-ups of the characters with lyrical long shots of Russia's vast expanse, her snowy plains, and her serene medieval settings.

When *Theme* was completed it did not pass the last censorship scrutiny. Obviously the subject of emigration was still considered too sensitive at that time. Panfilov may have staked his chances on the fact that Jewish exit visas had been steadily increasing to reach the record number of 51,320 in 1979. He could not have foreseen that a combination of unfortunate international events would prompt the

Soviet Union to reverse its policy and drastically curtail emigration (the decline reached its lowest level in 1984, when only 896 people left). But another, less topical reason may have played a role as well. The portrayal of an official playwright doubting the value of his own work, and consequently the values of the writers' community and of society at large, may have been seen as a threat to the cultural establishment. While *Theme* is a film of the 1970s, reflecting the nation's current issues in those years, its tardy release is a phenomenon of the 1980s, which testifies to a healthy change of policy and a willingness to face the nation's problems.

The work of another representative of the "Leningrad school," Dinara Asanova, is interesting in many respects. She was a Kirgiz who moved to Leningrad and worked at Lenfilm from the early 1970s until her untimely death in 1985. Her ethnic background is not apparent in her films, as she was able to assimilate the mood and the habits of her adoptive Russian city. Her films, in fact, fit well into the frame of the "Leningrad school," with their dry, unadorned style, and their difficult questions left unanswered. Asanova's style reveals her interest in the documentary, an interest that she inherited from her teacher Mikhail Romm, and which, in 1983, manifested itself in a TV series on juvenile delinquents.

She made her debut with the film *Woodpeckers Don't Get Headaches* (1975), from a screenplay by Yuri Klepikov, who wrote most of the scripts for her subsequent films. With this first work Asanova established the theme that became a constant feature of her films – the world of adolescents, with all the uncertainty and uneasiness of a time of transition, and their troubled relations to adults. In *Woodpeckers*, Asanova focuses on the idyll of two fourteen-year-olds, their discovery of unknown feelings, their awkward behavior, their naive happiness, their comic "serious" talks, and in the end, their all-encompassing grief. A train takes the girl away. The boy runs after it. The idyll ends, and with it, childhood. In the background, Asanova shows the adults' world, self-centered and often insensitive to the adolescents' precarious state of mind. Besides providing a dramatic tension, it also provides a backdrop of unromanticized everyday reality.

The gap between generations came to the foreground in her subsequent films, and Asanova did not conceal her contention that most of the blame lies with the parents. Referring to her film *The Restricted Key* (1977), set in a high school and dealing with the relationships between teachers and students, she said: "At sixteen . . . the human soul is especially fragile, defenseless, it needs to be treated extremely cautiously and tactfully . . . It is very painful to tenth-graders when they feel they are not trusted, looked down upon, patronized."[19] Following one of her favorite practices, in this film she mixed professional actors of a high caliber, such as Lidya Fedoseeva-Shukshina and Alexei Petrenko, with non-professional teenage performers. During the shooting, it turned out that the young people actually imposed their own point of view, giving the film a truthful ring. This, obviously, happened with the director's blessing. According to Asanova: "We had to give them freedom . . . This group of kids put us in a situation which excluded all lies, all taboos, even the slightest expedients which may be forgivable in a different situation." Given the subject of this film, which hinges on the right to privacy versus obedience to authority and poses the question of what constitutes honesty, the attitude of the adolescents seemed to fall perfectly in line with the director's design.

Asanova had been rather outspoken about social problems even before the age of glasnost, and yet none of her films was shelved. She made eight films in ten years, through which she has left a portrait of a generation, puzzling in its taste for Western music and punk attire and its search for a new identity. Asanova was not the only one to treat the theme of contemporary youth. The subject became a trend, sometimes attaining excellent results (for example, Sergei Solovev's *One Hundred Days After Childhood*, 1975), but more often producing undistinguished pictures for mass consumption (for example Pavel Lyubimov's box-office success *School Waltz*, 1979). The trend took up more dramatic accents in the late 1980s.

Women directors are rather scarce in Soviet cinema (as elsewhere). Educated women in Soviet society usually reach a comfortable midmanagerial level of employment but are rarely allowed to operate at the top of any industrial, cultural, or political establishments. In the film industry there are many female editors, costume designers, make-up artists, and actresses, but very few directors. Lana Gogoberidze, like Dinara Asanova, is one of those few. Before graduating from the State Institute of Cinema she already had a background in philosophy and poetry. A Georgian working at Gruziafilm in Tbilisi, she made documentary and feature films throughout the 1960s and 1970s. But it is with the film *Some Interviews on Personal Matters* (1979) that she gave full expression to her talent as a director and co-screenwriter. Her previous film, *Commotion* (1977) had already drawn praise, although of a peculiar kind, as she ironically reports: "After viewing my film . . . a well-known director told me: 'This is your first truly manly film,' assuming that to be 'manly' is the ultimate goal of a woman's art – manly films, manly poems, manly paintings. I smiled to myself at that boundless male presumption (can you imagine the opposite case, of a woman saying to a man: 'This is your first truly womanly film'?!)"[20]

Some Interviews, therefore, is the film of a woman about a woman. The part of the protagonist, Sofiko, was written expressly for the beautiful, sensitive, intelligent Sofiko Chaurieli, who distinguished herself in numerous Georgian films, including Paradzhanov's *The Colors of the Pomegranate* (1968). The fictional Sofiko is a woman in her early forties, a professional journalist, a devoted wife, a loving mother, an affectionate daughter, and an overall caring human being. She has it all, like the heroines of the many third-rate movies which exalt the woman as the keeper of family unity and as the model of civic responsibility, at the cost of her personal happiness. This detail, however, did not bother anyone because the sacrifice was presented as the ultimate virtue. But something unusual happens with Sofiko. She reaches a point where she is no longer able to reconcile all the different aspects of her life, to satisfy all the demands placed on her. One solution her husband suggests is to get a less demanding job, perhaps as a secretary. But Sofiko is not the kind of heroine willing to suppress her creativity. She can only live one kind of life, a life which involves all of herself. And so, her marriage falls apart as her husband finds himself a more convenient companion.

This film does not end with the apotheosis of the heroine, rather with a question: Who is to blame? The admirers of "manly" films would have no trouble pointing a finger at Sofiko. The script allows this presumptuous interpretation. But the camera does not. Throughout the film it conveys Sofiko's point of view or penetrates into her inner world by closing up on her dark, expressive eyes. There is sadness and happiness in those eyes, there is compassion, curiosity, humor, disbelief, pain, but not defeat. Sofiko is a feminine creature of extraordinary strength, because she has found a solid anchor in herself. And so, who is to blame? Perhaps, the habits and conventions of a society which places on the woman too many demands and expects too much from her. This point is also conveyed by the women Sofiko interviews as part of her assignment. Gogoberidze, through the journalist Sofiko, offers the viewer a fascinating and challenging gallery of women's portraits and, while focusing on "personal matters," points out a general social problem. The director continued to focus on the woman's worldview in her next film *The Day Is Longer Than the Night* (1984). Much more ambitious in scope, and aesthetically uneven, this film covers the life of the heroine from early youth to old age, tying it to half a century of recent national history.

These films reflect a general thematic trend. Since the early 1970s, short stories and novels about women have become more and more frequent. The press started debating women's issues, mostly concerning the double workload women had to carry – at work and at home – and the problems connected with shopping hours, queues, and poor service. By the middle of the decade the "woman theme" in film became fashionable. The titles were worded to appeal to the masses: *A Sweet Woman* (V. Fetin, 1977), *A Young Wife* (L. Menaker, 1979), *A Strange Woman* (Yu. Raizman, 1978), *The Wife Has Left* (Dinara Asanova, 1980). Most of these films focused on the psychology of the new woman, independent and self-sufficient, and the way her new status affected the traditional woman–man relationship. While simplistic films offered simplistic solutions, films like *A Strange Woman* and *The Wife Has Left* raised troubling questions. Are independence and love incompatible? What is the role of man? Is woman going to find happiness within herself? Other films outside of the specific "woman trend" touched on the same problems. For example *Five Evenings* (1979) and *Kinfolk* (1982), both by Nikita Mikhalkov, reflect women's material responsibilities and spiritual frustration.

At the opposite pole of the *bytovye* pictures, historical periods and exotic settings were prominent in the 1970s. Some of the most popular films in this category were foreign imports from India, which excited the popular imagination with inflated tales of love, death, magic, and heroic pursuits. The national production displayed a more serious approach to the genre. Nikita Mikhalkov, who had been acting in film since the early 1960s, made his debut as a director in 1975 with the film *At Home Among Strangers, A Stranger At Home*, a Soviet version of the "spaghetti Western." Here train robberies, horseback chases, and shootouts are set against the backdrop of the Reds and Whites in the Civil War. Mikhalkov himself plays the main role in a duster coat and hat *à la* Clint Eastwood. Mikhalkov's second film, *A Slave of Love* (1976), is set in the same period and, like the previous one, indulges in playing with cinematic genres. The self-reflexivity of genre is here even more explicit, since this film, in a Felliniesque vein, portrays the shooting of the silent melodrama, "A Slave of Love." But filmmaking is not the only concern of Mikhalkov, who intermingles with the melodrama the political events of the day – the conquest of the Crimea by the Red Army – and the tragic destinies of the protagonists. Thanks to a construction *en abîme* (a film within a film) the boundary between illusion and reality is blurred and, in the end, it is not possible to rely on facile assumptions.

Mikhalkov moved slightly back in time in his third film *Unfinished Piece for a Player Piano* (1977). The basis for the script was Chekhov's play *Platonov*, which lent the film the decadent atmosphere of a collapsing culture.[21] Disregarding class ideology, Mikhalkov transferred to the screen the neuroses of an aristocratic and *nouveau riche* milieu which were relevant to the upper circles of contemporary Soviet society. What the director emphasized was the spiritual bankruptcy and isolation of every character. The disintegration of society as a meaningful agglomerate was conveyed by placing particular emphasis on group games as an illusory means of keeping the social fabric together. But what is particularly important to Mikhalkov is neurotic alienation as a direct consequence of estrangement from nature and gradual identification with the machine. The player piano, with its mechanical, soulless performance, is obviously the central metaphor of the film. This theme recurs in *Some Days in the Life of I. I. Oblomov* (1980). The film is based on excerpts from the novel by Ivan Goncharov, *Oblomov* (1859), which raised heated debate among the contemporary critics, and whose protagonist became, in Russian radical criticism of the 1860s, the quintessential example of the "superfluous man."[22] Later, this view was adopted by the Bolshevik political propagandists. Mikhalkov, rather than following the official negative interpretation of Oblomov as the product of a parasitic aristocratic country estate, stresses his child-like poetic nature, his inclination toward daydreaming, his ties with nature and with the feminine life principle – the mother. By contrast, maleness, energy, progress, productivity, technology are attributes of Oblomov's childhood friend Andrei Stoltz. Born of a German father, Stoltz has inherited these "non-Russian" features, which were hailed by the progressive socialist critics of the past century, but are looked upon with apprehension by Mikhalkov's post-positivist, post-Stalinist generation.

A film with a vast historical background, *Siberiade* (1979), was made by Mikhalkov's older brother, Andrei Konchalovsky. An outspoken sustainer of the "American model" both in terms of filmmaking and marketing techniques, Konchalovsky was commissioned to produce

4   *Some Days in the Life of I. I. Oblomov* (1980) directed by Nikita
Mikhalkov

5   *Some Days in the Life of I. I. Oblomov* (1980) directed by Nikita
Mikhalkov

an anniversary film, an epic with popular appeal. The film did very well at the box office. Then, suddenly, it was withdrawn from circulation when Konchalovsky traveled to the West and rumors began that he was going to defect.[23] *Siberiade,* first conceived as the story of the development of Siberian oil wells, turned into a much more complex work, intertwining history and fiction. This cine-epos covers the events connected with the lives of two families in a small Siberian village, from the beginning of the century through the 1960s. The major historical events that shook the nation are presented in select documentary inserts, which introduce the fictional episodes as, so to speak, epigraphs. Besides chronicling half a century of the country's history, the film also raises questions of universal significance, as vast as the scope of the epos. These are questions about the eternal struggle of man against nature – man's drive to conquer and nature's power to annihilate, man's suffering and nature's impassivity, and most of all (as metaphorically conveyed by the character of Afanasy) man's irrepressible need to cut a road through the wilderness for no other reason than to pursue a dream.

Many historical films did not score high marks despite the efforts of reputable directors of the old guard, such as Sergei Yutkevich who made *Lenin in Paris* (1981) with all sorts of "poetic" embellishments. However, worthy of mention in the historical category is Elem Klimov's *Rasputin* (1975), which was released only in 1984. The version that has been circulated in the USSR and abroad was drastically cut and it is, therefore, difficult to judge the film with fairness. What remains is a glimpse of the Romanov family and their empire on the verge of collapse. The film offers an intriguing portrait of the two main figures, Rasputin and Tsar Nicholas, who, according to the original plan would have functioned as each other's doubles. As the film stands this point is unfortunately lost. What remains, and what led the film into trouble is the sympathetic portrait of Nicholas – the first in Soviet cinema.

Films about World War II have been the staple of Soviet cinema since the early 1940s. So many pictures have been made on that theme that they soon constituted a genre with its peculiar conventions. The treatment of war changed over the years in the works of a few creative directors who moved away from the celebration of victories and the cult of heros. The turning point was the beginning of the 1960s when there developed a new sensibility for the personal lives of human beings caught in the war catastrophe.[24] Nevertheless, dozens of conventional and insufferably flat war movies continued to be made throughout the 1970s. One exception was a film by Larisa Shepitko, *The Ascent* (1977) – a stylized parable full of biblical metaphors. Here, the war situation is used to test the moral stamina of the protagonist. The logic of the film, and the implacable will of the director, require that the protagonist ascend his "Golgotha" in order to restore mankind's hope in spiritual rebirth. Although rather heavy-handed in its symbolism, this film has been acclaimed by both domestic and foreign critics.

The best war movies of the period undoubtedly belong to Alexei German, whose latest film *My Friend Ivan Lapshin* (1983; released 1985) finally revealed him to be one of the most brilliant and innovative directors of his generation. German made only two films in the 1970s – *Trial on the Road* (1971; released 1986), based on motifs from the war stories of his father Yuri German, and *Twenty Days Without War* (1976), loosely adapted from a novel by a classic author of Soviet literature, Konstantin Simonov. Only the second film was released upon completion, and therefore German remained virtually unknown among the public at large until now. However, with that one film he already caught the attention of the critics.[25]

Although made in the early 1970s, *Trial on the Road* belongs in a discussion of the past fifteen years of Soviet cinema because of its recent release and also because it shows German's progression toward his latest brilliant achievement. The time is the winter of 1942; the setting, a Nazi-controlled region in northwestern Russia. Sergeant Lazarev (played by V. Zamansky), a POW suspected of having been a collaborator with the Nazis, lets himself be captured by a partisan division (as his name suggests, he comes back from the "dead"). As a reformed traitor, he must undergo several tests of courage and loyalty in order to win the trust of the officers and his comrades-in-arms. The leadership is represented by two officers whose opposite worldviews constantly clash and provide the plot's dramatic tension. The stiff-necked Major, played with cold precision by the gifted (now deceased) Anatoly Solonitsyn, is a fanatical doctrinaire who places ideology above human lives, while the commander of the partisan division, played with compassion and a touch of humor by Rolan Bykov (a Soviet audience favorite), is a simple man who relies on basic human feelings rather than military rules. After several trials and humiliations, Lazarev finally redeems himself in a hyperbolic military action, where he single-handedly guns down a detachment of Germans and dies in the process. Clearly, the censors objected to the unconventional treatment of the protagonist – the

6   *Trial on the Road* (1971/rel. 1986) directed by Alexei German

"traitor" turned "hero." This was a bold violation of the Soviet narrative canons, which showed German to be an innovator already in those early days. However, the style of the film does not match the boldness of its conception. German still uses the traditional stylistic devices of the Soviet war genre, albeit applied to unorthodox characters and situations. The director at that time had not yet found his true cinematic language.[26]

With his second film, *Twenty Days Without War*, German leaves the combat zone to concentrate on the lives of ordinary people in the rear. By moving away from the war, he also moves away from the rhetoric of the genre and displays an admirably restrained realistic style. It is December 1942. The newspaper correspondent Lopatin (Yu. Nikulin), on his way to the Caucasus front, stops in Tashkent, an evacuation point overcrowded with war refugees. The purpose of his trip is to see a film being made, based on his writings. There, he has a brief and meaningful affair. It is the fleeting encounter of two human beings brought together and soon separated by the cataclysm of war. Contrary to the melodramatics of the genre, this encounter is devoid of the fateful overtones which as a rule bear on the destinies of lovers.

In German's film, the encounter is a serene pause in a difficult journey, a poor but hospitable refuge to share the intimacy of each other's bodies and feelings. To avoid trite sentimentality, the camera maintains a controlled detachment throughout the film. One example is the scene of the morning after, where the two lovers are enjoying a chat over a cup of tea, containing their sadness with laughter before saying goodbye. The camera discreetly remains outside, watching them through the window panes and preventing the viewer from overhearing their conversation. Another example is the scene on the train, where Lopatin meets a pilot who tells him a long and melodramatic story of love and betrayal, involving himself, his wife, another man, and an illegitimate child. The story has all the elements of an ordinary tearjerker, and that is what it would have been, had German exploited the conventional devices of the melodrama. But he did not. The pilot pronounces his monologue in a static close-up of ten minutes' duration. The melodramatic effect is destroyed, and by dint of the interview-type shot the story acquires a ring of verisimilitude.[27]

On his journey Lopatin meets many victims of the war who share with him their personal tragedies, thus weaving a canvas of a larger common tragedy. The gloomy picture of life on the home front, shot in greyish tones and from neutral angles, is contrasted to Lopatin's visit to a movie set where they are shooting a typical war film of the period, imbued with phony heroism. The juxtaposition of the two styles makes a statement both about true heroism and true cinema. This introduces the theme of the interplay of reality and illusion which will be central to German's next film, *Ivan Lapshin*.

The poetic school and the village trend

Several films with a tendency toward lyricism and a highly metaphorical style left a mark on the 1960s and continued to be produced in the 1970s, although on a smaller scale. Their structure, based on analogical images rather than narrative logic, resembled that of a poem. In fact this trend was known as the "poetic school." It was also characterized as the "archaic school," because these films were often based on folk tales and legends.[28] The directors who belonged to this school were mostly from the Caucasus or the Ukraine, and regarded themselves as the heirs to Alexander Dovzhenko and the "poetic" style of his early films. Among them was the controversial Sergei Paradzhanov, himself an Armenian but working at the Ukrainian studio named after Dovzhenko (*Shadows of Our Forgotten Ancestors*, 1965; *The Colors of the Pomegranate*; and most recently *The Legend of the Suram Fortress*, 1984/released 1986 and *Ashik–Kerib*, 1989).[29] Others included the Ukrainian Yuri Ilenko (*On the Eve of Ivan Kupala*, 1969; and *White Bird with a Black Mark*, 1972); the Georgian Tengiz Abuladze (*The Prayer*, 1969; and *The Tree of Desire*, 1978); Otar Ioseliani, also from Georgia (*Pastorale*, 1977); and the Kirgiz Bolotbek Shamshiev (*The White Ship*, 1977). These films were never box-office successes, though they were highly regarded among cinema connoisseurs. Liberal critics expressed deep appreciation, while conservative ones attacked them in the press for being "difficult" and self-indulgent. As a consequence, those directors were only allowed to make a few films over the years.

This was the case with Andrei Tarkovsky, who may be regarded as a northern offshoot of the poetic school. The poetic elements already clearly present in his early films *My Name Is Ivan* (1962), *Andrei Rublev* (1965), and *Solaris* (1972) came to full bloom in his movies of the late 1970s, *Mirror* (1975) and *Stalker* (1980). *Mirror* reflects the director's search into his childhood for those fragments of experience which determined the course of his life. Memory brings into focus disconnected episodes, events out of chronological sequence, flashes of relationships charged with intense emotion, or simply visual and aural impressions. Recurrent images and poetry on the soundtrack (by Tarkovsky's father, the poet Arseny Tarkovsky) connect the protagonist's childhood to his adult life. The same actress (Margarita Terekhova) plays both the role of the young mother and later the wife, while Tarkovsky's real mother (Maria Vishnyakova) appears briefly at the end of the film. This poetic autobiography conveys the inner world of the child in relation to the surrounding reality – the parents' divorce, the hardships of war, life in the countryside, the mother's struggle for economic and political survival – as well as the effect of the child's experience on the adult protagonist. Tarkovsky fills his *Mirror* with a delicate canvas of aesthetic images and human emotions which both challenge and fascinate the viewer. But the director himself was not totally pleased with the result, judging by the following interview:

Many think that *Mirror* is my favorite film. But it's not my very favorite . . . It was very difficult to make it, almost impossible to edit it . . . I had to make nineteen versions of the editing, each one fundamentally different from the others, where each episode was moved back and forth before we achieved a satisfactory version . . . To me *Mirror* is too motley a picture to say it expresses my aesthetic taste.

7   *Stalker* (1980) directed by Andrei Tarkovsky

For his following film Tarkovsky found different formal solutions, as he stated in that same interview: "In *Stalker* . . . it seems to me that I achieved a simpler form, ascetism as a narrative form."[30]

Tarkovsky's statement seems to be true in view of the future developments of his "ascetic" style, in *Nostalghia* (1983) and in his last film *The Sacrifice* (1986). These two films were made abroad and are connected with Tarkovsky's last few years of painful exile and fatal illness.[31] Moreover, *Stalker* illustrates well the main theme that runs through most of Tarkovsky's films: the discrepancy between the spiritual and the material in the human being. The director's main concern is moral as well as philosophical. Tarkovsky goes beyond questions of ethical behavior to touch on the deeper problem of the spiritual essence of the human being. The protagonists of his films are engaged in a quest for a return to a state of grace, a recovery of the soul that was suffocated by matter. The Stalker is one of those marked creatures, blessed with a special sensibility (fools in Christ, or "poets"), that allows them to find the path to the hidden truth – the essence of things beyond their material appearance. The Stalker feels that he has a mission to help mankind achieve the ultimate vision. The characters in the film are symbolic of three states of mind: the Stalker as the visionary, the Professor as the positivist, and the Writer as the skeptic.[32] The action is a metaphoric voyage through a dangerous and mysterious "zone" filled with the material debris of our civilization, in order to reach the Chamber of Desires where the pilgrims would have their most intimate wishes fulfilled. Eventually, the mission fails because the Professor and the Writer do not undertake the quest with a pure heart, and are unable to enter the Chamber. The film ends with the Stalker crushed by failure. But a final note of hope is conveyed by the Stalker's daughter, whose glance is so powerful as to be able to impress a kinetic force on inanimate objects (an allusion to the "kino" artist?). *Stalker* is based on a science-fiction story by the brothers Strugatsky, "Picnic Along the Road" (*Piknik na ovchinei*), but Tarkovsky departed from the genre and created a philosophical parable of stunning visual beauty.

A major figure in the cinema as well as the literature of the early 1970s was Vasily Shukshin (deceased in 1974). First popular as a movie actor, he then had a large following of fans as a writer and film director. All his films, including the most popular – *Strange People* (1970), *Shop Crumbs* (1973), *The Red Guelder Rose* (1974) – are based on his own stories. As a writer, Shukshin belonged to the trend of "village prose," whose practitioners look at village life as an alternative to the loss of traditional values and spirituality caused by the big city. They oppose natural life cycles and folk rituals to the dehumanizing effects of technology.[33] Himself from a Siberian village, Shukshin transferred to the screen the thrust of his books, which emphasized going back to the roots in search of the real man. He did so in an original style which is at one time realistic and lyrical. His film *The Red Guelder Rose*, the only one which was known abroad, was extremely popular in the USSR and won the *Soviet Screen* contest for 1974. It tells the story of an ex-convict (played by Shukshin himself) who after serving time goes back to the village in order to cleanse his spirit of urban corruption. Eventually he is hunted down by his old gang and killed. Soviet audiences sympathized with the protagonist's rebellion against the system and his longing for spiritual rebirth. His tormented soul-searching is all the more poignant as it is set against a backdrop of petty bureaucrats and indolent workers.

The ecological theme is also the core of the film *Farewell* (1982), completed by Elem Klimov after the tragic death of his wife, Larisa Shepitko, who initiated the project.[34] Loosely based on a novel by the "village prose" writer Valentin Rasputin, *Farewell* is a moral–philosophical tale concerned with the biological, and sacred, ties

8 *The Red Guelder Rose* (1974) directed by Vasily Shukshin

between human beings and the place they call home. The film has practically no plot. The action consists of the evacuation of the small island of Matyora, which according to government plan is going to be flooded to create a water reservoir. We are again confronted with the dilemma of industrial progress disrupting the natural environment. But the film does not pretend to offer a solution. Its function is to focus on the other side, to show the villagers who live not *on* the island but *together with it*. With a stylistic restraint which defies the facile idealization of the peasant, Klimov conveys the organic, and at the same time reverent, relation of the people to the land (Darya praying in the woods), the water (the ritual of communal bathing in the lake), the house (Darya washing and decorating her room). Conversely, he puts more dramatic pathos in the scenes depicting the violence perpetrated on the land (the furious attack on the "tree of life" by the driver of the bulldozer). *Farewell* is ultimately a film about death. Whether justified or not in the name of progress, the flooding of Matyora is shown in the last sequence as the entombment of life under a still, cold, marble-like, black liquid expanse.

The years of transition

When the Brezhnev era came to an end it seemed that the country was headed for a period of moral and economic regeneration. Brezhnev's demise was expected and the new leadership had been positioning itself for at least one year.[35] The new General Secretary, Yuri Andropov, an enigmatic, ascetic man with the methods of a KGB chief and the mind of an intellectual, was quick to crack down on corruption and privilege. Many heads fell, including some that were very close to the Brezhnev family.[36] Andropov sought to renew Party and government cadres, at the highest as well as the lowest levels, and to inject energy and purpose into the stagnating economy. The country was at a turning point. Economic indicators were alarming, due in part to American punitive measures, and in part to another disastrous harvest, the fourth in a row. Furthermore, the war in Afghanistan, the Polish engagement, and other foreign misadventures were draining financial resources needed for domestic use. A new elite of technocrats, economists, and intellectuals was painfully aware of the current situation and looked to Andropov for leadership. The other two main sustainers of the new leader were the KGB, which Andropov had refurbished and brought to a new level of sophistication, and the armed forces. As a measure of social uplift, Andropov promoted campaigns against alcoholism, petty theft, and black marketeering, and encouraged discussions of these problems in the press. As for the arts, while censorship was firmly maintained, a movement towards constructive social criticism was favored. Cinema picked up the trend, and the most notable films of those years fall within these parameters.

When speaking of the period of transition, we cannot strictly adhere to chronology because films which appeared in 1983 must have been started at least one year earlier, before Andropov. Conversely, films planned under Andropov came out in 1984, when Chernenko was already trying to turn the clock back to the ways of the old regime. Nevertheless, Chernenko had hardly any impact on cultural life. The films discussed here, therefore, are characteristic of the end of the Brezhnev era and the dawning of a new period which later acquired more defined features under Gorbachev.

9   *Train Station for Two* (1983) directed by Eldar Riazanov

Underground economy and chamber films

Cinema turned its attention to the underground economy and offered the audience a gallery of portraits of a new social type: the enterprising middleman, or, depending on the point of view, the blackmarket profiteer. The film that anticipated this trend was *Train Station for Two* (1983), by Ryazanov and Braginsky. Extremely popular, and mostly well received by the critics, the film introduced black marketeering as a secondary motif. The focus of the story is on the encounter between a provincial waitress (interpreted by Ludmila Gurchenko, unfailingly good in all her roles) and an intellectual from the big city (played by Oleg Basilashvili). Both have serious problems with their lives and eventually find in each other love, compassion, mutual support, and the hope for improvement. The sentimental strand was responsible for the film's success. Nevertheless, like all of Ryazanov's works, this was a comedy with biting satirical elements. The action unfolds in a railroad station, a symbol for transitoriness, disorderly life, superficial relations, vagrancy, underground deals – in a word, anarchy. In that railroad station, it seems, social rules and the moral imperative are no longer operative. The main target of the satire is a train conductor, masterfully played by Nikita Mikhalkov with the cocky self-assurance of a successful rogue. He has established a profitable (and illegal) cantaloupe trade with the help of the waitress from the station cafe. When the train arrives from the south, the flamboyant macho conductor dumps a couple of suitcases full of cantaloupes on his waitress and even manages hurriedly to enjoy her favors in an empty compartment. This half-willing, half-misguided woman eventually finds a way out of the demeaning situation through her encounter with a gentle and sensitive man, himself the victim of unfortunate circumstances. Because of a car accident caused by his wife – a materialistic woman representative of the *nouveau riche* mentality – he is serving time in a labor camp, and is in fact hurrying back to prison after a brief leave. The labor camp setting with its rules, rigidity, law and order, conformism, and discipline is a metaphorical opposite to the train station, and both are seen as dehumanizing environments. Between is the private space of the two lovers, where they find the spiritual nourishment necessary to their survival.

Several films subsequently picked up on the rogue theme and offered an interesting social commentary, however superficial and wanting on the artistic side. Among them, *The Blonde Around the Corner* (1984), by Vladimir Bortko, tells the story of a pretty and frivolous food shop clerk who affords a life of affluence by privately trading in state-owned groceries, a long-established practice in Soviet life. Viktor Tregubovich's *A Rogue's Saga* (1984) is a satirical "epic poem" about the modern rogue. An amiable wheeler-dealer, an energetic, hard-working entrepreneur, he neglects his regular job in order to pursue his private business of trading favors, establishing connections, and providing services – placing someone's son in graduate school in exchange for a vacation on the Black Sea, in exchange for a role on stage, in exchange for a good deal on a car, and so on. This practice is known in Russian slang as *"blat."* As a result, he lives "above his salary," which means that his apartment is a consumer goods showcase. To press their case against the swindler (who, by the way, is able technically not to break the law, but to operate on the fringes), the film's authors suggest a parallel with the prototype of all Russian rogues: Chichikov from Gogol's *Dead Souls*.[37] Like Chichikov, who evaded his pursuers in a flying troika, our contemporary speeds away in his white Mercedes and vanishes into thin air.

A similar character is the protagonist of *Sincerely Yours . . .* (1985), by the woman director, Alla Surikova. The character's personality, the comedy situations, the consumeristic paradises, the bonanza of imported clothes and electronic gear, the petty concerns of a material-istic society – all of these are characteristics of the trend. However, we must note that in all these films the rogue is a person of medium social status, an average citizen in no position of power. The causes for the social malaise – the inefficiency of the economic system itself and the self-serving attitude of Party and government functionaries – are not discussed. The films simply show alarming symptoms, leav-ing it to the viewer to figure out the causes and the cure. Obviously, the filmmakers were just testing the new parameters of censorship, at the same time pushing for their expansion.

To soften the critical discourse and to make it more acceptable, many filmmakers added to their pictures elements of the fantastic. So much so, that a new term was found by the Soviet critics to charac-terize these films: "social fiction" (*sotsial'naia fantastika*), analogous to "science fiction" (*nauchnaia fantastika*). The fantastic element may be more or less prominent in certain films (*The Blonde Around the Corner* and *A Rogue's Saga* both have "fantastic" endings), but is rarely absent. In *One of a Kind* (1985), by Vitaly Melnikov, an employee of a scientific research center discovers that he has the mental power to transmit his dreams; he goes into show business, so to speak, establishing a profitable enterprise by selling his dreams to a sleeping audience.

One of the best achievements in this genre is the film by Eldar Shengelaia *Blue Mountains, or An Improbable Story* (1985). The "improbable story" occurs in an unidentified institution (a publishing house, a magazine's headquarters?) where extremely busy employees attend to their business with meticulous scrupulousness day after day. Unfortunately their business is not the same as the institution's. They study French, grind coffee, knit, play chess, or run in and out in between absorbing activities which take place somewhere else. As a result, the young writer who brings in his manuscript, "Blue Moun-tains," has to wait one year, only to learn that the manuscript has been lost. In the end, because of neglect, the institution's building collapses on the heads of its oblivious staff. But nobody is hurt (after all, this is a fantastic story), and the institution is moved to a modern building of glass and concrete. There everything is new – except the institute's operations, which resume as usual – knitting, coffee grind-ing, chess playing, French spelling, and so on. But the fantastic in this film extends beyond the narrative level. It is primarily conveyed by a style which is hyperbolic in its realism of detail. The discrepancy between the hyperrealism of the environment and the triviality of the action attains the level of the absurd. The institution becomes an empty shell, and the characters grotesque masks without souls. A few years later, another director, Yuri Mamin, will return to the theme of the collapsing building and to the grotesque style in the tragicomedy *Fountain* (1989).

Outside of the realm of the fantastic, but within the trend of social criticism, was the winner of the popularity contest for the year 1984. Once again, it was a film by Eldar Ryazanov, *A Ruthless Romance*, which is based on the nineteenth-century play by Alexander Ostrovsky, *Without a Dowry*. The merchant milieu, materially rich but spiritually poor, served Ryazanov well as a parallel to certain circles of the contemporary Soviet "bourgeoisie." But the audience was probably attracted by the tragic destiny of the heroine, who succumbs to the requirements of a tyrannical environment and to the romantic glamour of a refined swindler (another superb interpretation by Nikita Mikhalkov). To a certain extent the film *Vassa* (1983), by Gleb Panfilov, belongs to the same trend, inasmuch as it is about an industrialist's family of the early twentieth century and is based on the play *Vassa Zheleznova*, by Maksim Gorky. However, as in all of Panfilov's films, the figure of the heroine here is strong and positive. Notwithstanding the fact that she is the representative of the capitalist world on the verge of collapse, she fulfills her destiny with dignity and responsibility, and a lot of anger and pragmatism.[38]

Corruption and disillusionment in public life had a counterpart in films concerned with personal problems, family, and love. The peculiar themes of the so-called "chamber films" are reflected in titles such as *Private Life* (Raizman, 1983) and *Without Witnesses* (Mikhalkov, 1983). The former is about an executive going into retirement and discovering his true self through a closer contact with his family; the latter, about a divorced husband who visits his ex-wife and engages her in a bitter confrontation in order to gain psychological revenge. Another film by Yuli Raizman, *Time of Desires* (1984), is interesting as a sequel to the "woman films" of a few years earlier. The character type epitomized by the heroines of *Strange Woman* (also by Raizman) and *Moscow Does Not Believe in Tears* (Vera Alentova played the leading role in both *Moscow* and *Time of Desires*), independent but romantically disposed and seeking a true love relationship, has turned into a practical, efficient, energetic provider of material comfort, a woman of "useful" connections, whose aim is to fit her and her husband's lives into the fashionable mold of her desires – with catastrophic consequences.

Quite different in tone are the films of Pyotr Todorovsky, *Waiting for Love* (1983) and *A Wartime Romance* (1984). These are delightfully unpretentious comedies, humorous and touching at the same time. A *sui generis* "chamber film" was *Success* (1984), by Konstantin Khudiakov, telling the story of a strong-willed stage director possessed by a fanatic dedication to the theater and determined to achieve artistic perfection at all costs – even at the cost of trampling on human lives.

The film *Look Back* (1984), by Aida Manasarova, touches on the specific problem of the generation gap. More precisely, it portrays the drama of a mother whose teenage son has turned into an egotistical monster full of repressed fury. Although the film hints at the causes of the young man's troubles by vaguely suggesting that the mother in earlier years did not give her infant son enough love and attention, it finally seems to exonerate her because of her suffering and honest efforts to correct her mistakes. The viewer is left without a solution and with the uneasy feeling that a young life will be wasted.

Troubled youth

The issue of difficult youth, and often of outright juvenile delinquency, once a theme to be avoided, was singled out by the press in the early 1980s as one of the most pressing social problems. Newspapers, especially in the provinces, frequently reported stories of brutality among teenagers and showed that juvenile delinquency was on the rise. Both the stage and the screen reflected this trend.[39]

One film that had a vast following all over the country, but also raised a chorus of indignant protests, was *Scarecrow* (1984) by Rolan Bykov, a veteran actor eventually turned director. *Scarecrow* tells the story of a twelve-year-old girl, Lena Bessoltseva, who becomes the target of her schoolmates' vicious attacks.[40] Because of a banal incident she is unjustly accused of having betrayed the group, and after a period of ostracism and psychological abuse she is burned at the stake, in effigy. The metaphor of the burning dummy, with Lena watching it, is more eloquent of her suffering than any scene of explicit violence. Bykov probes an issue which is often hidden behind a neat facade of respectability. In this film the setting is a small Russian northern river town, with its pretty old houses, a church, a model school. It is, in fact, a tourist attraction. The schoolchildren

10   *Scarecrow* (1984) directed by Rolan Bykov

look as neat and pretty as the surrounding environment, but under the surface they hide disquieting personalities. They have a tendency to act as a collective, no doubt instilled by official education and upbringing and aggravated by the disintegration of the family. This would not be a bad thing *per se*, except that this collective, in order to have a *raison d'être*, needs a victim to hate and torment.

Thus, besides ventilating a current youth problem, this film carries deeper implications. Artistically woven into its texture is the idea that the collective can become a tyrant. In this teenage microcosm one can observe familiar patterns of denunciation, purge, demagogy, lack of moral stamina, and loss of individual integrity typical of behavior that – although most prominent in the Stalinist years – is not completely obsolete. One image that functions as a metaphorical link between past and present is that of the marching band. The omnipresent bands of the 1930s used to play their martial tunes in parks, city squares, workers' clubs, steamboats, train stations, and every other public place, in order to lift the people's morale and cover up the drab reality of the day with a cheerful note of optimism. In *Scarecrow*, the marching band, with its smart uniforms and shining brass, blends well with the rest of the neat town's facade. One would hardly notice it, if it were not for its conductor. Bykov himself makes a cameo appearance in this role and, simply by his expression of embarrassment and shame at performing the usual upbeat tune upon Lena's final departure, provides the viewer with the key to the entire film.

Another great success was the film by Dinara Asanova *Tough Kids* (1983). Based on real-life episodes and characters (Asanova eventually turned her research materials into a documentary for television), this film is set in a correctional institute, more precisely a summer camp for male teenage offenders. The camp director, Pavel Antonov (simply Pasha to the boys), rejects abstract pedagogical principles in favor of spontaneous human relations. In other words, he believes that his young friends can be reformed not through regulations but through love and understanding. He establishes a big-brother relationship with each of the boys and pursues his mission with total dedication. Eventually, the experiment fails when the kids suddenly go on a rampage of violence and vandalism. One of the merits of Asanova's films is that they never idealize heroes or vilify villains. Pasha is neither a saint nor a guru, just a decent man with strengths and weaknesses. His weakness, in fact, is brought into focus when he vents his rage and frustration on the youths for having failed him. In a dramatic scene, where the boys, sincerely sorry for their deeds of the previous night, come to Pasha to apologize, he repeatedly shouts at them in a crescendo of fury: "I will *not* forgive you!" In the end, it is clear that Pasha will not give up his mission. But it is also clear that he is shaken and does not have any concrete answers. Thus, the film raises once more the problem of the generation gap, poses the question of how to reach out to youth and reestablish the missing link.[41]

Asanova's next and last film, *Dear, Dearest, Beloved* . . . (1984),[42] touches on the same problem, but in a different setting and mood. This film was not as popular as *Tough Kids* because of its "difficult" structure – allusions, innuendoes, bits and pieces of information that the viewer had to reorganize in order to make sense of the story. One can even say that the film borders on "social fiction," given the absurd (and yet, totally believable) mind set of the young heroine. A nineteen-year-old, in the eccentric attire of the latest counterculture fad, holding an infant in her arms, jumps into the car of a stranger and asks him to "rescue" her. The driver, a good-natured fellow a generation older, is taken by surprise and willing to help. Driving around Leningrad in the course of the night, he tries to establish a dialogue with the young woman. He wants to understand her problems, to assist her and the baby. But all he gets is a confused story about her "dear, dearest, beloved" who kicked her out of the house. Ultimately, it turns out that she is being chased by the police for having stolen the baby from another woman. Her motive? To blackmail her estranged lover by having him believe that the baby was their own. The kind "rescuer" (played by Valery Premykhov, who also played Pasha in *Tough Kids* and wrote the script for this film) in the end is totally baffled and, while discussing the incident at the police station, he offers the audience a question to ponder:

What can I teach them? You, yourself, do you understand anything about these . . . kids? For me this is the first time I have run into one of them. Who are they? What do they want? Before, when there was famine around, they engaged in theft, vandalism . . . this was understandable, justified. But now, what do they want? Do you, yourself, know?[43]

Asanova does not pretend to know what they want, but in the course of the film she suggests what is wanting: a family environment, loving parents, and the transmission of values – all things that the pitiful heroine of this story did not get.[44]

A film about orphaned children growing up in an institution in the wake of World War II was made by Nikolay Gubenko. *Orphans* (1977) deals with the urchins that roamed the streets and the devastated countryside for a loaf of bread (like their predecessors during the Civil War, known as *"bezprisorniki"*) and are finally put in a special school. The protagonist, now an established writer, looks back at those years from the perspective of one of the kids. The flashbacks are recounted largely in the nostalgic mood of the memoirs genre, which softens the trials and tribulations of the little hero. It is a mood reminiscent of Fellini's *Amarcord* (1974), which is directly quoted by specific visual associations and evoked by the music score. Often humor and comedy situations overlap with the harsh reality of hunger, loneliness, and abuse. But on two occasions, tragedy and drama, still fresh in the narrator's mind, are conveyed to the viewer with great emotional impact. One episode deals with the accidental death of a Jewish boy, whose parents perished in a Nazi camp. Seeking revenge, the boy engineers a bomb to blow up the German POWs held in the woods not far from the institute. Tragically, the bomb explodes in his hands. The second episode pits the protagonist against a schoolteacher, a war veteran with a violent disposition (played by Gubenko himself). Having been slapped, the boy calls the teacher "a fascist." The political implications are significant. The condemnation of fascism as an ideology that leads to war and destruction is pervasive of the whole movie. By applying the epithet to a Soviet war hero (and one that wears a mustache *à la* Stalin) the connection with the national ideology becomes obvious. This was the first time the connection was made explicit, although in a few other cases denunciation of fascism was meant to evoke associations wth totalitarianism at home – most notably in the documentary compilation *Ordinary Fascism* (Mikhail Romm, 1966).

Escapism and politics

As a pendant to the serious genres engaged in social criticism, the Soviet audiences were offered a good number of light musicals. Some of them were bound to be popular in spite of weak plots and poor production values, simply because they featured celebrities from the musical world. Among them were *Don't Get Married, Girls* (Evgeny Gerasimov, 1985), with the pop singer Valery Leontiev, and *I Came to Talk* (N. Ardashnikov, 1985), with the pop queen Alla Pugacheva. Others had more substance and were made with taste and ingenuity; for example, the films of Karen Shakhnazarov, *Jazzman* (1983) and *A Winter Evening in Gagry* (1985).

Escapist, but with a clear political slant, was a series of movies belonging to the detective genre. In the early 1980s, when the period of international *détente* came to an end, the Soviet leadership intensified anti-Western propaganda (anti-American, in particular) in the mass media and in film. This marked the beginning of a new trend which exploited the entertainment value of the detective genre borrowed from the West, while presenting an image of the West that suited the current political mood. And so, the audience got a taste of "James Bondism" Soviet style, with less explicit violence and no sex, but with enough intrigue, chases, stunts, and karate chops to please the popular taste. Eloquent examples of this genre are *Unmarked Freight* (V. Popkov, 1985), *Cancan in Englischen Garten* (V. Pidpalyi, 1985),[45] *Two Versions of One Accident* (V. Novak, 1985), *European Story* (Igor Gostev, 1984), and the television adaptation of Yulian Semyonov's novel, *TASS Is Authorized to Announce* (Valery Fokin, 1984), dealing with CIA and US capitalist atrocities in Africa.[46]

Less adventurous but just as propagandistic are the films *We Accuse*

(T. Levchuk, 1985), a dramatization of the trial of the American pilot Gary Powers in the sixties; and *Flight 222* (by Sergei Mikaelian, 1985), based on a real-life incident involving a Soviet ballerina who, upon departure from New York, was detained by the Immigration Service, together with an Aeroflot jet full of passengers, in order to ascertain whether she was going back of her free will. As expected, in these films the Americans are the villains. However, one must note that the targets of Soviet criticism are generally government officials or people somewhat connected with the "military–industrial complex." Not infrequently, the average American citizen comes across as a good fellow, although naive and misguided. On balance, the Hollywood producers of similar hits have concocted a much more monstrous image of the enemy.[47]

The flow of anti-American political escapism died out toward the end of 1985, together with the vitriolic cartoons that for a couple of years had enlivened the world news page of *Pravda*, depicting "Ronnie the Cowboy" with a swastika sign in place of the sheriff star. After the Geneva summit that year a new image of the US was being shaped by the Soviet media. Cinema made its contribution with the documentary *Geneva: The Beginning of a Dialogue* (Oleg Uralov, 1986). The film not only records the events of the summit but sounds a note of hope in a future of cooperation and peaceful coexistence. It presents "the other" – a good-looking, good-natured, and good-humored President Reagan – as a reasonable partner and an indispensable ally in the search for a solution to the nuclear menace. More anecdotal in terms of changing politics is an episode connected with the Moscow summit of 1988. Early in February, a festival of American films took place in Moscow and Leningrad, which included *King's Row*, starring Ronald Reagan.[48] There is no information on whether the Soviet public appreciated the film or the performer. But it is certain that Reagan's cinematic image – as the honest, clean, all-American hero – was used by the press to generate positive feelings in the population. In the May issue of the magazine *Soviet Screen* – which very appropriately came out one week before the summit – there was an extensive article dedicated to Reagan, complete with attractive stills from his most popular films. The title of the article, "Some Day I Will Amaze This City," refers to the prophetic words of Drake McHugh, the protagonist of *King's Row*. The many virtues of the typical Reagan hero are listed in detail: "He is a business-like type with a practical side. A conservative in the good sense of the word . . . with solid habits, firm ideals. He is a patriot and a good family man.

And, most important, he is a simple fellow, just like everyone else. Which means that everyone can achieve what he has achieved."[49] The author underlines that, while this is Reagan's screen image, he is actually this same "nice fellow . . . both on film and in life." The film critic is also taken by Reagan's acting talent: "In the highly dramatic scene when Drake McHugh wakes up after the surgery and looks down there, where his legs used to be, he shouts, horrified: 'And where is the rest?' – the actor here is simply magnificent." About the less magnificent side of Reagan's career – his involvement with the Screen Actors Guild administration in the years of McCarthyism – the article is silent. That period is dismissed in a very short sentence: "Notwithstanding the fact that from 1947 to 1952, and later in 1959–1960, Reagan served as the president of the Screen Actors Guild, he could no longer get any good roles."

A dash of surrealism

The works of Vadim Abdrashitov (director) and Alexander Mindadze (screenwriter) do not fall neatly into any of the categories discussed above, but they do belong widely to the trend of social criticism of the late 1970s and early 1980s. Both Georgian but working at Mosfilm, Abdrashitov and Mindadze have been collaborating since the late 1970s and their co-signature has always been a guarantee of aesthetic achievement and moral commitment. Thanks to the support of their mentor, Yuli Raizman, they were able to overcome considerable opposition. Their early films include *Speech for the Defense* (1977), *The Turning Point* (1979), and *Fox Hunt* (1980). Each in its own way is concerned with the protagonist's sudden awareness of a reality that transcends the illusory world of social conventions. The consequences of the awakening are not pleasant, as the individuals in question are alienated from what was previously their environment.[50]

This theme has remained a constant in more recent films, such as *The Train Stopped* (1982). Here, an investigator pursuing the causes of a train accident struggles to break through a shield of lies and indifference in the working community where the accident occurred. The search for the truth becomes the focal point of his life, but he has to give up when he realizes that the community resents the investigation, whose results are bound to disturb the quiet flow of life. Hypocrisy and comfort are preferable to turmoil and truth. Their next film, *Parade of Planets* (1984), treats the same theme in an allegorical form, and marks a departure from the realistic style. In the opening titles,

11   *Parade of Planets* (1984) Abdrashitov (director) and Mindadze (screenwriter)

the authors announce that this is "a quasi-fantastic story." Indeed, the story, although justified on a realistic level, is set in environments which destroy the perception of everyday reality. Not only the viewers but the film's protagonists themselves have the impression of having stepped into an uncanny world. The six protagonists are forty-year-old reservists called up for the last time to play war games. In the course of the maneuvers, they are "killed," and subsequently dismissed. Wanting to prolong the game for a couple of days before going back to their jobs and families, the "ghosts" set out on a journey that takes them first to "the city of women" (a textile factory town), an idyllic and sensuous spot inhabited exclusively by charming and hospitable females, and then to the "old people's world" (an institution for senior citizens), where semi-surrealist figures of gentle octogenarians bring them in touch with history. The voyage for the six reservists has been an exploration into the self, the experience of a reality which seems illusory only from an ordinary point of view. Now they know that the illusion is on the other side, the positivist world of social conventions and conformism. Will they be able to readjust? The viewer does not know. At parting, the men disperse in the city shouting military passwords to each other, which now sound like nonsensical playwords.[51] *Parade of Planets* gets its title from an episode in the film. One of the reservists, an astronomer, explains that when a certain configuration appears in the sky, the so-called "parade of planets," something wondrous is bound to happen. This occurs only once in a thousand years. The scene when the protagonists watch the phenomenon, together with the dwellers of the old people's house, is one of the most evocative and visually engaging. The sense of awe and foreboding is almost palpable, achieved through sweeping camera movements that connect earth and sky.

In retrospect, that scene was prophetic. 1984 has indeed been the end of an era. The cultural world was ready for a fresh start. When the new policy of glasnost made it possible, public opinion turned against the odious past and labeled a whole epoch with the contemptuous term, "the period of stagnation." It was clear, however, that within the general climate of artistic repression creativity did not die. Significant achievements in film could be counted in the otherwise dull production of those years. While Western cinema in the 1960s and 1970s has been characterized by a number of "new waves" (French, Italian, German, and even American) sharing some common traits, Soviet cinema followed its own course. The outspoken political protest of Western filmmakers and their formal experimentation would not have passed the scrutiny of censorship. But a number of Soviet directors found an indirect way to express dissent. They were able to communicate with the audience through allusions, oblique references, evocative images, suggestive juxtapositions. They developed an aesthetic code, known as "Aesopian language," which evaded the censor and enabled the audience to read between the lines, or, more precisely, between the images.[52] The best films discussed in this chapter display the use of Aesopian language and its subversive intention to a greater or lesser degree. It is fair to say, therefore, that if in the 1970s cinema was no longer the "most important art," it was perhaps the least stagnating.

2   Perestroika in the film factory

Glasnost in the air

The spring of 1985 will go down in history as the time when the wind of reform began to blow new life into the progressive forces of Soviet society. Nobody could have predicted at that time that four years later that wind would gather momentum and hit the adjacent countries of Eastern Europe with the strength of a tornado, overturning governments and institutions, and leaving a trail of debris along the Iron Curtain borderline. In the Soviet Union the developments were not so sudden, and therefore not so spectacular, but the movement toward radical changes in all spheres of public life was steady and significant. This statement, and others that follow, would have been different, had the book been written after the events of August 1991. But at the time of writing, they were accurate.

The art fields responded enthusiastically to Gorbachev's initial directives for perestroika and glasnost.[1] As it is often the case, the first daring voices denouncing the previous administration's "mistakes" and abuses of power, and calling for a global renewal, were those of poets, filmmakers, artists, and exponents of the intelligentsia in general. It was from the pages of *Iskusstvo kino*, *Literaturnaia gazeta*, *Ogonek*, *Novyi mir*, rather than from military intelligence data, that the keen Western analyst could have sensed the magnitude of the process that was going to transform the Soviet Union and the Eastern world. Open criticism of censorship in art and literature, negative allusions to the Stalinist terror, the camp system and the policy of collectivization, calls for rehabilitation of cultural and political figures in the official press, could not have happened at that early stage without a green light from the Central Committee.[2] But the initiative came from the very top, from "the man at the helm," who believed that he could not succeed in his ambitious program of economic and political reforms without the support of the intellectual elite.[3] Traditionally regarded as the voice of the nation, the Soviet intelligentsia was to lend credibility to Gorbachev's policies in the eyes of the people, and to mobilize public support. While this task, with time, turned out to be extremely difficult if not impossible on a massive scale, at the outset Gorbachev could not have found a more devoted ally. Hampered by two decades of adverse policies, artists and intellectuals were suddenly provided with a much needed outlet for their repressed creativity. Words, images, and sounds, until then unheard and unseen, began to trickle down to the public, at first cautiously testing the limits, then pushing further and further beyond the frontier of the permissible, and finally turning into an irrepressible flood, gushing out of the printed page, the screen, the stage, and the exhibition halls.

Together with glasnost, and the encouragement for independent thinking and individual action, came the need to reshape the administrative structures of the cultural institutions and the creative Unions. The filmmakers were the first to realize the importance of consolidating their gains through institutionalization of the new policy, in order to ensure continuity and prevent a setback. The Filmmakers Union took a leading role in the restructuring process, providing other fields with an example to follow.[4]

A new strategic balance: the Filmmakers Union and Goskino

A major administrative shakeup took place in May 1986, at the V Congress of the Filmmakers Union. Three-fourths of the Union's leadership were replaced with progressive members from the creative ranks rather than from the bureaucratic apparatus. For the first time, nominations to official posts were not prearranged by the bosses, which allowed the controversial film director, Elem Klimov, to be elected First Secretary of the Union, ousting Lev Kulidzhanov who had afflicted the filmmakers with two decades (1965–1986) of repressive policies.[5] This event has been characterized in some Western circles as a small revolution; but, actually, Klimov's election had been prepared from above. It was the result of a backstage strategy devised by the new political forces. After extensive preliminary caucusing to exclude the most objectionable Union leaders from even attending the Congress, Klimov was nominated by Alexander Yakovlev, who at that time was the head of the Central Committee's Propaganda Department, and who is credited with being the main architect of glasnost.[6] The election, by hand vote from the floor, confirmed the nomination. Klimov's victory may have been helped by the official attention he received in the year preceding the Congress. In 1985, his film, *Rasputin*, censored under the Brezhnev regime and shelved for a decade, was suddenly distributed; and in the summer, his latest film, *Come and See*, won first prize at the Moscow Film Festival, after its production had been blocked by Goskino for eight years. Klimov was perceived by the majority of the delegates as a strong figure capable of leading the film industry out of a debilitating state of stagnation. Many also identified with his longtime struggle against Goskino for the right to freedom of artistic expression, and sympathized with him for his uncompromising stance in the face of adversity. His unbending nature later proved to be an obstacle to smooth relations with associates and the membership at large, but at the time of the Congress it was exactly the right asset.

Very few critical voices rose in opposition to the methods employed in the conduct of the Congress. Nikita Mikhalkov, while sustaining the principles of the glasnost revolution, worried about the Jacobin spirit that moved a number of filmmakers eager to settle accounts. Having never experienced the frustrations of political persecution, he expressed the point of view of a privileged son of the Soviet aristocracy, fond of certain charms of the *ancien régime*. But there was some wisdom in his warning against a nihilistic rejection of tradition, and in his appeal to honoring past achievements. He defended colleagues, such as the renowned actor and director Sergei Bondarchuk who was not even chosen as a delegate to the Congress, because many resented his despotic ways. Mikhalkov was sharply rebutted and, to no one's surprise, not elected to the Union's Secretariat.[7]

In line with Gorbachev's policies, therefore, the Filmmakers Union acquired a dynamic and progressive leadership. It would not be superfluous to look at the composition of the new Secretariat, and compare it to the outgoing one.[8] Not a single incumbent was reelected, and the Secretaries' number was dramatically increased, from twenty to fifty-one, with the percentage of Party members reduced from 77 percent to 46 percent. The sharp turnover shows how the new forces relied on a quick preemptive strike to eliminate the old guard and acquire a large power base – a strategic move that Gorbachev himself masterfully employed. The expansion of the Secretariat was intended to achieve that end as well as to "democratize" the Union. Nevertheless, for all its progressiveness, the new Secretariat, with one exception, once more excluded women. It is a persistent feature of Soviet life that participation in leading positions is still mainly a man's prerogative.[9] Perestroika, however, has affected society in many areas, including the perception of gender roles. At the next Congress of the Filmmakers Union (four years later), a woman was finally elected to the very top.

The renewal of the film industry was facilitated by the sweep of the top cultural heads, starting with the replacement of the Minister of Culture himself. In August 1986, P. N. Demichev, occupying that post since 1974, was replaced by V. Zakharov, at the time the deputy to Moscow Party chief Boris Yeltsin. But this was only a temporary appointment. Two years later, possibly as a side-effect of the "Yeltsin affair," possibly just to stress the concern for a competent leadership in the art field, the film and stage director–actor, Nikolai Gubenko became the new Minister of Culture of the USSR.[10] But the most significant step toward the revival of film creativity was the reform of Goskino. An old pillar of conservatism, Filipp Ermash, Goskino's head since 1972, was removed without the official mention of appreciation, and was publicly blamed for the stagnation of cinema during his long years of service. His replacement, Alexander Kamshalov, came from the same bureaucratic background. Like Ermash, Kamshalov headed the Cultural Section of the Central Committee. He was also a film specialist and the author of a number of books, and was obviously selected to represent the ongoing changes in the party policy on cinema. He was expected to establish a viable relationship with the Filmmakers Union, fostering collaboration rather than confrontation.[11] Where in the past Goskino was responsible for all aspects of film production and distribution, and exercised ideological and financial control, the reshuffling of the administration balanced the scales by increasing the filmmakers' decision-making power. The republics' Goskinos were abolished, and the republican studios were placed under the jurisdiction of the local Ministries of Culture. All studios acquired the right to plan their own yearly productions and to decide on scripts and shooting schedules; and, more important, to move toward self-financing. Furthermore, censorship was virtually dismantled as an institution.

When asked whether Goskino had been stripped of its functions, in February 1987, Klimov answered: "Certainly not. The state agency still has a large range of very important functions, that can be fulfilled only by the state . . . Goskino must work out the strategic projections of development for the industry as a whole, coordinate the production planning of the studios, process the orders for state-commissioned films, handle film printing and distribution, establish foreign relations, conduct export–import affairs, and guarantee the industry's material and technical development. And finally, Goskino retains the right to decide whether a film, once completed, may be released . . . [But] in case of a dispute concerning a specific film, a solution will be worked out jointly by Goskino's Collegium and the Secretariat of the Filmmakers Union."[12]

In the course of the next three years, Goskino *de facto* lost most of its prerogatives, in a measure that was unimaginable at the beginning of the reforms. Goskino no longer has a monopoly on the international market. Gradually, studios and independent producers entered into direct negotiations with foreign partners and signed their own contracts. This eventually caused the demise of Sovinfilm, Goskino's branch for co-production ventures, that folded up in May 1989. Its functions were taken over by Sovexportfilm, which continued to operate as the state agency for film foreign trade, although on a par with all other enterprises. Goskino has so far maintained its grip on domestic distribution. But the distribution market, like the production sector, is expected to become autonomous in the near future, with the major studios as well as the small cooperatives selling their films directly, outside of the central umbrella of the Main Film Distribution Board.

Down with censorship!

In the summer of 1990, the Law on the Press was approved by the Supreme Soviet. With that act, the institution of censorship was legally abolished. Restrictions could still be enforced in three cases: to protect state and military secrets, to prevent pornography, and to impair the promotion of war and ethnic conflict.[13] But since the beginning of glasnost it has been virtually impossible to block the circulation of a film if the Union pressed for its release. Even before the law took effect, most filmmakers were confident that glasnost meant freedom of expression, as illustrated by the following statement: "WE, the film artists, enjoy 100 percent glasnost. We make movies about labor camps, about the mafia that infiltrates the highest echelons of power, about drug addicts and prostitutes, about speculators and robbers, about corruption within the organs of the Ministry of Interior Affairs, and about moral degradation in the army, the Komsomol, and . . . you name it!" – and all this was said in an article critical of the recent developments.[14]

Others, however, think that censorship still operates in subtle ways. Screenwriter Leonid Gurevich said that while 90 percent of the films that are made nowadays would never have been approved before, some of the most daring are still running into trouble. The film *Countersuit*, for example, from a script by Ales Adamovich, about the "enemies" of perestroika was held in bureaucratic limbo for quite some time, notwithstanding the fact that it received the First Prize at the Leningrad Documentary Film Festival, in 1989. Other films that ran into the same difficulties show a wide range of topics, from the role of the militia at spontaneous gatherings and unapproved rallies, to agricultural reforms. According to Gurevich, "the opinions expressed in those films did not suit some of the most conservative leaders." The situation is one of dialectical tension, where Goskino no longer has unconditional control over the film industry and cannot make any final decision without the consensus of the Filmmakers Union. When asked who would have the final word in case of an unsolvable dispute, Gurevich said: "The Central Committee, as usual."[15]

To promote the liquidation of censorship, one of Klimov's first moves (literally, two days after the V Congress) was to create the Conflict Commission, consisting of critics, directors, script writers, actors and representatives of Goskino to review the inventory of banned films, and to decide on controversial new ones. In order to protect the rights of filmmakers far removed from Moscow, conflict commissions were also established in several republics, and they kept close ties with the central body. The total number of films to be rescued was not known to the Commission members when they first tackled the job. The president of the Commission, Andrei Plakhov, at first thought that the number was "around twenty, then fifty," and finally it became clear that "the figure was well over 100," including feature films, documentaries, TV movies, and animation.[16] The procedure was rather simple. After screening and deliberation, the Commission made its recommendation to Goskino for a prompt release. By the end of the decade, all the films that had been censored over the years were taken off the shelf. The Commission was also designed to investigate the reasons behind the ostracism of some directors who were expelled from the Union and prevented from working. The cases that attracted the most attention in the West were those of Kira Muratova and Alexander Askoldov.[17] But several other lesser known directors were reinstated in the ranks and returned to their professional status. Another positive development is the fact that Soviet directors were no longer harassed for making films abroad, and those who had emigrated in search of artistic freedom were being invited back to the motherland. The internationally renowned director Andrei Tarkovsky, once stripped of his Soviet passport for refusing to return upon expiration of his visa, has been posthumously rehabilitated, and virtually turned into a national hero.[18]

Having completed the first stage of its activities, the Commission turned to the current problems and faced the first conflicts of the era of glasnost. Those arose primarily in connection with documentary films that were the first to deal with sharp issues of political and social life. One case in point was the documentary *Theater in the Time of Perestroika and Glasnost*, made by Arkady Ruderman for Belarusfilm, in 1988. For reasons unknown the filmmaking process was terminated before completion. The studio's administration claimed that the actual shooting did not correspond to the script that was previously approved. The director insisted that the script was the same, but it became necessary to add new materials as the film was progressing. The new materials had to do with an editor of the Belorussian Soviet Encyclopedia, a woman by the name of L. Shelenkova, who wrote an article on Marc Chagall in pre-perestroika times, and was fired. She brought a lawsuit against the administration, but the judge dismissed it. Interviewed in the film, the judge says that he was not hostile to the plaintiff, but had to yield to pressure "from above." Notwithstanding a resolution of the Conflict Commission in favor of the film, and numerous requests from the FU and Goskino, Belarusfilm has closed its door to the director. The film's rough cut, however, has been shown at some festivals, and even on television.[19]

Occasionally feature films are involved as well. Such was the case of *Assuage My Sorrow* (1989), stopped by the artistic council of the Mosfilm association that produced it. The council found it "too gloomy," about disillusioned people who have lost all faith. The film was also criticized for two scenes "in bad taste," where the hero makes love to a woman still wearing his socks, and later performs a dance in a state of drunkenness with his pants unzipped. The council required forty-three corrections, and the authors firmly refused. The case was taken to the Conflict Commission, which did not find "anything in the film's ideological content, or in its aesthetic form that would prevent it being shown to the viewer," and ruled in favor of the filmmakers. There was also a little slap on the wrist for the council: "With the absolute majority of votes, the Commission found that the demands of the management are based on taste and not on aesthetic values." As a result, the film was released in its original form.[20] The Commission is keenly aware of its role as arbiter, and emphatically rejects any censorial functions. Plakhov explained: "We do not pretend to pass judgement on artistic matters, we do not assess value," on the other hand "we will not defend those films that we find obviously weak, or tendentious."[21]

Another case in point is the film *Tragedy in the Rock Style* (1989), by director Savva Kulish. Blocked by Mosfilm managers upon completion because its depiction of drug abuse and sex orgies was considered too crude, it had to wait one month before the conflict was resolved. This, however, occurred without the help of the Conflict Commission. The order to release the film came directly from Goskino's first deputy chairman, Armen Medvedev. The film *Little Doll* was also the object of a dispute between the director Isaac Friedberg and the head of the production unit "Youth," Rolan Bykov. Friedberg added a sex scene that was not in the script. It involved a relation between a female schoolteacher and one of her male students. Bykov felt it was inappropriate for a children's movie, but the director did not budge, and the Conflict Commission supported him. The film was moved to another Mosfilm unit, and soon released. More recently, Kira Muratova's latest film, *The Asthenic Syndrome* (1990), was released only because of considerable pressure from the Filmmakers Union. Goskino objected in particular to the use of foul language by a woman character. She uses the so-called *"mat'*," which is verbal abuse referring to sexual relations with the mother.

Another step was to eliminate the endless number of checkpoints involved in the mechanics of censorship under the old system.[22] Before perestroika, a script had first to pass the scrutiny of Glavlit, the watchdog of all printed materials, and possibly undergo subsequent checks by the military, the Ministry of Defense, and the KGB, if the plot involved one of those institutions. Once the film was in production, its course was monitored by the studios' internal security organs, euphemistically called artistic councils and editorial boards. After completion, the film had to be cleared by the central Repertory Control for release, and if it failed the test it was sent back to the studio for cuts and revisions. In case the revisions were not satisfactory, the film could be condemned to the "shelf." As if this routine procedure were not enough, a film had to undergo other occasional screenings within the Party's various departments of culture, from the city level up to the Central Committee. While this encumbering process is no longer in place, the Repertory Control has retained a perfunctory function in the release of films. Any negative decision, however, would be severely undermined by the filmmakers' right to appeal to the Conflict Commission.

The arbitrary editing of foreign films by the Editing and Dubbing Section of Goskino has also been under attack. Cavalier treatment of foreign imports started a long time ago. Some critics of this practice remind us that in the early 1920s none other than Eisenstein recklessly chopped up Fritz Lang's masterpiece, *Dr. Mabuse der Spieler*, and turned the three-hour-long feature into an hour-and-a-half propaganda piece (*agitka*) titled *The Gilded Rot*.[23] But for Eisenstein this was an isolated episode dictated by the harsh conditions of the time. More reprehensible, in the eyes of today's critics, are the bureaucratic scissors that have been at work in the following decades. Foreign films were placed into three categories by length: two hours and ten minutes, those in two parts; one and a half hours, the popular films; one hour and fifteen minutes, the "difficult" films. Therefore, besides ideological reasons for the cuts, most of the time the films were shortened for practical considerations. Another practice was to strike most of the prints in black and white, to economize on color film stock. *Tess*, by Roman Polanski was circulated in black and white and shortened by half an hour. Akira Kurosawa's *Dodescaden* (1970) was renamed *Under the Trolley's Wheels*; originally two hours and twenty minutes long, it was reduced to one and a half hours, and also circulated in black and white although it was Kurosawa's first experiment with color. *The Conformist*, by Bernardo Bertolucci, was cut down to one hour and twenty-five minutes from one hour fifty-five minutes, in a way that "it was impossible to connect one episode with another, and make sense of the action on the black and white screen."[24]

Perestroika, however, has improved the situation on this front as well. The current director of the Editing and Dubbing Section, G. Inozemtsev, maintained that reckless cutting is a practice of the past. "Not a single meter will be taken off" the films acquired since 1987 – Coppola's *The Conversation*, Forman's *Amadeus*, Fellini's *Ginger and Fred*, and others – said Inozemtsev. "If *The Conformist* were to appear today, it would be released in its original form." Goskino director, A. Kamshalov, later confirmed this statement on the TV show "Direct Line."[25]

The Union's centrifugal spin

While Goskino and the Filmmakers Union were able to find a working accommodation and live in peaceful coexistence, there was
infighting within the Union itself. From the outset, those that were
excluded from power formed an opposition front that shunned the
Union and undermined the work of the leadership from the outside.
There was also some dissatisfaction in the rank and file. Many complained that too much power had again been concentrated in a few
hands. As in the past, a number of the Union's Secretaries were also
chairmen of the studios' production units, members of Goskino's
Collegium, and held other key posts concomitantly. Here is the hypothetical, but quite possible, description of the plight of an unfortunate
filmmaker: "If a young director of children's films does not agree with
the position of Rolan Bykov, no matter where he turns for help, he
will bump into Bykov again and again: at Goskino (Bykov is a member of the Collegium), at the Filmmakers Union (a secretary and the
president of a commission), at Mosfilm (the artistic director of the
creative association for children's films), at the Children's Fund (a
member of the Presidium). He is even at the Academy of Pedagogical
Sciences."[26] The difference with past practices, however, is that these
are elected positions, rotating every five years, and not lifelong
appointments as they used to be.

   In an effort to respond to these concerns and reach out to the
members, the Union established some new general practices. The
membership was polled on a regular basis, and the results were taken
into account in making decisions. In addition, periodic open meetings
involving the Secretariat and the membership at large started taking
place in the main auditorium of the House of Cinema, in December
1987. The purpose of these meetings was for all film workers "to ask
the Union's leaders any question, and to share opinions on any troubling problem."[27] Upon request by the Union members, the leaders of
Goskino, too, agreed to share the podium. Judging by the steno-
graphic reports that periodically appear in the bulletin of the Union,
the leadership was under heavy fire from both the radical and the
conservative wings, with the floor delighting in an exercise of
glasnost not unlike the one displayed in the People's Congress.

   Among the leaders, too, there was some uneasiness. Worn out by
the political struggle and the everyday concerns of the office, Elem
Klimov decided to take a leave of absence, in January 1988, in order to
return to filmmaking. Another director of Klimov's generation,

Andrei Smirnov, agreed to act as First Secretary until the next election. Whatever the real reasons for Klimov's retreat, he seemed to have lost some popularity at the time of the Union's election of its representatives to the People's Congress. In January 1989, Klimov was nominated as a candidate, together with seventeen other colleagues. Two months later, however, he was not elected.[28] Goskino, too, was somehow shaken at the top when Alexander Kamshalov was accused of plagiarism on the page of *Komsomol'skaia Pravda*, on the eve of the XVI Moscow International Film Festival (1989). But the scandal caused only some painful embarrassment to Goskino's head, rather than triggering a change of cadres.[29]

In an effort to expand the support basis in the country at large, the All-Union Society of the Friends of Cinema was established, in 1988. It includes three sections: the federation of cine-amateurs, the federation of cineclubs, and the association of cine-educators. In Moscow, the public was offered new facilities with the inauguration of the Kino Center, also in 1988. The complex includes concert and lecture halls, movie houses, a Film Museum, and a press. The Film Museum's operations are totally funded by the Filmmakers Union. It is, therefore, not a state institution but a social organization. There was a project to open branches in all the republics. The aim of the Museum was "to raise the cultural level among viewers and film professionals, spread true humanistic ideals and democratic principles, instill socialist morals, patriotism, and internationalism."[30] While the aim was admirable, the rhetoric was a bit stiff, smacking of the old Bolshevik impulse to educate and uplift the masses. In the current situation, however, the reasons may also be economic since publicity is the first source of revenue. Finally, to reach out to the world, the FU established the Council on International Relations, whose functions include the selection of films for festivals in the USSR, and consultation on Soviet films to be sent to festivals abroad.

Within the Union the drive toward decentralization became gradually more pronounced. Professional guilds were organized to defend the interests of specific groups: actors, directors, screenwriters, critics, cinematographers, and others. As part of the Union, the guilds have an obligation to submit to the Union's statute and follow the resolutions of the Secretariat. At the same time, they were recognized as individual legal bodies, with the right to act on occasion independently from the Union. This was supposed, on one hand, to satisfy the inclination of certain guilds to dispense completely with the Union's leadership, and on the other, to maintain a solid united front.

The most serious challenge to the Union's cohesion, however, came from the republican unions and their secessionist tendencies. In order to involve the various republics in the general management, a group of representatives was invited to participate in all meetings of the Secretariat. Furthermore, a special commission monitored the problems arising in the republics, and provided help and advice. Nevertheless, fragmentation occurred when several republican unions approved their own new bylaws independently from the center. Ethnic nationalities and their sensibilities have been a thorn in the body of Gorbachev's reforms toward perestroika, and the general situation was reflected within the Union.

The issue of the nationalities was at the center of the filmmakers attention at their V Plenum (November 1988), titled "Democratization of the Community and Ways for the Development of the National Cinemas." On that occasion, it was decided to established a Filmmakers Union of the Russian Republic (RSFSR), in view of the projected reorganization of the central Union on a federative basis.[31] An appointed committee worked for one year on the preparation of the founding documents that were then approved in December 1989, at a meeting in Repino, a resort on the Gulf of Finland. Finally, the constituent Congress of the FU of the RSFSR took place in February 1990, and established the union's legal status. Igor Maslennikov of Leningrad was elected to the post of President, and he immediately invited Sergei Solovev of Moscow to cover the post of Co-president. Said Maslennikov: "I do not want to be called First Secretary because I intend to share the power of my mandate with my comrades."[32] The choice of the title was an indication that the new leaders were shunning the labels associated with the rule of the Communist Party, a practice that was then confirmed at the VI Congress, four months later. The establishment of the union of the Russian Republic paralleled the movement toward political sovereignty sought by the RSFSR under the leadership of Boris Yeltsin. The feelings of the Russian filmmakers matched those of the Russian population at large. They felt that "the development of Russian self-awareness occurred mostly as a gradual acknowledgment of having been exploited and neglected."[33] There was also a side opposed to the creation of a Russian republican union. The opponents argued that this would only increase the bureaucratic apparatus, favor the self-serving "games" of the present administration, and finally lead to the disintegration of the central Union. These sentiments were fueled when further fragmentation occurred with the creation of the Moscow Organization of the FU and the Leningrad Organization of the FU, which were granted the status of republican unions in recognition of their numbers (Leningrad is the second largest with 520 members).

The final act of the decentralization process unfolded at the VI Congress of the FU (June 5–7, 1990), that took place one year before the regular five-year term. On the eve of the Congress, the revolutionary moment seemed to be over. The jubilant mood that marked the historical meeting four years earlier had been replaced by anxiety and frustration. The state of the industry from an economic point of view was generally described as being "catastrophic" – those with a sense of black humor labeled it "katastroika."[34] In July 1989, after consultation with a number of republican unions, the Secretariat voted to anticipate the Congress by one year, and the decision was then confirmed at the next Plenum, in November. This fact revealed a sense of urgency. On the other hand, the decision was met with some resistance by a number of filmmakers, including some of the Union Secretaries, who thought that four years were not enough to implement fully the New Model.[35] But First Secretary Elem Klimov, who resumed his office in January 1990, maintained that "the time was ripe" for discussion of some pressing issues. First among them, the drafting of a new statute. "The present statute," Klimov said, "is a kind of Stalinist Constitution" that does not reflect the situation that developed in the economy and in society.[36] Other items on the agenda were: the assessment of accomplishments in the implementation of the New Model; the drafting of a new platform; the proposal for a Law on Cinema; and the election of a new leadership.

Hundreds of delegates from all the republics convened in Moscow for the opening of the Congress. Given the situation that had developed in the Baltic regions, the Lithuanians chose not to send an official delegation, but an unofficial group was granted observer status. After three days of emotional reports and heated debates that looked and sounded like democracy on the verge of anarchy, the delegates fulfilled their mandate.

The Union will be reorganized as a federation of independent republican unions, and to this effect a commission was charged with drafting a new statute. The central governing body, that changed its name from Secretariat to Council of Representatives, will consist of one representative for each union plus a President and two Vice-

Presidents. In practice, this means that the administrative apparatus will be greatly reduced, from a Secretariat of fifty-one members to a Council of Representatives of twenty.[37] More important in the eyes of many, no more than three representatives will be from Moscow. The new federative structure reflects the mood of the country at large, striving for autonomy from the center and for freedom of initiative.

The election of the three top leaders for the first time was held by secret ballot. Outgoing First Secretary Elem Klimov, who was nominated but firmly declined, was replaced by Dovlat Khudonazarov who, following the latest trend, assumed the title of President. The election of Khudonazarov was revealing of the Union's direction in two significant ways. Firstly, the new President came from the republic of Tadzhikistan, and was therefore emblematic of the movement toward decentralization of power. Secondly, he had been involved in politics for a number of years and at the time of the election he was a deputy of the People's Congress and a member of the Supreme Soviet. He will be able to defend the interests of the filmmakers at the highest level. A film director by profession, Khudonazarov had not been working in film for several years, but judging by the applause from the floor during his position statement he was popular with the electorate. He is young, handsome in an unassuming way, and came across as being an honest, solid, and reliable leader. At the VI Congress, revolutionary charisma was out, business and politics were in. As vice-presidents, the Congress elected Andrei Razumovsky, the head of the Association of Independent Cinema and of a private enterprise, and Maria Zvereva, a young and respected screenwriter. Joked Razumovsky, "This Congress was no less revolutionary than the previous one. Think about it, they elected a Tadzhik as President, and as Vice-Presidents, a woman and a capitalist."[38]

Khudonazarov pledged to continue the work of the previous leadership that, although often criticized in recent times, had the undeniable merit of giving the film industry a great impetus and of playing a major role in the implementation of glasnost. The new Union, however, will play a lesser role, having released considerable power to the federative constituents. Instead of exercising centralized control, it will serve as a coordinating and representative body.

Education, research, the press

The filmmakers' reformist spirit suffered a setback in the education sector – the All–Union State Institute of Cinema (VGIK) that prepares the future generation of directors, actors, technical personnel, and critics, and that operates under the jurisdiction of Goskino. The impulse for change came from the students themselves, who as early as April 1986 started questioning the dismal state of instruction, the lack of management, and the practice of clientelism in deciding on admissions. Subsequently, the Filmmakers Union established a commission to help the students in their effort to restructure the academic curriculum and dismiss lethargic administrators and teachers. The results were not worth the struggle, though. The Institute head, Vitali Zhdan, was sent into retirement, only to be replaced by his deputy, Alexander Novikov.[39] The academic council dismissed the demand of the students and of some progressive professors that vacant administration positions be filled with filmmakers of renown – creative people with actual work experience. One such candidate for the post of rector was Sergei Solovev, film director, Union Secretary, and head of one of Mosfilm creative associations. But his candidacy was vetoed by the academic council and the Ministry of Education. In the summer of 1989, the situation at VGIK was officially evaluated by a joint commission of Goskino's Collegium and the Filmmakers Union. The Institute was found wanting in many areas, and sharply reprimanded in the final resolution. The evaluating commission noted that "neither the rectorate, or the VGIK Soviet were able to spearhead the perestroika of the institute, and did not achieve any serious, positive results in the educational, scholarly, and creative activities of all the departments." The commentary to this statement acknowledged that it was "the first time that a resolution of such severity was adopted to designate the work of the institute as unsatisfactory."[40]

Less resistant to perestroika was the All-Union Scientific Research Institute of Film Art (VNIIK), the main Goskino agency for scholarly research and publications. The staunch conservative Vladimir Baskakov, formerly deputy director of Goskino and the Institute director for thirteen years, was replaced by the writer-screenwriter Ales Adamovich in 1987. Adamovich was one of Klimov's close associates and the scriptwriter for his film *Come and See*. Two years later, Adamovich was elected to the People's Congress together with nine other representatives of the Filmmakers Union, and joined the most radical wing, the Interregional Group. The turnover among the staff was not so dramatic. Many of the Institute's researchers kept their jobs, but the change at the top generated a new dynamism and an entrepreneurial spirit that resulted in scholarly exchanges and projects with Western partners.

Another focus of the filmmakers' reforms was the specialized press. The two main film journals, the popular *Soviet Screen* and the scholarly *Film Art*, had been published jointly by Goskino and the Filmmakers Union for decades. Now the Union argued that the filmmakers needed a forum of their own, in order to acquire a distinct voice in the political arena. After a three-year struggle the filmmakers scored a major victory. In January 1989, *Film Art* became the sole organ of the Filmmakers Union. The event, however, did not signal a split between the two leading institutions, rather a fair territorial division. According to an announcement in the *Information Bulletin*, the project was approved by the Central Committee with the full support of Goskino.[41] Already in January 1988, the section, *Screen*, started appearing in the newspaper *Soviet Culture*; later, in 1990, it became a weekly publication called *Screen and Stage*. Furthermore, in 1989, the Union received permission to proceed with the plan for the publication of its own newspaper, a request that had been turned down three years earlier; the first issue of the monthly, *House of Cinema*, was released in 1990.

With the elimination of censorship, independent publishers entered the domain of the periodical press, once exclusively under state control. The independent film periodicals today are: *Film Art* (*Iskusstvo kino*; organ of the Filmmakers Union of the USSR; monthly; 60,000 copies; illustrated, scholarly/intellectual bent; covers Soviet and foreign film, history, theory, culture, and sociology); *House of Cinema* (*Dom kino*; organ of the Central House of Filmmakers; monthly bulletin; 50,000 copies; popular bent with a taste for sensationalism, the mass audience orientation is due to commercial considerations because the publication is self-supporting); *Cine-Phantom* (*Sine-fantom*; individual publishers, as opposed to organizations; irregularly issued; number of copies varies; avant-garde orientation, with an aesthetic and psychoanalytic bent; covers "parallel cinema" and foreign film; unique in its genre in the USSR; started in 1989).

But most film periodicals are still state-run. Among them are: *Film Research Notes* (*Kinovedcheskie zapiski*; published by VNIIK; quarterly; 2,000 copies; scholarly research in film history and theory; started in 1989); *Screen* (*Ekran*; published by VNIIK; yearly; 50,000 copies; illustrated journal for a general educated audience; covers Soviet and foreign film; reviews, criticism, profiles, festivals, events); *Soviet*

Screen (*Sovetskii ekran*; organ of Goskino and the Filmmakers Union; eighteen issues per year; 1,000,000 copies; illustrated journal for a mass audience; covers Soviet and foreign film; various topics in simplified form, events, criticism, reviews, history, celebrity profiles, statistics; runs popular contest and readers' mail; since January 1991, it changed its name to *Screen*); *Screen and Stage* (*Ekran i stsena*; supplement to *Soviet Culture*, the organ of the Central Committee of the CPSU; same mass orientation as *Soviet Screen*, but shorter; started in 1990); *The Film Viewer Companion* (*Sputnik kinozritelia*; published by Soiuzinformkino; monthly; 800,000 copies; caters to a general audience; provides reviews and evaluation of current releases, and recommendation based on viewers' groupings); *New Films* (*Novye fil'my*; published by Soiuzinformkino; monthly; 100,000 copies; designed for distributors and theater managers; information on current repertory, film summary, commentary, credits, suggested target audience; started in 1964); *Opinions* (*Mneniia*; published by Soiuzinformkino; quarterly; 25,000 copies; covers only Soviet cinema; runs longer reviews of the current releases, presenting the same film from the point of view of various critics; film analysis is bland and more focused on content than form; started in 1989); *Lens* (*Ob'ektiv*; published by Soiuzinformkino; 23,000 copies; same as *Opinions*, but covers only films from the socialist countries; after the changes in Eastern Europe, however, the journal has lost its focus); *Soviet Film* (ceased to exist in January 1991; it was published in Russian, English, French, German, and Spanish; a publication of Sovexportfilm; monthly; illustrated journal intended for foreign audiences; covered Soviet and foreign film; events, festivals, reviews, profiles, criticism, analysis); *Cinema* (*Kino*; published jointly by the Latvian Filmmakers Union and the Latvian Ministry of Culture, in Riga; monthly; 10,000 copies; the best known of the republican film journals for its "liberal" orientation already in pre-perestroika times; used to publish articles barred from Moscow journals; still hosts prominent Moscow and Leningrad critics; orientation similar to *Film Art*).[42]

In the first four years of perestroika, the filmmakers took up a heavy political and administrative burden, within the industry and in the government. Thanks to their dedication, and to Gorbachev's favorable policies, which spearheaded the reform of Goskino and the abolition of censorship, the Soviet film industry acquired the potential for artistic development and economic expansion. The period between the two Congresses of the Filmmakers Union witnessed an experiment in the industry's financial structure, from the idealistic and impractical New Model of production and distribution to the concrete realization of independent enterprises. Many problems remained unresolved at the closing of the VI Congress – distribution being the most pressing one. The new course was only sketched rather than precisely mapped out, as was the case in the past. This reflected the aspiration of the members toward decentralization and autonomy, and therefore signaled a strength rather than a weakness. The relationship with Goskino has become increasingly more tense, although not strained, due to the fact that the state committee has lost so many of its prerogatives and is struggling to preserve some functions in order to justify its survival. Whatever developments the next decade will bring, at the beginning of the 1990s the filmmakers have stated their goals loud and clear: private initiative, free market, foreign participation.

3   Learning a new game:
khozraschet

The New Model

In the euphoria of the revolutionary moment the newly-elected
Union's Secretariat put forth a number of resolutions designed to
change radically the system of production and distribution in the
cinema industry, according to a "New Model" consistent with Gorbachev's vision of a global perestroika. This was reflected in the final
report of the V Congress, "On the Ideological–Artistic Tasks of Soviet
Cinema in the Light of the Decisions of the XXVII Congress of the
CPSU," and reaffirmed less than one year later, at the II Plenum of
the Filmmakers Union. In his opening speech, Elem Klimov made it
clear that "the first plenary session after the V Congress must be
devoted . . . to the most complex and the hottest issue of our
cinematography – the issue of its fundamental, radical perestroika,"
and added that the revolutionary directives announced by Gorbachev
at the XXVII Congress "created the political, ideological, and psychological preconditions" for a sharp turn.[1] An article in *Pravda* officially
sanctioned the filmmakers' position. It read:

The new model is a moral one . . . Although in our Constitution there are
good pronouncements on creative freedom, this freedom has not yet been
implemented in practice. As soon as the studios become autonomous and
self-supporting . . . the artist whose thoughts are shaped through suffering
and who is in touch with his time will acquire a greater weight . . . The V
Congress of the Filmmakers has started a struggle against routine thinking . . .
and has marked a change of style in Soviet cinema.[2]

The foundation of the New Model was built on a few simple
principles: freedom of expression, managerial decentralization, self-
financing economy, free market.[3] While the principles were sound,
the goals proved to be too ambitious given the critical state of the
country at large, and remained partly unfulfilled at the end of the
decade. Already in November 1988, the participants in the V Plenum

of the Union, noted that "some three years ago there was more optimism and faith, now there is a prevalent feeling of alarm, because virtually not a single one of the resolutions of the V Congress has been completely implemented."[4] And one year later, a prominent screenwriter–playwright complained that "after all the disputes and discussions about perestroika . . . there are no concrete results."[5] The major successes were registered in the area of artistic freedom, thanks to the policy of glasnost and the virtual elimination of censorship. Decentralization and democratization of the administrative apparatus also had some momentum, and deeply affected the nerve centers of the film industry – Goskino, the Filmmakers Union, the studios. The economic sector, however, proved to be more resistant to reforms, being strictly interconnected with the state of the country's economy overall. Some significant steps were taken in the direction of independent production and market-oriented distribution, but as a rule the studios still relied on Goskino as the major source of funds.

The difficult path walked by the reformers has been punctuated by numerous drafts of the original document, "A Model and Structure of Cinematography: Basic Principles and Mechanisms," also known as the Base Model, that was first approved at the II Plenum (January 1987). By the spring of 1988, when a new version was officially approved by Goskino and the Filmmakers Union, the document had been amended forty-two times.[6] Even so, the process was not over. One year later, at the VII Plenum (March 1989), the leaders were saying that the Model "was moving toward its realization" (A. Gerasimov), that "the Model has been worked out" (Ibragim-bekov), that "it is ready" (Lotianu), that "there is hope that soon the New Model will be signed" (Lebeshev), that "the base has been laid for a production–economic experiment: the New Model" (Plakhov). There were already warnings that the Model as it was worked out "was not a perfect one" (Chernykh). In general, the film leadership stressed the flexible nature of the New Model, that kept adjusting to the everchanging reality, and made a point to reiterate at every opportunity that the Model "is not a dogma."[7] The last version of the Model, called "Perestroika in Filmmaking," was approved by the Council of Ministers in June 1989. But, after the VI Congress, with the drafting of a new platform and a strong push toward privatization, the Model lost momentum and became history.[8]

Restructuring the studios

The implementation of the New Model started within the studios. The main reform was the revamping of the creative associations (*tvorcheskie ob'edineniia*), or production units, that were first established in the 1960s. Although in those early years the idea was to improve the production process by decentralization, until the recent perestroika the artistic directors had dictatorial power, and the creative associations were strictly controlled by Goskino through a chain of command staffed with bureaucrats and Party officials. Under the New Model, the composition of the creative associations, their status within the studios, their relations with Goskino, and the function of the artistic directors have been reassessed.

The number of creative associations varies according to the studio size, from two or three in the smaller studios to around ten in the larger ones. Of the thirty-nine studios nationwide, Mosfilm is by far the largest, with 4,000 workers, eleven creative associations and a yearly production of approximately fifty features. In principle, the associations are organized on a thematic basis – genre films, psychological dramas, literary adaptations, children's films, and others – but often the dividing line is blurred. The changes that took place there are typical of the reform in the other studios as well. Six of the artistic directors at Mosfilm came from the ranks of the new leadership that took over the major film institutions, with the other five reconfirmed in their posts by election.

The association "Comrade," for example, headed by the renowned film director Yuli Raizman, was established some twenty years ago. Its name was subsequently changed to the Third Association, and recently restored to the original. It specializes in social–psychological drama, which Raizman considers the most promising trend in film – and with good reason, because as a prolific author in that genre he has never failed to reach a large audience. Another twenty-year-old association, "Time," previously called the First Association, is headed by Sergei Bondarchuk. One of the most popular leading actors of the 1960s, turned film director, Bondarchuk was perceived as a right-winger at the inception of perestroika, and removed from the Secretariat of the Filmmakers Union. Because of his artistic reputation, however, he maintained his position in the studio. His association specializes in films based on literary classics and historical themes. The veteran film director Vladimir Naumov is still the head of "Union," an association that he managed for two decades together with his late colleague, Alexander Alov. Formerly called "The Writer and the Film Worker," the association can boast of no small achievement, having produced more than a hundred films over the years, including three masterpieces by Andrei Tarkovsky (*Andrei Rublev*, *Mirror*, and *Solaris*). It also hosted Klimov and Smirnov at the beginning of their careers, and today favors the cooperation of young authors with established ones. The aim of the association is to raise the visual standards of modern cinema, and focus on a wide range of pictures, from philosophical subjects to satirical comedies. The association that has been probably the most successful at the box office in recent years is "Rhythm," headed by another seasoned and talented director, Georgi Danelia. Its specialty is "serious" comedies in which social problems are treated with a light touch. Last of the old-time associations is the "Association of Television Films," headed by Sergei Kolosov, and devoted entirely to the production of TV serials and features.

Among the new associations is "Youth," under the leadership of actor and director Rolan Bykov. Its mission is to restore the production of children's films that was virtually halted in the 1970s with the liquidation of the original Youth association at Mosfilm. Other associations of the time of perestroika are "The Circle," headed by Sergei Solovev and dealing with a variety of styles and subjects, from documentaries to literary adaptations; "Genre," headed by Vladimir Menshov, specializing in established genres – the comedy, the melodrama, the thriller; "The Word," headed by screenwriter and playwright Valentin Chernykh, focusing on outstanding scripts on controversial moral and social problems; "Start," headed by Karen Shakhnazarov, designed to launch young filmmakers, and to provide them with the freedom to work on themes and genres of their choice. Finally, the association "Debut," that has operated for many years in very sad conditions, was revamped under the leadership of the young screenwriter Yuri Arabov. As its name implies, the association sponsors debutante filmmakers, but on a national scale. The administrative office, located at Mosfilm, funds productions and provides general supervision, but the films are actually shot in the studios of the republics.[9]

Within his own creative association, each artistic director serves as the chair of an artistic council, that is responsible for the unit's financial and administrative management. His function is similar to that of a Western producer, although it involves fewer risks. All these administrative positions are elective and renewable every five years, to ensure efficiency, stimulate initiatives, and avoid the creation of a permanent bureaucracy. The artistic directors are automatically members of Mosfilm Board of Directors and participate in the general management of the studio-relations with state organs, financial supervision, maintenance of facilities and equipment – together with the heads of the administrative departments and the Director of the studio, appointed by Goskino and the Filmmakers Union. Mosfilm Board consists now of sixteen people, down from an overstaffed body of sixty-two, and is chaired by Mosfilm general director, Vladimir Dostal.[10]

Each association employs a team of workers, technicians, support staff, and artistic personnel. The composition of the production team varies by the demands of a specific film project. Directors, actors, costume and set designers, cameramen, and others are hired on contract for the duration of the project. In the past, studio personnel were hired on a permanent basis, and kept on the payroll regardless of whether they were actually engaged in a production. Now the associations will retain a small core, and draw according to their needs from a "creative reserve" of available specialists who would move freely from production to production. This is to encourage competition and to thin down the ranks of ineffectual workers. The application of this capitalist principle, though, has been received with some hostility, stirring fears of unemployment in a society where everyone has a constitutional right to a job. To ease anxiety, the Filmmakers Union established Kinofond, in 1987, a well-endowed financial institution that provides for the social needs of the membership, including unemployment compensation in between jobs.[11] On the other hand, Mosfilm as well as the other studios felt the pinch of rising production costs. As soon as the technical departments and services became autonomous, the studios had to rent equipment, costumes, transportation, and props for steep prices. In addition, technical and artistic personnel fees went up considerably due to the competition from independent producers. Often, the studios have trouble retaining the best specialists because they cannot match the fees.

The Gorky film studio, also in Moscow, is worthy of note for being in the vanguard of the reforms. It hosts five creative associations, and produces about twenty films a year. The most controversial association within the studio is Lad'ia ("The Boat"), that produced and distributed the blockbuster *Kings of Crime* (1988) about mafia organizations in the USSR. This was the first instance when a studio got to manage the distribution of a film directly, on a large scale, bypassing the government-run network. Once specializing in pictures for youth, the Gorky studio is expanding its repertoire, because of the economic necessities. The studio also rented out its facilities to the independent film cooperative Podarok ("The Gift"), for the production of Vasily Pichul's second film *Dark Nights in Sochi* (1989). This kind of arrangement was another first.

Lenfilm in Leningrad employs 2,600 people. The studio is articulated into eight creative associations, and a Videofilm unit (headed by Alexander Sokurov). The studio produces fifteen to twenty feature films a year, and just as many TV programs. Only three of the creative associations were operating on a self-financing basis by the end of 1989, and 30 percent of the studio's budget came from Goskino to make films on order by state agencies.

The restructuring of the republican studios was precipitated by the liquidation of the local Goskinos. Under the jurisdiction of the republic's Ministry of Culture, the studios are still subjected to a certain degree of regulation, but most regard the switch as an improvement of their autonomy – especially in the case of the smaller republics, where the Goskino apparatus had weighed down on only one studio. Some studios feel even too confident of their newly acquired status. One paradoxical case occurred at Belarusfilm (Minsk), where the studio's administration, behaving according to the "old model," arbitrarily stopped the production of a film near completion, confiscated the existing footage from the creative association, and fired the film director. Appeals to the Moscow central authorities on the part of the filmmaker and the artistic council resulted in official resolutions from both the FU Secretariat and Goskino, ordering the studio to return the materials. But the response was a disdainful *nyet*, implying that Moscow should not meddle in local affairs. Democratization in this particular case has tied the hands of the central powers that, ironically, wanted to enforce individual rights.[12]

Radical thinkers argued that the reform did not go far enough. The artistic director of Mosfilm association "The Word," Valentin Chernykh, voiced his concerns on the pages of *Film Art*. He maintained that although in theory the artistic directors now have to compete for election on the basis of individual talent, in practice the election results are predictable.

A few film directors got together and nominated some candidates, or the candidate put forth himself, having ensured the support of a number of major film directors who were promised contracts with the given creative association. Then, the candidates were discussed and confirmed by Mosfilm Party Committee, the Goskino Collegium, and the Filmmakers Union Secretariat . . . But in the past, too, the candidates to the post of artistic director were discussed at the Party Committee, the Collegium, and the Secretariat. Now confirmation is based on personal value, rather than on a program . . . But all in all, there has been no revolutionary perestroika in the electoral system of the artistic directors, the old ones decreased in number, new ones appeared (there are more creative associations now), and basically all the new ones are Union secretaries. I am one of them. Other Union secretaries are also on the Goskino Collegium. We are faced again with the old principle of the administrative–managerial apparatus, where the same individual occupies both an appointing and an appointed post.[13]

While this was generally true for the major studios in the initial stage, independent cooperatives and associations soon started operating as free enterprises, marking the beginning of a new and more significant phase of economic restructuring.

Freeing the market

The most optimistic forecast of the Soviet economists soon after the rise of Gorbachev put all production enterprises on a self-financing system (*khozraschet*) by January 1988.[14] Filmmakers were eager to meet the deadline, regardless of the difficulties involved in the transition for such a complex organism as the film industry. The task was unrealistic, as was the projected pace of the general perestroika. Notwithstanding the impatient claims of the left-wingers, the country was not prepared to sustain a sudden economic shock. Change, however, occurred and reforms were gradually implemented. By the beginning of 1990, the film industry was already transformed in many respects, and steadily moving toward the realization of full *khozraschet*.

When the filmmakers produced the first version of the Base Model, they had already a precedent to cite. At the II Plenum, where the original document was first approved, several speakers reminded the audience of the Experimental Creative Studio established in 1963, in the wake of the short-lived new economic policy introduced by Kosygin. Most of the speakers, belonging to the generation of the turbulent 1960s, stressed the connection between the New Model principles and the ideals and activism of those years. The story of the ECS is virtually unknown outside the inner circles, and, given its relevance today, it deserves to be sketched.

A threesome of enterprising young fellows, fed up with the shortcomings of the state management, and convinced of the advantages of an economy regulated by supply and demand, drafted a plan for an experimental studio based on a new production system. They submitted the plan to the Council of Ministers of the USSR. The Council, by special decree, ordered Goskino to test the idea with a practical experiment. As a result, the Experimental Creative Studio was established, under the sole management of the three original founders – Grigory Chukhrai, as artistic director; Konstantin Simonov, as head of the script department; and Vladimir Pozner, Sr., as executive director.[15] The technical facilities remained under the jurisdiction of Goskino, but in every other respect the ECS was independent. Recently, Chukhrai highlighted the connection between that enterprise and the present situation: "The principles of our new system were the same as those being introduced today in the most disparate sectors of the economy: *khozraschet*, evaluation of work according to the results, pay in relation to the workload." In addition, he stressed the point that is at the core of the current perestroika: "We did not have any financial sources, except for the revenues from the distribution of our films."[16] The studio, therefore, was compelled to produce films, that would guarantee large audiences and long runs. The danger of going bankrupt prevented the production of "grey" pictures.

The experiment was extraordinarily successful. Productivity rose sharply, waste was cut drastically, the profits were astronomical in comparison with the average state-subsidized production – more than three million rubles of profit over the financial plan for each film. Attendance was constantly at the highest level – an average of 32 million viewers over one year circulation for each film. "These are fantastic figures," said Chukhrai, "not only for that time but for the present time as well."[17] The leaders of the ECS prepared a report on the results, and worked out a project for the gradual introduction of the system in other studios. But personal success is more often resented than rewarded, especially in a system that promotes mediocrity. In fact the activities of the ECS were perceived as a threat to the comfortable routine of the untalented and apathetic majority. The ECS collective was accused of pocketing big profits, a fact that has always stirred the jealousy of those who are incapable of individual initiative. But the charge was unwarranted, according to Chukhrai. "We made big profits for the industry, but our personal income in comparison to the income of the present co-op entrepreneurs was rather meager."[18] In 1967, the studio produced the controversial film, *The Beginning of an Unknown Era*, censored and shelved for the next twenty years. This provided fuel for a campaign against the studio's activities. With the appointment of Filipp Ermash at the head of Goskino (1972), the ECS was officially suppressed. It was renamed Mosfilm Experimental Creative Association, was incorporated in the regular production process, and ceased to be experimental. Chukhrai reminisced about that sad moment: "'The experiment has been successfully carried out,' said Ermash, 'but an experiment cannot go on forever.' This was tantamount to a deliberate and premeditated murder of a healthy, blooming organism."[19] Of the three founders, only Chukhrai remained at Mosfilm, until the very recent perestroika of the studios. Over those years, though, he made only three films. Looking back on his career from today's perspective, Chukhrai focused on the positive rather than the negative. The Brezhnev time did not inspire him, he said. "But the problem was not only with the epoch, it was also with me . . . I do not want to be perceived as a victim of the System, and in fact I was not a victim. I was in a constant fight with the System, and the one who fights both hits and gets hit. This is normal."[20]

The first stage toward the implementation of *khozraschet* was to change the mechanics of allotments from the Goskino yearly budget for film production. Starting with 1988, each creative association within the studios received a bulk sum, based on a production program submitted to Goskino. The association is then responsible for producing the films of its choice and returning the original sum at the end of the first year after release. If there is profit after expenses, the association has a right to keep it, and reinvest it in the production of new films. The association may also use the profits to update the studio's technological base, which in most instances is in dire need of renewal. The second stage – *khozraschet* on a full basis – will begin when the associations no longer need to "borrow" the initial capital from the state, but will be able to plan and finance their films from profits alone. This cannot happen, as a rule, before three to four years from the beginning of the reform, allowing two and a half years for production time and one year circulation.

However, some daring pioneers in the uncharted territory of capitalist enterprise emerged almost immediately. Radical financial innovations occurred with the numerous production and distribution cooperatives that have mushroomed all over the country, soon after the Law on Cooperatives became effective (July 1, 1988).[21] An attempt by the Council of Ministers to outlaw them, in December 1988, was defeated a few months later with the support of the Filmmakers Union, that defended the rights of the cooperatives at an official hearing. The controversy that followed the crackdown was sharp and pointed, as reported by several media. The authorities offered a moralistic reason: "The censors were afraid of the anarchy bugaboo; they would say, you make a small concession and everybody rushes to shoot porno flicks and anti-Soviet movies."[22] But the real reason was probably economic, or a matter of prestige, since many cooperatives soon became quite competitive.

Most of the cooperative organizers saw their firms as a necessary development in film production and distribution. They thought their enterprises were "the only salvation for the cinema industry, agonizing under an excessive workload and a lack of production means."[23] The number of independents grew steadily in the next two years. Their presence soon became a major factor in the economic reshaping of the film industry, and required a clear identity. The Association of Independent Cinema (ANK) was therefore established and officially registered with the Moscow City Council, in May 1990. At the time, the Association included fifty-five organizations nationwide (by the time of the VI Congress, June 1990, they were already seventy-eight), involved in production, distribution, and social activities. The members covered a wide range, from small cooperatives, relatively unknown, to major enterprises headed by top directors, such as Sergei Solovev, Nikita Mikhalkov, Vasily Pichul, and Yuri Kara. It also includes the Filmmakers Union and Kinofond. The Association was meant to provide its members with legal, social, and political protection, and help securing financing and establishing business relations with foreign firms.[24]

ANK foresaw production of thirty features in 1990, and sixty in the next year, plus hundreds of documentaries, educational, and animation pictures (up to now, the average yearly output was 150 features for the whole industry). ANK's president, Andrei Razumovsky, who is also the head of the independent production firm Fora Film, saw the task of the Association as the creation of a system of production and distribution alternative to the state system. "We are not against Goskino," said Razumovsky, "we are against Goskino's monopoly," and added that ANK is ready to welcome as members any of the studios that will choose to leave Goskino.[25]

Among the independents, the cooperative Podarok ("The Gift") is the best known abroad. At the head of the enterprise is the young director Vasily Pichul, whose first film, *Little Vera*, brought him international recognition. Together with a core of collaborators from the previous film – screenwriter Maria Khmelik (his wife), cameraman Efim Reznivov, editor Elena Zabolotskaia, and manager Mark Levin – Pichul produced the feature *Dark Nights in Sochi* (1989) financed by a bank loan. With a distribution deal with Italy's RAI as guarantee, Podarok obtained a 500,000 ruble loan from the Bank for Social Innovation (Zhilsotsbank). The agreement provided for the profits to be split between the bank and Podarok, with the RAI sales division "Sacis" handling foreign sales worldwide. Pichul's cooperative rented space and facilities at the Gorky Studio in Moscow, and received technical assistance in production and post-production from Italian producer Silvia D'Amico.[26]

An episode revealing a lively entrepreneurial spirit occurred in Leningrad. Writer Gennady Begelov appeared on TV to raise money in order to make a movie out of his autobiographical novel, *A File On Me*, telling of his ordeal in a labor camp. The viewers responded generously. With the donations – approximately 50,000 rubles – he made a short and presented it to the Lenfilm council. The studio was impressed and decided to include a full-length feature project in their next production plan.

The film industry, like other industries, benefited from the Law on State Enterprises, passed in 1987. The studios and the independent producers acquired the right to negotiate foreign deals directly without going through the state channels. This was a major breakthrough that shattered the monopoly of Sovexportfilm on the international market, and gave individual associations the opportunity to deal with foreign currency. In most cases, this was a real necessity because one of the main benefits resulting from foreign sales is the possibility to purchase Western equipment and film stock of better quality. Foreign deals and joint ventures can now be sought not only in marketing a film abroad, but also in the form of co-productions. At first, the prospective foreign partners were a little disoriented by the changes in the administrative structure. Used to dealing with a monolithic and predictable bureaucracy, they were suddenly faced with a plethora of independent organizations. Disorientation and enthusiasm were initially responsible for a huge number of projects and negotiations. But because of the financial complexities involved only a few concrete deals were actually struck by the end of 1989.

A few examples will better illustrate the situation. The film corporation Interdet, representing five major Soviet studios, produces films in all categories and manages a substantial distribution network in the USSR. Its Western branch, Primodessa Film, is a joint-venture company with 50 percent German ownership. It handles Soviet movies in the West and Western-made movies in the USSR, and provides equipment and personnel for films produced in the USSR. The Italian presence in the Soviet film industry has been prominent since the early 1960s. The trend has only been reinforced in recent times. Among dozens of new projects were *The Barber of Siberia* (produced by Angelo Rizzoli's Erre Produzioni, directed by Nikita Mikhalkov, starring Meryl Streep), *Mother* (based on M. Gorky's novel, produced by Nello Santi, directed by Gleb Panfilov, starring Inna Churikova), and *Drums of Fire* (co-produced by Italy, Morocco, Spain, and the USSR). International Cinema Co. (ICC), headed by producers Rispoli and Colombo, has specialized in mega-co-productions with foreign partners since its beginnings, in 1986. As new opportunities opened up in the Soviet Union, ICC started negotiating historical blockbusters, such as *Genghiz Khan* (with Kirghizfilm, directed by T. Okeev), *And Quiet Flows the Don* (with Mosfilm, directed by S. Bondarchuk of *War and Peace* fame), and *Tamerlane* (with Uzbekfilm, directed by A. Khamraev). Most of the deals with the state agencies involve merely buying services from the Soviets, rather than a real 50 percent split of costs and profits. The financial structure for such deals remains rather complex, and seldom profitable, because of the non-convertibility of the ruble. Soiuzkinoservice, which has evolved out of the defunct Sovinfilm, is authorized to finance foreign and Soviet film production, and distribute its products in the USSR, but its main function is to provide services to foreign producers. The latter included, among others, CCC Filmkunst (West Berlin) for thirteen TV episodes and two feature films based on Jack London's novels, called *Alaska Stories*; South Carolina Educational Communications (US), together with Yorkshire TV (UK), for *The History of the Soviet State*; and even Lorimar (US) for an episode of *Dallas*. Soiuzkinoservice also launched a joint venture with Greek Varas Video and a Dutch company to build a video production facility and market their products.

With few exceptions, the American film industry does not seem to be able to deal effectively with the Soviets. Eager to get a foothold in a potentially very lucrative market, American producers are held back by the uncertainties of the political situation and by the impossibility of making a profit in hard currency. Only a very few are willing to accept revenues in rubles, open an account in a Soviet bank, and wait until the day the ruble becomes convertible. According to film director Savva Kulish, "it was easier for Reagan and Gorbachev to make an agreement than it is for a Soviet and an American studio."[27] Nevertheless, in the summer of 1989, a delegation of the American Film Marketing Association participated in the Moscow Film Festival, displaying their products at the film market. That trip produced some results: an agreement for three pictures paid for in US dollars, and a percentage distribution arrangement in rubles. After recovery of costs, 50 percent of the ruble revenues will be deposited in the Soviet Union, waiting for more favorable times.[28] Another US–Soviet joint venture is the agreement between Sovexportfilm and Time Warner Inc., to build and operate multiplex theaters in the Soviet Union (March 1990).

State agencies are by no means absent from the scene. Challenged by the competition, Sovexportfilm quickly adjusted to the new times, skillfully using its massive organization and considerable resources. According to reports in *Variety*, as of the summer of 1989, Sovexportfilm cooperated with some 300 film, television, and video companies in 110 countries. Sovexportfilm "sells about 500 Soviet feature films annually, showing in theaters, TV, and video. In 1988, export champs were *The Cold Summer of '53* (26 countries), *Commissar* (25), *Little Vera* (22), *Assa* (16), *Before Dawn* (14), and *Forgotten Melody for Flute* (12) . . . About 150 foreign features, half from Socialist nations, are bought every year for showing in the Soviet Union."[29] In one of its sleek brochures, it claimed to be still "the biggest company specializing in export and import of films and a reliable partner You can trust." Indeed, some foreign partners preferred to deal with a solid and well-established organization, rather than take risks with inexperienced newcomers. Sovexportfilm participated in a Soviet–German joint venture, together with Berlin-based Films Cosmos and Munich-based Futura/Filmverlag. The new company, called Felix Film will have a branch office in Moscow to deal with distribution of German and Soviet films in the other country, and to provide support, assistance, and technology to Soviet producers. Goskino has struck a deal with Finland's Finnkino, by which the Tallin movie theater, "President," will show exclusively Finnish films, and the USSR-owned "Kosmos" theater, in Helsinki, will show only Soviet films. Moreover, profits from the Tallin box office have been earmarked for the production of a Finno-Soviet documentary, *The Caribbean Crisis*.

Sovexportfilm, however, lost its most valuable asset. At the Cannes Film Festival (May 1990), Mosfilm declared its complete independence from Sovexportfilm. In practice, this meant that Mosfilm "is now the sole owner of its 2500-film library and its current productions."[30] The studio participated in the Cannes market for the first time as a private firm, represented by its director, Vladimir Dostal, and its agent for the US, AFRA Film Enterprises. The story had an unexpected twist when, a few days later, Sovexportfilm declared Mosfilm's action illegal. After lengthy negotiations, Goskino was willing to recognize Mosfilm's ownership of the films produced on a self-financing basis, but insisted on retaining copyrights of films made before 1988.[31] The Filmmakers Union contacted government authorities to seek a solution to the problem, and after months of deliberation Mosfilm won the dispute.

Reforming distribution

While the ways and means of production changed, domestic distribution remained the last bastion of state monopoly. Adjusting to the new economic reality, Goskino introduced some cosmetic changes, but in practice maintained control of the distribution networks. The Main Film Distribution Board, once the sole institution responsible for setting prices and making decisions on the number of prints and the geography of distribution, has entered into a more cooperative relation with the studios. The Board has taken a first step on the way to reforms by establishing a national film market (Soiuzkinorynok), to be held quarterly. The first market took place in Moscow late in 1988, and on that occasion representatives of the distribution networks of the republics, regions, and cities of the USSR were faced for the first time with the new task of actually choosing the movies. They were suddenly responsible to the local soviets, which put up the initial purchase funds, but, even more, they were responsible to the audiences. The public demand has never been so seriously considered as it is under the new system. The films must attract a large enough public to generate revenues, or the movie theaters, and the studios alike, will face the possibility of bankruptcy. Lacking statistical data and market studies, price ranges at the first market were set on the basis of attendance forecasts made by a panel of experts – sociologists, critics, scholars, film directors, distributors, and the like. But scientific data were being gathered, and prices will eventually reflect the realities of the market. The projection was that by 1990 every studio would set its own prices and package deals. Under the new system, the theaters, too, will benefit if managed properly. They will be allowed to keep whatever income is left after expenses, and reallocate it to their immediate needs. Normally, theater expenses include the price of the film, the money that may be borrowed from the Main Distribution Board, publicity, and operation of the facilities.[32]

In addition to the film market, Goskino also established 154 cinevideo organizations (KVO), which are republican and regional associations representing the theaters under their jurisdiction. The results, however, have been disappointing. It soon became clear that the KVOs were controlling the theaters rather than representing them, and were themselves controlled from above. United under the umbrella of the Distributors Association (AKP), the KVOs amount to another monopoly.[33] The Filmmakers Union has fought the establishment of the Distributors Association, that nevertheless came into being on March 27, 1990. The FU Secretariat warned that it was the distributors' intention to create a "national trust, comprising government agencies and powerful regional cinevideo associations with the goal of monopolizing production and distribution nationwide." The statement from the Secretariat outlined the consequences of such a move: "This will undoubtedly be a hard blow to the condition of free creativity and economic independence that has just been born in our cinema, it will again place our national cinematography in a state of humiliating dependence on the new 'center', and will allow the distributors to favor imported foreign films at the expense of our national productions . . . The establishment of such an association contradicts the spirit and the letter of perestroika, the work of the FU and Goskino, and in particular the resolution of the Council of Ministers of the USSR of November 18, 1989 (No. 1003)." After the establishment of the Distributors Association, the FU retained for itself "the right to further opposing the creation of an organization that monopolizes distribution."[34]

Studios that are seeking alternative forms of distribution have serious difficulties in placing their films with the KVOs. The Gorky studio, for example, which was successful in dealing directly with a number of theaters, was blacklisted by the Distributors Association. Its 1990 pictures, *The Feast of Balthazar*, and *Voyage to Wiesbaden*, were purchased by only one KVO. Similar is the case of Solovev's *Black Rose*. The production unit "The Circle" which produced the film at Mosfilm, bought distribution rights with a loan from the Moscow

Innovation Commerce Bank (Mosinkombank) and, through the newly created group "Producer," organized its own publicity and distribution independently from the official channels. KVO leaders, who objected to the "commercial" price of the film, higher than the regular state-subsidized prices on the film market, responded by blocking its circulation in a number of cities and regions. The boycott included a range of tactics, from petty harassment to criminal acts. In Kiev, the private firm, Art–Impex, booked the facilities in the Palace of Culture for the film screening. Tickets were sold out for all-day showings over three days. But on the eve of the opening, a commission from the distribution bureau declared the auditorium unsuitable for film screening, and shut it down. In Magadan, cooperative distributors organized screenings of *Black Rose* in the cultural clubs of mines and excavation sites. But on the appointed night, the projectionists received an order from the administration to cancel the show and return the ticket money. And the people who came from several miles away, braving the Siberian snowstorm, had to go back home disappointed. Still another similar episode took place in Dnepropetrovsk: representatives of the local KVO raided the projection booth, attacked the projectionist, and stole a good half of the film. But in other regions, where distribution officials did not interfere, the film enjoyed significant success. The film did well in Krasnoyarsk, Irkutsk, and especially in Estonia, where the viewers were happy to pay three times the price of a regular ticket in order to see something that was part of the struggle against the central power.[35] *Black Rose* is not alone on the KVO's blacklist. Recently, a peculiar festival took place in Podolsk, near Moscow, the Festival of Unbought Films, featuring those movies that were boycotted or simply neglected by the buyer.[36]

Many pictures are simply not bought because the distributors prefer to spend their money on foreign films that bring in higher returns. "Most of our national pictures are not seen by the viewer, not even on a poster. There are entire cities where for many years Soviet movies have not been shown at all," complained Andrei Smirnov.[37] Yet, the national production has grown by leaps and bounds. With the consolidation of the independent enterprises last year, the number of feature films doubled in 1989. The vice-director of Mosfilm, V. A. Malkov, in his speech at the VI Congress, complained that Goskino is responsible for the saturation of the market with foreign films. At the last film market, Mosfilm offered seven national pictures, while

Soiuzkinorynok introduced a package that included thirty foreign films. Malkov is not alone in supporting a quota on imports, and the imposition of a protectionist tax on foreign films.

At the beginning of 1990, at the sixth film market, strong competition among the sellers occurred for the first time. On that occasion more sellers than usual showed up: Soiuzkinorynok, which recently became a company distinct from Goskino, studios, and independent associations. The buyers were KVOs, regional professional unions, youth clubs. Soiuzkinorynok had a showcase of eighty-one pictures. The tendency was to buy mostly foreign films: *Doomed to Loneliness* (Japan), dedicated to a karate master (856 prints); *Cocoon* (USA, 809 prints); *The Nets of Love* (India) a musical (665); Soviet films performed very poorly: *The Day of the Fish* (Lithuania, 10 prints); *Lifting* (Tallinfilm, 17 prints); *Days of the Human Being* (Riga, 20 prints). Eastern Europe did not fare well either: *The Prosecutor* (Bulgaria, 19 prints); *The Rooster Will Not Crow* (Czechoslovakia, 15 prints). The worst score was *Send me to the Front* (Mongolia, 3 prints). The only Soviet film that ended up within the first ten, unexpectedly even for its authors, was the fantastic comedy *Doping for the Angels* (Ukraine, N. Popkov, 551 prints), whose hero has alternating visions of mafioso-tormentors and guardian-angels. Many films of artistic merit were also neglected by the buyers; for example, *The Lost Bus*, by Yu. Kheifits (30 prints), and the Kazak film *Revenge*, by E. Shinarbaev (38 prints), notwithstanding the deliberate lowering of the prices as an inducement.[38]

Resentment for this state of affairs kept mounting. Producers and studio managers see the future of Soviet cinema in the total deregulation of exhibition and the elimination of intermediary distributing organizations. This point was reiterated by virtually all the speakers at the VI Congress. The general consensus was that the theaters must be in private hands if a real connection between producer and consumer is to be achieved.

The KVOs supply theaters and also fill the orders of other clients, such as clubs, trade unions, and educational institutions. They take a percentage of the box office to run the business and buy new films. The KVOs are increasingly being challenged by the cooperative distributors, completely independent from any state institution, that have set up shop in major cities and provincial centers. The independents started at a disadvantage with respect to the established networks, because they had no theaters of their own. But they deal effectively with social organizations, youth clubs, workers' clubs, schools, and trade unions. Their main asset, that in the long run may become a real advantage, was an entrepreneurial staff, as opposed to the entrenched clerks of the state-run channels. The "*kooperatory*" may even start from scratch, producing blockbusters and detective films on the American model, but reflecting the national reality, and then distribute them directly. Regardless of the quality, which may be of a higher or lesser degree, these films attract large audiences, "significantly larger than those gathered by the state distribution system." But even when dealing with films bought from a regular studio, their distribution system works better. "They achieve significantly greater results than the state distributors, and the film's producers receive from the independent distributors an amount of money that is infinitely larger than what they receive from the state system."[39]

The same entrepreneurial spirit moves some of the major studios, that have decided to dispense with the distribution networks altogether and go directly to the customers. Control over prices and revenues allows the studios to compensate film authors more fairly (on a percentage basis), and also to allocate funds where they are more needed (for example, for the renewal of the technical base). One of the most adventurous in this area is the experimental creative association Lad'ia, at the Gorky studio. The association manager, Mark Ryss, explains how they revolutionized the business: "We sent out 650 letters, offering our products and our conditions. We received a lot of answers; one of the first to answer was the management of the cine–concert hall, Cosmos, in Sverdlovsk, a complex of 2500 seats. They bought our film *Kings of Crime*, and they recouped the cost with showings in just that one theater."[40] *Kings of Crime* has generated significant profits for Lad'ia as well. The film director, Yuri Kara, plans to pursue this line of business, notwithstanding the accusations of commercialism and betrayal of high artistic principles that poured in from the official establishment and the intellectual circles alike. Kara went on to produce *The Feast of Balthazar, or A Night With Stalin*, partly shot on location at Yalta. Although the director's intentions were to produce a popular movie of some substance, some exponents of Soviet film criticism were worried "by the possibility of turning the fine and sacred theme of the personality cult into a common thriller, of which the director appears capable."[41]

Goskino's hands-off policy prevented direct interference with the private initiatives in the distribution sector. The Gorky studio, however, encountered significant resistance from the managers of the state distribution organizations. The artistic director of Lad'ia, Pavel Arsenov, complains: "The most difficult thing was to find a common language with the top distribution managers. The reason is that our system upsets the working methods they employed for so many years . . . Well, the distribution managers say that, of course, they stand behind us. But in practice . . . I'd better illustrate this with an image. Here, our 'Boat' is sailing. We drop our divers into the water to scan the bottom of the sea. And someone sits on the shore and cuts off their oxygen supply, and at the same time encourages them, 'How're you doing down there, guys? Keep on going!'"[42] The journal *Soviet Screen* provided a forum for the polemic between Lad'ia and the Main Film Distribution Board, letting both sides voice their views. From the establishment we heard that "Lad'ia constantly and, as we see it, tendentiously, keeps expounding one and the same idea – namely, that the Board hinders Lad'ia's experiment because its success would make one question the very existence of the Board." This view is too simplistic, according to the chairman of the Board, A. Suzdalev, who claims there is a huge number of interconnected issues that must be taken into consideration. Most of all, "it was impossible to sign a contract with Lad'ia, because the association asked for 14 percent of the gross . . . almost double of what we make."

This is what prompted Lad'ia to start its own distribution business, which turned out to be successful and profitable. The Board in response, while defending its position with some valid figures and facts, also uses some trite moralistic arguments against the dangers of capitalist exploitation. "Many regional distribution organizations at present do not have the means to buy directly from Lad'ia in the amount they need, because of the high prices. This is true even for the very popular film *Kings of Crime* . . . The important thing is that, in the final analysis, the viewer be the winner . . . that cinema in general, and the distribution sector, in particular, not succumb to commercialization."[43] Lad'ia, however, claims that it has a responsible policy in setting the prices. In fact, the studio differentiates between clients, taking into consideration the size of their business. "One thing is the amount of ticket sales at the Palace of Culture, with an auditorium of 2000 seats; another is a small children's theater in a provincial town," says Mark Ryss. The studio also offers package deals that may include a box-office hit, a children's tale, a family picture, a movie based on a Soviet or foreign classic, and other variants. The package is put together to the client's specifications. In any case, the studio has exclusive copyright on all of its films.

Not surprisingly given the Russian propensity for polemics, studios and cooperatives have accused the state distributors of the same sin they are decrying: commercialization. Screenwriter Eduard Volodarsky expressed the opinion of many when he stated that the present "criminally ungifted state distribution network" must be completely restructured, because most managers are "cinematically illiterate." For example, he continues, "the regional managers that come to the film market buy mostly, and at high prices, foreign and Soviet box-office hits (detective, adventure, erotic movies) . . . and only reluctantly take some of the films that in their opinion are difficult, philosophical, boring."[44] Other voices echoed this concern: "With the exception of a few agencies that work creatively, and are not afraid of the difficult, non-commercial movies, and that know how to turn their screenings into cultural events, the distribution system generally prefers the blockbuster, the hit, such as *King Kong* and *The Disco Dancer*."[45]

Many problems stem from the fact that there are no laws governing the movie business. The Filmmakers Union has prepared a bill to be submitted to the Supreme Soviet, but until then all initiatives are at the mercy of the competent authorities. A favorable measure was taken on January 1, 1991 with the elimination of the tax on movie theaters. According to a law dating from Stalinist times, the theaters were compelled to pay the state a heavy percentage of their revenues. The abrogation of that law opened possibilities for profitable business. This advantage, however, may be offset by another law that took effect on July 1, 1990 – the income tax law. The Filmmakers Union, at its latest Congress, drafted a resolution to seek exemption for the theaters. The theaters could also benefit from the deregulation of ticket prices. Still controlled by the state, they have not been raised since the 1920s. The average price in 1990 is approximately 50 cents.

To compound the problem, theaters are half empty today, as "attendance is dropping by 100–200 million tickets a year."[46] Filmmakers are actively pursuing popular pictures that would turn the wave around, at the same time challenging the still widespread notion that profitable pursuits are incompatible with art, and even with morals. Pragmatism has become a requirement of every entrepreneur under the new conditions, and many are concerned that the gold rush triggered by the free-market economy would distract the best talents from aesthetic endeavors.

The independents, eager to avoid charges of ruthless commercialism, have come up with their own solution. Fora Film, in the past two years has produced a number of art films thanks to the money it made with successful commercial productions. Revenues from commercial pictures allowed Paritet to make the prestige film *Sphinx*, with a cast of first-rate actors. The same is true for Perspectiva, which produced the educational movie *Eisenstein, Lessons on Montage*. The Association of Independent Cinema also uses revenues from commercial movies for benefits and planning of major projects. Among them, the Inform Video Bank, an international cinema data base; a TV cable network; and a school for film industry managers and legal counsels.[47] Besides, ANK wants "to participate in the education process at VGIK." To this end, Fora Film has already started financing the education of two students, so that "in four to five years we will acquire two new film directors."[48]

The concept of *khozraschet* has sent shock waves through the stagnating economy nationwide and has raised fears and hopes. Though rather conservative as an actual reform measure, and certainly short of capitalism, it has had a deep psychological effect. Right-wing political forces, together with the more conservative segments of the population were alarmed by the prospect of speculators and profiteers depleting their pocketbooks and undermining the foundation of the socialist system. The ghost of the late NEPman came back to disturb the sleep of bureaucrats and average citizens. The idea that entrepreneurs could make more money than salaried people was troublesome; it ran contrary to Soviet ethics as well as the Russian peasant mentality. Unlike the American dream of being able to match the color of one's neighbor's lawn, the Russian wish is to have one's neighbor's cow destroyed, if the cow happens to be fatter than one's own. *Khozraschet* came under fire also from the opposite side. Radical thinkers were unhappy with the limitations of the plan and the narrow parameters of operation it afforded. But it was a beginning, and if it did not produce the expected results, it served to foster public discussion and steer private initiative. The film industry took advantage of the new opportunities and laid the foundation for the development of a full free-market system.

4   Serving the Muse or the people?

The theme of the VIII Plenum of the Filmmakers Union in May 1989 was "Cinema: The Renewal of Artistic Awareness." After three years of administrative reshuffling and economic restructuring that distracted the best talent from aesthetic pursuits, the filmmakers felt the need to turn their attention to art. Some prominent figures were invited from abroad to take part in the discussion. Among them were Andrey Siniavsky, whose appearance marked his rehabilitation as a Soviet writer of stature, Polish director Konstantin Zanussi, and English producer David Puttnam. The main concern that emerged from that meeting was that, notwithstanding the endless possibilities granted by the new freedom of expression, no new masterpiece has appeared. Worse, in the opinion of many, not even plain good films have materialized in substantial numbers. Two causes were pinpointed: conformism of thought, due to long years of ideological brainwashing, and commercialization, or the gold rush triggered by the free market economy.

The demise of Socialist Realism

As for the first issue, Andrei Smirnov suggested that the average filmmaker "was and remained a toady and a lackey of power, ready to celebrate the latest directives."[1] In his opinion, supported by many other voices, the majority of the filmmakers simply made a 180 degree turnabout, substituting one set of values with another, and kept marching in compact rows. The bottom line was that there is a frightening lack of people "capable of going against the current – that very breed of people on which culture is founded." Disappointment with the current state of affairs ran so deep that someone was prompted to compare favorably the period of stagnation to the present one, pointing out that in those years some masterpieces were indeed produced, because "as everybody knows, they are born not thanks to, but in spite of, the main line of development of the cultural processes." Today, no filmmaker would dare release a film that does not include at least a sprinkle (and more often, an avalanche) of "sharp social issues" – organized crime, rackets, drugs, prostitution, youth violence, suicide, rape, corruption, alcoholism, shortages of housing and food, speculation, blackmail – and of political denunciation, mostly of the horrors of Stalinism and Brezhnevism but occasionally of Marxism–Leninism itself and the Communist Party. The critic, Irina Shilova, passed a severe judgement on this widespread mode: "In these detached accusations, in these cold condemnations, these emphatic acts of repentance, these contemporary games there is as much truth as in the sugary fairy tales of the early 1940s, full of unrestrained optimism. Then, the viewers expected reassurance. Now, they expect denunciation and revenge. Cinema responds to these expectations and, bluntly speaking, speculates on them." What is lacking, she said, is the human compassion that permeated the movies of the 1960s (and even the 1970s, to a certain extent), and touched a deep chord in the viewer's heart.

While there was a large consensus for this critic's view, the critics themselves received a fair share of criticism. It was generally agreed that they need to work out new evaluating criteria, "stemming not from the latest ideological or political situation, but from the very nature of art." The emphasis was on the need for an aesthetic discourse, and for a method of structural analysis, rather than schematic evaluation according to a scale of social values. In other words, most of today's critics evaluate a film "exclusively in measure of its degree of perestroika-ness or antiperestroika-ness," revealing a "pathetic blindness," when not tendentiousness. The fact is that as long as the old evaluating criteria are not rejected, old myths are merely replaced by new ones, and this is why "between the innovative conceptions and the old dogmas one can see more similarities than differences." The roots of this evil, as the prominent critic Viktor Dyomin emphasized, is the legacy of Socialist Realism that has left a thick encrustation on the minds and souls of all the people connected with the arts. "We must address art as art, without bowing to politics or the Party," he said. And in the conclusion of his speech, he proposed amending the statute of the Filmmakers Union and abolishing the clause that upholds Socialist Realism as the official style. In fact, the statute provides that "only those filmmakers that stand for the principles of Socialist Realism may be members of the Union." Dyomin's suggestion resulted in a resolution of the Plenum to discuss the matter at the next Congress of the FU, the only venue where the statute may be amended. "But," the resolution said, "as of today we consider it necessary to reject – and erase from life – that clause of the statute that, in substance, prescribes that the filmmakers work according to the laws of Socialist Realism." The recommendation was then upheld by unanimous vote at the VI Congress, in June 1990. By this action, the filmmakers dealt the last blow to the monumental facade that, like an ornate and mendacious effigy of the regime, for fifty years concealed its ugly face. If the other creative unions follow suit, Socialist Realism will be struck from the books and, hopefully, "from life."

Art films and popular movies

Besides ideology the other enemy of art is considered to be economic pragmatism. To many this second danger is even more upsetting because while ideology is, at least in theory, on its way out, pragmatism is, most concretely, on its way in, becoming a requirement of every entrepreneur under the new conditions. This issue has been amply debated since the very beginning of perestroika in the film industry. The argument went like this: with the transition to khozraschet, studios and production cooperatives must either make a profit or go bankrupt. The so-called "difficult" films, conveying a deep spiritual message through a poetic visual form, may collect international prizes, have an intellectual following, and acquire great prestige, but inevitably they will fail at the box office. This would make it impossible for the true artists to pursue their aesthetic fulfillment, while it would encourage a trend of cheap commercialism. Possible solutions to the problem have been proposed. It was reasonable to expect from the major studios that they would produce a number of films at a loss for purposes of prestige (not unlike the Hollywood studios of the 1940s). But to rely only on chance was too risky in a society where art is a public institution (even in the time of perestroika and glasnost), and not simply a private pursuit. The best solution was found with the establishment of Kinofond, whose functions include "providing financial help to individual studios and creative filmmakers producing experimental films, that have a substantial significance for the development of the aesthetic language of cinema, which daringly forces its way into the new layers of history and contemporary reality."[2]

But it was obvious from the very beginning that even the economic debate had an ideological component, expressed in the form of an idealistic concern for mass education, and of a highbrow dismissal of the commercial movie. Throughout the history of this century, the liberal elites (among filmmakers and viewers) have always expected cinema to be educational, i.e. to offer the audience spiritual and moral uplift through art.[3] The government, too, insisted on the educational function of cinema, although in a cruder sense. But the masses have always been attracted by popular genres, melodrama, adventure, detective, musicals – and today is no exception.[4] A crucial point of the current debate among the filmmakers is the difficulty of producing films of aesthetic and moral value that would also have a mass appeal.

Sociological studies of the tastes of the Soviet mass audience are being conducted at the Scientific Research Institute of Film Art (VNIIK).[5] A senior fellow of the Institute, film scholar Maya Turovskaya, having established that melodrama is the all-time box-office hit genre, decided to undertake her own personal "psychological experiment," at an ordinary show of the film *Eseniia* – a Mexican picture released in the USSR in 1975, that attracted millions of viewers. "I went to the movie theater – she recounts – that was full of women, for the most part. What's *Eseniia* all about? A gypsy woman steals a baby girl and brings her up in the gypsy settlement. Then a handsome officer marries her, and after many adventures someone recognizes her, through the medallion she is wearing, as the once-kidnapped daughter of a rich *hacienda* owner. Happy ending. The women in the audience are all in tears. The one next to me wipes her eyes. 'Did you like the movie?' 'Yes, very much so!' 'Why did you like it?' 'It was all about me.'" Here Turovskaya asked herself a question: "What does it mean, about me? Was this woman kidnapped by a gypsy? Or, did she wear a medallion? Or, was she married to an officer (well, maybe she was married to one of our officers, but this is not it)? And yet, she cries because it's all about her!"[6] In an earlier essay, Turovskaya had already tried to answer this question: "Let us assume that the taste of the masses is based on criteria that are closer to folklore than art . . . Then, *Eseniia*'s 'archaic' quality, the fact that it corresponds to a 'thematic model,' its stereotypes, the repetition of its narrative functions, while constituting a limitation on the artistic level are crucial factors in terms of communicability." She maintained that the cinematic melodrama as an aspect of modern urban folklore utilizes "the most ancient archetypes of human civilization," and therefore "allows an immediate participation, or even identification, touching simultaneously on three emotional chords: laughter, pain, and horror."[7]

To those who maintain that the artist's mission is to uplift the popular taste, Turovskaya retorted:

For a long time and without appeal we have expressed a utopian idea coming from the enlightened eighteenth century, which was actually already exhausted in the nineteenth century: the idea that we will educate everyone, and that everyone will then seek the "high" in art. We thought that if a person learned how to play Vivaldi on the violin, this would automatically be a moral person . . . It is time to say goodbye to the absolutism of these ideas, and take a good look at what is happening in real life. Then we will know what we should discuss with the artists, and what a popular film is.[8]

The difference of opinions as to what the masses need fueled numerous discussions. In January 1987 a special conference, on the theme "Artistic Value and Popular Success of Films," was organized jointly by the Filmmakers Union and VNIIK. One year later, the III Plenum of the FU, dedicated to "Perestroika and Perspectives of Creative Development in Soviet Cinema," indirectly addressed the issue. Finally, early in 1989 the Council for feature films, "The Lumière Brothers," was established, whose function is "to evaluate systematically all new films, and to discuss the questions of film aesthetics."[9] The Council seems to represent both ends of the spectrum, since its co-chairmen are Eldar Ryazanov, a prolific author of very popular films, and Valentin Tolstykh, an eminent philosopher and a specialist on film aesthetics.

More than once Tolstykh blamed filmmakers and distributors for feeding the public "cinematic trash (*kinoshka*)." He has been emphatic about it: "I want to stress this point: *first* the cinema turns into *kinoshka*, and *then* the viewer begins to look at cinema as just a means to satisfy his needs for leisure and entertainment." What is needed today, he said, is "a social cinema, that would shape the citizens into truly social human beings."[10] Although Tolstykh's idealism may be a bit out of touch with reality, he had a point in that particular case, because he was referring to two fourth-rate musicals (*Don't Get Married, Girls*, and *I Came to Talk*) and an adventure–espionage movie of the "Rambo" type, *Solo Voyage*. But in the opinion of the critic, Kirill Razlogov, the success of the commercial genres is a natural phenomenon rather than the result of faulty education. In a public debate with Tolstykh, he echoed Turovskaya's view. "Actually," he wrote, "the understanding of art – and of cinema in particular – among the masses is substantially different from our professional

understanding. It is based on psychological mechanisms of identification, on a direct juxtaposition of art and life . . . especially at the
emotional level; in this light, films like *The Disco Dancer* and *Eseniia* are
'the most truthful films,' they are films 'about me.'"[11]

There is also a third approach to the issue, which is less theoretical
and more practical. In the early days of perestroika, Elem Klimov took
a realistic look at the situation and concluded that "the problem
facing our cinema today is not that vulgar films attract big audiences
. . . the problem is the constant flow of dull films that do not attract
anyone." He suggested: "Let the 'difficult' films find their own
audience, however small, and let good comedies attract millions. The
crucial point is to stop the flow of 'greyish' pictures."[12] Indeed. Why
worry about the commercialization of cinema, some argue, when "we
are not even able to make good commercial films?"[13] The film scholar
Mikhail Yampol'skii, assessing the situation in 1988, maintained that
the current "bulk of film productions attract neither those who
appreciate art nor those who seek entertainment." His conclusions
were rather pessimistic: "From the point of view of the viewer's
demand the majority of our films are films for no one."[14]

The voice of the people

Nevertheless, the movies in the Soviet Union still attract a huge
audience, in comparison to the other industrialized countries. While
there has been a steady decline in attendance, starting from the mid
1970s, the average citizen even today goes to the movies fourteen
times a year.[15] At the same time, the intellectual level of some genre
films has been raised considerably. Statistics from Soviet and American sources show that the most successful films at the box office were
those that offered sociopolitical issues, relevant to the present day, in
the form of classical popular genres.[16] It is revealing that the top two
pictures for 1988, in terms of the box office, were *Little Vera* and *The
Cold Summer of '53*. The secret of their success – a success that equaled
American imports usually favored by the Soviet audiences – was a
combination of entertainment and substance. The American best-
sellers of the year were *King Kong* and *Short Circuit*.[17]

The Cold Summer of '53, by director Alexander Proshkin, was also
the winner of the popularity contest organized yearly by the
magazine *Soviet Screen*, pushing *Little Vera* down to the second place.
The film deals with a serious subject, the immediate aftermath of the
Stalin regime and its devastating consequences, and has the breadth

of a tragic epos. But the dynamic editing, emotional camera work, and harrowing musical track cast a dramatic episode of national history into the mold of the adventurous western. *Little Vera* is a realistic commentary on the disintegration of the social and moral fabric within the working class, and offers all the situations of the conventional melodrama. It also has the distinction of featuring an explicit sex scene – the very first on the Soviet screen.

Further confirmation of this trend comes from data relative to the 1987 releases. A film like *Repentance*, by the Georgian director Tengiz Abuladze, became an immediate sensation in the Moscow intellectual circles and international festivals because of its daring political content and highly artistic values, but had only a modest impact on the masses. Its explosive denunciation of the Stalinist terror, couched in the idiom of phantasmagoric surrealism, was not accessible to the general public. The younger generation, in particular, which makes up the majority of moviegoers, missed the point.[18] Conversely, *The Man from Boulevard des Capucines*, by director Alla Surikova, a light-hearted comedy patterned on the model of the American western, turned out to be the most successful film of the year, with an attendance of 50.6 million viewers in fifteen months.[19] *Capucines* did not touch upon political history or social issues, but offered a commentary on cinema itself, providing the audience with some food for thought sandwiched between adventure and slapstick. *Soviet Screen*'s popular contest, however, shows *The Messenger*, by Karen Shakhnazarov, at the top of the list – a discrepancy that may be explained by the relatively small number of respondents (31,012). The actual number of viewers, in twelve months, for this film was 34,438,000 – some 10 million less than *Capucines*.[20]

The year 1989 yielded mixed results. The winner of the *Soviet Screen* contest was *Intergirl*, by Pyotr Todorovsky, the story of a top-level prostitute combining sentimental and realistic elements in a well-balanced formula, and offering the viewer good production values. The protagonist, Elena Yakovleva, also scored first as best actress of the year. In second place the viewers put the documentary *Solovki Power*, by Marina Goldovskaya, the reconstructed chronicle of life in one of the harshest camps of the Gulag. Neither by its theme nor by its technical qualities could the film have any appeal as entertainment. It scored very high because it was an act of civic denunciation. The largest age group among the respondents comprised people between eighteen and twenty-four (49 percent). This was clearly the center, with two polarized groups on each side, teenagers – fourteen to seventeen (19.7 percent) – more likely to vote for entertainment, and young adults – twenty-five to thirty (17.2 percent) more likely to appreciate the significance of historical revelations.[21]

The contest, which has been held for the past thirty-four years, draws in an average of 30,000 answers. In addition, *Soviet Screen* receives approximately 40,000 letters a year from readers interested in discussing all aspects of the film industry, from opinions on specific movies, to requests for information on directors and actors, to suggestions on how to improve the quality of production and distribution, to complaints about the shortcomings of exhibition, the poor condition of the theater in provincial towns and villages, and the dismal repertoire selections. In the last three years, the complaints have become more vocal, the language more belligerent. The editor who handles the readers' correspondence observed that often he detects a stern, commanding tone – "we do not want, we demand, we are fed up." The readers nowadays are also critical of the critics, which is a good and useful thing, thinks that same editor. Too bad that a large number are more interested in nasty polemics than in constructive dialogue. This attitude pertains to those who dislike the current trend of films of social denunciation and resent the critics' support for showing "the ugly side of life."[22] Even *Intergirl*, whose version of truth was somehow varnished, had its detractors. A reader from Moscow writes: "In earlier times, the film heros were workers, peasants, intellectuals, Red Army soldiers. And now? The film heros are prostitutes and pimps, organized hooligans, bandits and speculators, impotents . . . One should not make movies about them, but give them a hack and send them to work in the mine. And your intergirl must be sent to the construction works; if she refuses, kick her out of the country!"[23]

Never before perestroika had public opinion played such an important role in the planning of the film repertoire. In early 1987, the Moscow movie theater Zvezdny started a regular program of preliminary screenings accompanied by questionnaires, designed to gather data on matters of popular taste. That same year, Mosfilm together with the Moscow City Council's Film Distribution Bureau conducted a sociological poll. *The Messenger* was shown in five city theaters well in advance of its official opening. After the screening, the audience met with the film's crew, discussed the film, and was asked to fill out a questionnaire. The results were useful for projections and planning. Teenagers turned out to comprise the bulk of the projected audience. Thus, the time for the film release, already set for June, was moved to the fall, since in the summer young people tend to engage in outdoor activities or leave town.[24]

In September 1988, at the request of Goskino, VNIIK conducted an opinion poll among the audience of the first Festival of Popular Genre Films, held in Odessa. Contrary to expectations, the results showed that the viewers' preferences were not exclusively for entertainment and escapism, but there was a demand for some added ingredients. Fifty-five percent of the respondents identified the theme they considered most important today as the honest discussion of historical facts relative to the Revolution and World War II, and revelations on the heros of those years whose lives have been tragically destroyed. The reporter of the poll commented that before perestroika this category of thematic preferences did not exist. 51 percent indicated a preference for movies about love, the family, and people's private lives, and 47 percent favored pictures on contemporary social problems and the topical issues of perestroika. Apart from thematic considerations, the poll revealed preferences of style and form in the following order: (1) "films rich in content, honest, based on life"; (2) films "capable of exciting the imagination, stirring deep emotions, generating happy feelings"; (3) films of highly artistic value in direction, acting, cinematography, etc.; (4) films that are just pleasant to watch, "that don't have anything in common with life, and that are geared primarily toward leisure and entertainment." Not surprisingly, at the very bottom of this long list one finds the "difficult" films, favored by only 17 percent of the audience.

The assessment of cinema in the time of perestroika was generally positive. Fifty-six percent thought that recent films played an important role in the moral and political renaissance of the country, but some felt that there is still room for improvement. In conclusion, the commentator thought that the poll showed "a growing politicization, not only of cinema but of the mass consciousness that addresses it."[25]

The video boom

The video industry has become a booming business, and in this area state enterprises compete with the legitimate private sector and with an aggressive black market. Goskino's division, Videofilm, is the largest producer and distributor, with studios in many republics and regions. It produces a variety of films in all categories – documentaries, entertainment, cartoons, current affairs, music and ballet, drama – but its main business, as for the independents, is distribution. Videofilm has also been involved in co-productions, providing services for the shooting of the American adventure picture, *Red Heat*, with Arnold Schwarzenegger performing his feats against an authentic Moscow background. Videofilm's ambitious program of expansion envisions also a commercial TV channel that would compete with central Gosteleradio for the public's favor. So far, Videofilm has opened about one thousand "video-salons" around the country, where customers can rent or watch cassettes. In remote villages, video wagons and trains have been set up *in lieu* of theaters, following in the tradition of the revolutionary agit-trains of the 1920s that brought motion pictures to the rural areas for propaganda and educational purposes. This time, however, the purpose was purely commercial. Videofilm's top executive, Oleg Uralov, runs the firm as a self-financing enterprise, taking risks and aiming at profits. One of Videofilm's goals in the next few years is to turn 100,000 village cinemas into high definition video theaters, possibly with the input of Japanese technology.[26]

Such projects are part of Goskino's strategy to contain the tremendous expansion of the independent sector. In the past two years, the independents have become formidable competitors. As a protectionist measure, private video cooperatives were excluded from the Law on Cooperatives of July 1988, that granted legal status to small business enterprises. Unlike film cooperatives, which were subsequently legalized, video cooperatives are still outlawed. But imaginative ways were found to circumvent the ruling. Today, the independent sector is officially organized by a number of institutions and social organizations, but actually run locally by private entrepreneurs.

How does it work? The Ministry of Culture is officially responsible for video showings in those cultural centers and museums that once sheltered only high culture and political education; the Ministry of Social Services, for showings in state-owned restaurants and cafes; the local soviets, for showings in public buildings, parks, and railroad stations; the workers' unions, for showings in factory clubs and recreational centers; and the Young Communist League (Komsomol), for showings in youth clubs and private apartments. The sponsoring organization is only nominally involved. It is at the lower level that the actual business takes place, with the managers of the video-salons raking in the cash and paying the sponsor a share of 15–20 percent.

By far the most aggressive among the sponsors, the Komsomol controls a vast net of video-salons. Its facilities vary from big video screens in large auditoriums to simple TV sets and VCRs in private living rooms, accommodating some thirty seats. A family that runs a video business grosses an estimated 12,000 to 15,000 rubles a month – an enormous sum considering that the average monthly salary is 250 rubles. Even after expenses, which take a substantial toll – including bribes for officials, buying the cassettes from video pirates at stiff prices, maintaining facilities and equipment, advertising, and paying the Komsomol's share – the profits are exorbitant by Soviet standards.[27]

Falling behind in the video race, Goskino has had to strike back. In fact, Goskino was hindered by restrictions that did not apply to the independent organizations. While Videofilm showed mostly Soviet classics and a few old foreign films, the independents showed the latest foreign hits, pirated on the international market and distributed only one week after release of the cassette abroad.[28] Complaints have been pouring in from foreign producers about violation of copyrights, but nothing could be done legally to stop the rampant video piracy since the USSR did not sign the Berne copyright convention. Besides, according to insiders, if the business is forbidden it would go underground, the ticket price would triple, and the annual gross would amount to something close to 70 billion rubles per year – which would equal the entire defense budget of the USSR! Today, the estimated yearly gross of the video industry is 10–20 billion rubles, which is fifteen times higher than global film industry revenues. These gigantic profits, however, are not reinvested in the industry. "They simply disappear into other spheres of the economy," complained a film sociologist.[29]

The first step to balance the scales and give Goskino an equal opportunity was to eliminate all restrictions. Starting in 1989, the state-owned video-salons were allowed to show the same pirated films as the independents. This was a big boost for Goskino, and Videofilm quickly revised its repertoire to conform to the most popular trends.

When in the early 1930s the then Minister of Cinema, Boris Shumyatsky, ordered the film industry to produce "movies for the millions" he had a dream of conquering the mass audience with entertainment laced with ideology. It worked for a while, since everything else was banned in those years.[30] Today, however, Shumyatsky's dream has turned into a nightmare, as the masses, oblivious of ideology, flock to the video-salons to watch the latest feats of Arnold Schwarzenegger or the erotic adventures of "Emmanuelle" and her likes. The typical video repertoire consists of three main categories: (1) American action movies, especially the Stallone, Schwarzenegger, and Chuck Norris offerings; (2) Kung-fu movies from Hong Kong and their American clones: (3) Western European erotica, although "pornography" is still officially censored. Other favorites, in the Asian republics, are exotic melodramas of Indian production. Exceptions to these trends are occasional old and recent classics, such as *Gone With the Wind* and *Last Tango in Paris*. Soviet productions are totally absent from the repertoire, both the classics and the glasnost films. Soft-core and hard-core pornography constitute the bulk of the illegal, underground video business that charges as high as twenty-five rubles a ticket for a glimpse of the forbidden fruit. Compare it to two to three rubles a ticket for the regular video-salons, and to the unrealistic, state-controlled ticket price for the movie theaters still at fifty cents, and one gets an idea of what sells.[31]

Not everybody can afford to spend twenty-five rubles for a porno flick, but the average citizen is willing to pay four times the price of a movie for a viewing at the video-salon. An American scholar of popular culture, Richard Stites, offered this eyewitness account of his experience in a Leningrad workers' club. "Looking for the latest fad in Soviet society, I decided to spend an afternoon at the video-club of the 'Elektrosila' factory. The small room was crowded with some fifty people from all age groups, from grandmother to little Ivan, basically the workers' families. The equipment consisted of a simple TV monitor and VCR, and the feature that day was a Kung-fu movie in Chinese with Russian voice-over. The cassette was of decent quality, but the film itself was a silly story full of senseless violence. And yet the audience was glued to the screen."[32] Video-clubs and video-salons offer five showings a day, and they are usually sold out. The audience profile varies according to the establishment affiliation, but the overall majority of the viewers are teenagers.

The second government measure aimed at increasing state revenues through the video business was the levy of a 70 percent tax on the video-salons and other showing places. As soon as the law took effect, in July 1990, the independent sector launched a counterattack. The emerging enterprise with the greatest potential for profits is now the video-cafe, which is already changing the existing setup of the video network. As a private cooperative, the cafe pays the regular 30 percent tax on beverage and food sales. However, it advertises video entertainment as an extra feature, and charges three rubles "for coffee."

One observer concluded that in this era of high technology it is virtually impossible to monopolize and control the use of the electronic media, unless one envisions a "specific type of government . . . that will never come back in this country," and predicts that "in the present situation, any ban in this sphere would only lead to the stimulation of underground business."[33] The Soviet authorities should not be overly concerned about the pirating business. According to data released by UNESCO, world sales of blank videocassettes total 400–500 million a year, the sales of prerecorded videocassettes total 70 million. On the world market, video pirating is rampant. In the Philippines and Indonesia 90–95 percent of the sales are pirated cassettes. In Venezuela and Brazil, the percentage of pirated cassettes is 70–75 percent. In Holland and Italy, 30–60 percent. Data for the Soviet Union are unavailable.[34]

Soviet analysts of the video market were quick to sound an alarming note at the inception of the phenomenon (1987), but they saw the remedy in a better run state industry, rather than in the expansion of the legitimate independent enterprises. They stated that the government was bound to provide adequate facilities, which would otherwise be provided by "some dealers, charging for video shows in their privately owned minitheaters: living rooms, dachas, cafes and bars (after hours), and even (as the press reported) at the morgue."[35] In 1989, the Soviet customs established a special division for the control of videocassettes. This became a necessity because the number of cassettes smuggled into the country rose dramatically in recent years. In 1988, the customs checked more than 80,000 prerecorded videocassettes at the Sheremetevo International Airport, and confiscated about 9,000. Those that are commonly allowed in are subjected to a stiff tax. According to division chief, Vladimir Karyzhsky, reasons for confiscating the materials are "pornography, and films publicizing sadism, cruelty, and anti-Soviet feelings."[36] But in an era that tends toward democratization of institutions, the customs officers do not want to appear as arbitrary rulers on matters of "art." So, in order to be able to pass a fair judgement on what constitutes pornography, they attend special seminars of "the Scientific Council on problems of philosophy, culture, and contemporary ideological currents of the Academy of Sciences, and special courses at VNIIK, and at the All-Union Institute for the advancement of workers in the cultural field." Not only that, but if the officer-turned-specialist is challenged by a stubborn citizen determined not to part with his cassettes, the customs "will gather an arbitration commission of art scholars, philosophers, physicians, social workers, and Party representatives"! So far, however, the customs were able to handle all problems by themselves. Nowadays, *Rambo I. First Blood* is on the list of allowed materials.[37] The division chief thinks that even the scene where the Vietnamese patriots torture the hero is not disparaging of the Vietnamese people, because "it is rescued by the pathos of the social idea." *Red Heat* is not only allowed, but it is officially distributed by Videofilm, notwithstanding the fact that it contains some cold war clichés. Other popular pictures, however, are still on the blacklist. *Cobra* and *The Predator* are routinely confiscated. But there is hope for further leniency in the future, because "the customs cannot ignore the changes in the public opinion." Thanks to the customs' "new thinking," it is easy to predict that the video business will soar to even higher spheres.

An estimate puts the global figure of VCRs currently in use in the USSR at two and a half million, with 500,000 in the commercial video system, both state-owned and independent, and the rest in private homes. As of 1988, there was one VCR for every eighty to ninety families – mostly of foreign make, due to the illegal imports of electronic equipment that began in the late 1970s. But the number of video users in private homes is much higher, since people tend to watch movies with friends and relatives. An estimate put it at 5–7 million watchers.[38] The same happened when the first TV sets hit the market in the 1960s, and were in scarce supply. Government imports of Japanese VCRs are in the plans, as are increases in the production of Soviet-built recorders. The USSR Council of Ministers passed a resolution (September 1988) calling for a production goal of 500,000 recorders by the end of 1990, and 2 million by 1995.[39]

The price of a VCR for the average citizen is rather steep. If the buyer is lucky enough to find any equipment in the regular shops, the price of a Soviet-made VCR would be around 1,200 rubles, while Japanese imports would be priced at 3,000–4,000 rubles. But, most of the time, the buyer is faced with empty shelves and has to resort to the black market, where the price is at least three times as high. A Japanese multisystem recorder cannot be acquired for less than 9,000 rubles, and a TV set with a big screen, for 20,000. Like the VCRs, foreign-made blank cassettes are available on the black market for dollars or for the ruble equivalent.

Prerecorded pirated cassettes are now for sale in state-owned electronic shops. They sell for 100 rubles, which leaves a good margin for the government. With no royalties to pay, the cost of producing a cassette is minimal. Razlogov described how it is done: "An executive buys a cassette abroad in a regular video shop, takes it home, and the firm makes 500 copies of it. Some go to the stores for sale, some circulate in the video-salons. Usually in video-salons they show twenty-fifth generation cassettes, and the image definition is terrible. Another way is to bring into the country cassettes lifted from foreign TV." Resentment against this practice is mounting, both in Western Europe and the US. American film industry representatives have been calling on the Soviets for years to get tough on the video pirates. But now that the Soviet government itself is in the business the picture has become messier.

The effect of video on the film industry is a matter of great concern. The decline in movie attendance, that had quietly started in the mid 1970s with the development of television, has now intensified. The people do not mind spending more for video. Since there is little on the market they can buy, average citizens have a lot of extra rubles and little use for them. As a consequence, video-salons around the country outnumber the movie theaters ten to one. Since there are about 5,000 movie theaters in the USSR, the estimated number of video-salons is 50,000, with 1,000 in a big city like Moscow, and 100 to 200 in smaller towns.

On the other hand, the video boom has generated new business in parallel fields, such as journal publications. In early 1989, *Soviet Screen* started a section called "Videocompass," whose purpose was "to give the viewers an orientation in the stream of video-production that has flooded the private video market."[40] This was done at the request of the readers. Given the limitation of space, only four films could be accommodated in each issue. They are selected and discussed by a number of prominent critics that rate the films according to their own judgement. It is interesting to note that all four films featured in the first "Videocompass" were American. They included, in order of preference, *The French Connection (1971)*, *Being There* (1979), *Trading Places* (1983), and *Cobra* (1986). In the following issue the selection was again mostly American, with one exception: *Last Tango in Paris* (Italy/France, 1972), *the Warriors* (1979), *9½ Weeks* (1986), *The Class of 1984* (1982). This pattern was consistently repeated in subsequent issues, with Italy trailing the USA one to four, and other nations appearing only in insignificant numbers. One exception was the issue dedicated to James Bond (No. 4, 1990), where seventeen movies of the charismatic 007 were briefly reviewed. Not a single Soviet film appeared in the "Videocompass" selection.

As the demand for information grew, a number of video journals sprang up. The video buffs are willing to pay three to five rubles for an issue of their favorite magazine. Besides the independent *Video-Ass*, a Soviet–Swiss joint-venture magazine, and *Russkoe Video*, published in Leningrad, there is also a journal of the State Research Institute of Film Art, *Video Digest*. In this area, too, state enterprises try not to lose any ground.

Video-Ass started appearing in early 1990. The first issue was printed in 100,000 copies that were instantly sold. Chief editor, Vladimir Borev described it as an independent magazine that reflects the "democratic character of the videoculture." By that he meant that the videoculture cannot be regimented into "bureaucratic frames." On the contrary, "the videoculture actively undermines the remnants of the command-administrative system in society." Therefore, "the magazine too, takes an independent position."[41] The magazine is designed to provide information on the video market both "black" and "white," foreign and national, and to conduct viewer polls. Information comes from a data bank, NITs Videokultura (Independent Information Center Videoculture), that gathers data from foreign publications and information agencies.

NITs Videokultura conducted a poll in the Ukraine, in 1989, to determine what film genre was the viewers' favorite. Out of a sample of 692 people, 466 were in favor of horror films and science fiction – notably two genres that have not developed in Soviet cinema. In response to the readers' interest, *Video-Ass* (No. 2, 1990) published a filmography of ninety horror and science-fiction films that appeared on the foreign screens in recent years. This provided valuable information to both viewers and business, because videocassettes reach the Soviet market with a one and a half years delay after the release of the original film. The list included *Batman*, *The Terminator*, *They Live Among Us*, *Dracula's Widow*, *Moonwalker*, and others.

One of the paradoxes of the new era is that having acquired freedom of artistic expression most filmmakers are unable to bring it to fruition. The law of the market turned out to be more tyrannical than the state censor. In the Brezhnev years, it was difficult to get funds for controversial films. Nevertheless, the funds were there and, knowing how to manipulate the system, they could be obtained. Several masterpieces came out of the dark days of stagnation, shaped by the struggle between the creative spirit and bureaucratic regulations. But since the beginning of perestroika the Muse has been silent.[42] The people, on the other hand, have been offered a long overdue repertoire of naked truth, naked bodies, and naked violence. They have signaled their support by taking their rubles to the box office and supplying the producers with funds. The authors of art films found themselves in the same predicament as their Western colleagues, with the disadvantage that they do not have any experience in fund raising. As perestroika in the film industry enters its second phase, the future of film art and the means to protect it will be the objects of great concern.

Part II

Spring waters and mud

5   Off the shelf

Together with a new crop of films, glasnost brought to the screen an array of unknown, or forgotten, pictures that had been sitting on the censor's shelf for years. The Conflict Commission of the Filmmakers Union was able to rehabilitate virtually all the films that were previously banned, and negotiate their release with Goskino. In retrospect, it was hard to understand what could have triggered the unfavorable decisions, since most of those films look quite bland today from a political standpoint. Even the members of the Goskino Collegium that reinstated some sixty films were amazed at their findings, as reported by Rolan Bykov:

> The Collegium's world-wise members shook their heads mournfully: "What? *Kuban Cossacks* is banned! And *Eugene Onegin* and *Loyal Friends!*"
> The long list was read. Yes, all these films were banned. In the case of *Kuban Cossacks*, it was because one of the actors, Yuri Lyubimov later went abroad. *Eugene Onegin* was banned because of Galina Vishnevskaya who played Tatyana – and also misbehaved. Aleksander Galich, a scriptwriter of *Loyal Friends*, was responsible for that film being relegated to the shelf. The stories are similar for all the sixty films.[1]

There were also more serious reasons, to be sure, based on ideology, touchy subjects, or mistrust of poetic form. This seems to have been the case with the masterpieces of Kira Muratova, always held in great esteem by her colleagues, but banned for some twenty years. In the fall of 1986, during an emotional evening dedicated to Muratova's works at the House of Cinema, the director received a standing ovation from the representatives of the film world. "I had always known," Muratova told the audience, "that my films will come out some day. Only I did not believe that I myself would live to see that day."[2]

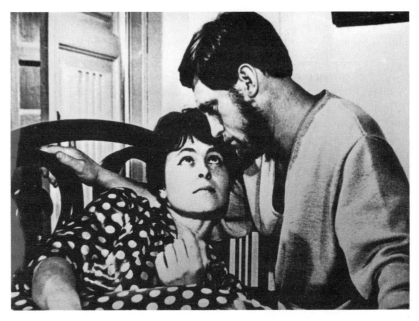

12   *Brief Encounters* (1967/rel. 1986) directed by Kira Muratova

Captive beauties of the late 1960s and 1970s

After a brilliant debut with *Our Daily Bread* (1965), co-directed with her husband Alexander Muratov, Muratova was allowed to make her own film, *Brief Encounters* (1967). On the surface the story was simple enough. Valentina, a conscientious civil servant in charge of the regional housing office, and Maxim, a geologist–prospector and guitar player devoted to an itinerant and adventurous life, have a difficult relationship – a series of brief encounters and lengthy separations. Their episodic meetings bring into focus their love and need for each other, but also their basic differences, disappointments, and resentment. There is a third character in this love triangle, Nadya, a country girl Valentina hires as a maid without knowing of her past relation with Maxim. Muratova, who also wrote the script and played the role of Valentina, succeeded in conveying the subtlest nuances of feminine psychology, placing both romances in the past, and presenting the idealized figure of the man only through flashbacks of the women's recollections. Through superb camera work, daring editing, and richness of visual detail, the women's world acquires sharp definition in juxtaposition to the world of the man, played by late legendary Vladimir Vysotsky – juvenile, irresponsible, and yet charismatic.

The censors may have objected precisely to this character, a free spirit, declaring without apologies his aversion to the nine-to-five routine of the bureaucrat. Besides, Vysotsky's role in real life had always been a thorn in the side of the cultural establishment. He was an idol of the masses, as the author and performer of the semilegal and underground songs that became the conscience of the nation in the 1960s and 1970s.[3] They may also have taken exception to Valentina's character, which denies the traditional Russian values associated with the woman. Valentina is unmarried, without children, and interested in romantic love rather than in the family. Or was it the film's background that disturbed the bureaucrats' sensibilities? Life in Valentina's provincial town is rather shabby. Her cozy apartment is an elegant oasis of *fin-de-siècle* furniture and leather-bound books in an otherwise barren cityscape. Valentina's job brings to the fore problems with poor construction work, water supply, and housing shortages, which she tries to solve. But her attitude toward work is mechanically dutiful, rather than enthusiastic. Emotionally, she does not relate to "the people," and she is more devoted to her private life than to the cause. On the one hand, she is a representative of the new Soviet bourgeoisie, a *nomenklatura* lady, comfortable with her position; on the other, she longs for the romantic, anti-establishment hero who stirs her imagination and her passions. The decor of her apartment underlines her psychology. It looks oddly anachronistic, more fit for a Chekhovian anti-heroine than for a Party executive.

The treatment of the countryside may also have been problematic for the censor, showing how village girls are pushed into the humiliating position of housemaids to city dwellers by the lack of jobs and opportunities at home. It is an exodus from the utopian land of plenty that never materialized into an alien world. The relationship between Nadya and Valentina functions as an indicator of the traditional gap between the peasants and the urban intelligentsia. Notwithstanding her good intentions, Valentina is unable to communicate with the country girl, who remains suspicious and hostile. Even more revealing is Nadya's relation with Maxim. A lover of nature and the wild, he is no less a stranger in Nadya's village than Pushkin's Aleko was in the gypsy camp. In spite of his boots, beard, and work clothes, he relies on the comforts of civilization – good camping gear, canned food, and a jeep – and feels closer to the woman that he jokingly calls "madam" than to unworldly Nadya.

The last scene is a director's master stroke. Having realized the inner bond between Valentina and Maxim, Nadya sets the dinner table for the couple with meticulous accuracy, before leaving the house forever. The camera lingers on the table, covered with crystal, silver, and lace, symmetrically framed by two elegantly carved chairs, awaiting the happy lovers. Then the frame goes black. The focus of the film, as the concluding image suggests, is on the individual's inner space – the space that Valentina values, pampers and guards against interference from outside. If the censor was able to read Muratova's cinematic language, one has to give him credit, because it is from the aesthetic manipulation of space, framing, and *mise-en-scène* that a potentially disturbing picture emerges – the picture of the *embourgeoisement* of the Party cadres, and the search for fulfillment in the individual's private world.

Muratova's second film, *Long Farewells* (1971), also unmercifully condemned, deals with a difficult relationship between mother and son and the disintegration of family ties. Bored with a life at home that he finds too prosaic, the teenage boy dreams of joining his father in Siberia. The father (another Maxim), moved by a spirit of adventure, had deserted the family and joined an archaeological expedition. The boy gives vent to his frustration by responding to his mother's solicitous cares with deliberately callous treatment. As in the previous film, it is Muratova's keen sense of cinematic aesthetics that conveys the depths of feelings and themes, as in the scene when the boy "nails" his mother to the wall by projecting on her body slides of exotic places and wild beasts. A few humorous touches do not alter the tragic tone of the film. A Soviet critic recently called it "one of the few tragedies of the twentieth century which affords the viewer the possibility of supreme catharsis."[4] And British film scholar Ian Christie characterized it as "the finest of all modern Soviet films."[5]

Muratova's career was paved with obstacles and frustrations. Her next picture, *Getting to Know the Wide World* (1979) was also shelved. Then, in 1983, the film *Among the Grey Stones* was so grossly reedited without Muratova's permission that she had to withdraw her name, and the film was released under the pseudonym of Ivan Sidorov. Whatever the reasons behind the censor's consistently harsh judgement, the Odessa Studio where Muratova made most of her films was not an adequate venue for her talent. A Soviet critic offered this explanation: "In a studio that produced a flood of insignificant movies Muratova was a misfit. She was advised to drop directing.

She knew that."[6] Finally, having been rehabilitated, Muratova was able to work at ease on her latest films, *Change of Fortune* (1987) and *Asthenic Syndrome* (1990).

Another victim of the wave of repression that hit the film industry in the late 1960s was the film *Commissar* (1967), by director Alexander Askoldov. Not only was the film victimized, but the director himself, who was barred from filming altogether, was expelled from the Film-makers Union and even from the Party.[7] Askoldov's film was a daring act of courage, besides being the expression of an accomplished artist. Despite twenty years of captivity in Goskino's vault, the film has not aged. When it appeared on the wide screen, in the summer of 1987, it stunned the audience with its freshness of thought and the still vigorous impact of its black-and-white images.

The script, also by Askoldov, is based on Vasily Grossman's story, "In the Town of Berdichev," but is larger in scope and implications. The story contains elements that are *per se* controversial. A woman commissar attached to the Red Army during the Civil War becomes pregnant in the middle of a bloody campaign. She takes leave to give birth to a son and is sheltered by a Jewish family. In that humble abode she finds assistance, love, and human compassion. As a result,

13 *Commissar* (1967/rel. 1987) directed by Alexander Askoldov

the commissar uniform is shed to reveal the essence of womanhood that emerges from the rough military greatcoat like a butterfly from her cocoon. But the call of duty, in the end, prompts the commissar to abandon her child and return to the battlefield.

This was not a sound treatment of the Civil War. According to Soviet canons, commissars were not supposed to have romances, much less to get pregnant. The focus should not have been on individual lives, but on the historical destiny of the nation. Furthermore, the Jewish question, which has always been a touchy subject for the Soviet authorities, became even touchier with the Arab–Israeli Six-Day War that broke out when *Commissar* was due for release. The sympathetic treatment of a Jewish family, and the flash-forward to a Holocaust scene that connects past and present and indirectly points at Soviet responsibilities and racist biases, was sure to trigger the censor's reaction.[8]

These factors contributed to the final banning of the film. But beyond the obvious and simplistic explanations there was a deeper reason for keeping *Commissar* out of circulation. As several Soviet critics nowadays have noted, the film looked at the historical events that shaped the Soviet state from an unorthodox point of view – a retrospective view, charged with the knowledge of fifty years of tragic developments, that shook the foundation of the dogma.[9] In *Commissar*, the Civil War is not the heroic epos that marked the beginning of a great era. Rather it is a gigantic cataclysm that devastated the social fabric and even affected human nature, generating distorted personalities. Klavdia Vavilova, the commissar, is one of those, her womanhood having been stifled by the harsh code of revolutionary ethics. A 1989 review in *Pravda* carried the eloquent title, "A Bolshevik Madonna," which effectively captured the intrinsic dichotomy underpinning the whole film.[10] Askoldov conveys the feeling of two irreconcilable concepts by a set of recurrent images: at the opening, the long, winding line of the Red Cavalry passing by the statue of a Madonna, while a lullaby is heard on the soundtrack; the mixing of blood and milk, when a deserter holding a jug of milk is shot on the commissar's orders; Klavdia's surrealist visions of war and death while giving birth; Klavdia, in peasant woman's clothes, walking with her child through a symbolic religious landscape, suddenly confronted by soldiers from her unit; Jewish children from a loving and caring family watching the cannons roll through the street of their town, and later engaging in a violent "pogrom game" where the victim is the little sister; and, finally, the feeble notes of the "Internationale," reminiscent of the opening lullaby, played by a solo trumpet over a snowy wasteland.

The camera observes, comments, guides the viewer's eye, and stirs emotions, projecting the drama of ordinary life against the grand romantic canvas of the revolution. But it does not judge. It does not raise issues of good and bad, or right and wrong. It does not even condemn the all-sweeping war tornado, ravaging the country with the frightening beauty of a natural disaster. It simply invites the viewer to look anew at preconceived notions that were no longer viable in the late 1960s.

After its release, *Commissar* has been shown worldwide, including Europe, the USA, Canada, Japan, Israel, Tunisia, Australia, and New Zealand. The main actors, already stars in their own country, acquired international fame – Nonna Mordyukova (Klavdia), Rolan Bykov (Yefim, the Jewish tinker), Vasily Shukshin (the regimental commander), Raisa Nedashkovskaya (Yefim's wife, Maria). But to get *Commissar* off the shelf was not easy, not even in the time of perestroika.

In September 1986, the Conflict Commission decided to restore the film to its original form and release it, but no action was taken by Goskino. Even in the Filmmakers Union, rumors had it, someone at the top was blocking the film. In the meantime, the International Moscow Film Festival (July 1987) was approaching, and promised to be a true and happy celebration of glasnost. Unearthed masterpieces and new features were going to be shown side by side. Only Askoldov's film did not figure in the program. At that point, he decided to take the matter in his own hands. No one can tell this story better than he himself:

I was not invited to the festival, and learned about the events only in the press. When I found out that Klimov said: "We must not show this film at the festival," I realized that I had been silent for too long, for twenty years, and I decided that it was time to open my mouth . . . I went to the Filmmakers Union, where the new leadership was having a press conference . . . I sat in a corner of the large room and listened as my comrades were proudly telling about their accomplishments in the restructuring of our cinema. Unexpectedly, a journalist from Brazil asked Klimov: "Have all the films been taken off the shelf?" . . . At that moment, my eyes and Klimov's met. Obviously, my eyes spelled trouble. And Klimov said: "Well, for the most part the job is done. Everything is alright. We have already excellent relations with Hollywood. And, generally speaking, we have accomplished a lot. But, to be frank, there is a problem with one picture. Personally, I think it is lacking in artistic qualities . . . This happens, you know. It happens that a film may not be so good, and in addition it may have some problems . . ." Here, something uncanny happened. As if someone poked me in the back, I walked across the room, stopped before Klimov, and told him that I wanted to address the audience directly. Even Klimov was taken aback. I was handed the microphone, and delivered a very short speech.[11]

The next day, the film was shown to a crowd of journalists and festival guests. After the viewing, the director of the San Francisco Film Festival, Peter Scarlet, publicly invited the film and its author to the USA, signaling the support of the international community. The film was restored at Mosfilm from a tattered copy that had been stashed away at the State Film Archives. It was reconstructed from bits and pieces, but it was not possible to make a new soundtrack. Askoldov was not unhappy about it, because he "wanted the picture to be seen as it was made in 1967."[12] When the work was completed, the picture was promptly sent abroad. But it was not released in the USSR until the end of 1988. Askoldov traveled all over the world with his film, gathering prizes and a significant amount of hard currency for Goskino, but he himself has not been compensated for his work. According to a Soviet scholar, "so far he, and the whole production crew, have not received any money for the film."[13]

Andrei Konchalovsky, too, was penalized for his film *The Story of Asya Klyachina Who Loved But Did Not Get Married* (1967), although less severely. The film was subjected to close scrutiny, and renamed *Asya's Happiness* after the original title was found unsuitable. But even with that change it could not be released. Twenty years later, Soviet and foreign audiences had a taste of what could have been a new direction in Soviet cinema's aesthetics.

When the film was shown at the House of Cinema, soon after its completion, it created a sensation. "The film was still being edited, polished, some scenes were still being shot, and it was already the subject of conversations, discussions . . . In the inner circles, there were rumors of an oncoming event . . . And after the screening, the unanimous judgement was: *Asya Klyachina* is an event."[14]

Konchalovsky shot the film in a documentary style, bringing the camera to a collective farm, and using the farmers to play themselves. He chose professional actors for the two leading roles only – Iya Savvina as Asya, and A. Surin as her boorish lover Stepan. Even the character of Asya's devoted suitor and Stepan's rival, Sasha Chirkunov, was played by one of the farm dwellers, G. Egorychev with plain, moving honesty.

And yet, the film is not a documentary but a well crafted drama,

14 *The Story of Asya Klyachina Who Loved But Did Not Get Married*
(1967/rel. 1987) directed by Andrei Konchalovsky

where the dramatic pivot is Asya herself. This character required technical skill and deep sensibility. "Without Savvina, this movie would not have been possible," said Konchalovsky, at the film's viewing at the House of Cinema in 1967.[15] Savvina was able to bring to the surface the inner qualities of a poor peasant girl, one of those humble creatures who in the tradition of the great Russian novel are the repository of goodness, love, and truth. The portrait of such a peculiar "positive hero," in the opinion of one Soviet critic, makes *Asya Klyachina* "the key film of the 1970s."[16]

Asya is in love with Stepan and is expecting his child. Stepan, a rural bully with a rugged sex appeal, takes advantage of the homely, lame girl, and shuns his responsibilities. A knight in white armor comes to the village in the person of Sasha, a solid and handsome tractor driver, who is taken by Asya's spiritual beauty, her shining eyes and blond ringlets, and proposes to her. He offers a secure and serene life for Asya and her unborn baby. Although moved by his devotion, Asya rejects him because, simply put, she "does not love him." Contrary to social conventions, marriage without love would be for Asya a debasing compromise. By the same token, her relationship with Stepan, humiliating according to common thinking, in her eyes is redeemed by love. And yet, when Stepan finally decides to honor his duties after the child is born Asya rejects him as well, out of pride, but also out of the realization that her passion for the man has now turned into something deeper and more substantial, the love for her son.

Asya realizes all this intuitively, rather than rationally, and acts spontaneously. She is proud and independent, not in a calculating way, rather as a natural being possessing an inner dignity. Asya's link with nature is underlined in the dramatic scene where she gives birth to her son in a ravine by the roadside, clumsily assisted by Stepan, but basically alone with her pain and elation – with the mystery of life that blends her body with the earth and the trees.

In this film Konchalovsky used the documentary style to strip characters and sets of all artificiality, and probe into the substance of things. The revelation of ideal beauty through unglamorous Asya is matched by the revelation of the spirit of Russia and the soul of her people through an unsentimental, unvarnished portrait of the collective farm. Here, the camera records the hardships of work during the harvest days, under a scorching sun, with sweating farmers covered with dust and dirt, shouting at each other in the realistic language of the workplace. This was a deliberate blow on the director's part at one of the most cherished myths of Socialist Realism, the country idyll. In the 1930s and 1940s, images of swaying prairies and limpid skies, of plump melons and turgid wheat-ears, of rural beauties in embroidered blouses and smart fellows in shiny boots singing and dancing to folkish accordion tunes were intended to afford the people a glimpse of the promised land. Mythmaking was used to pacify desires and to foster dreams. But even before Konchalovsky made this film, the dream was long gone, exposed by Khrushchev's "secret speech" at the XX Party Congress.

Konchalovsky's merit, and his disgrace with the censors, was not so much to reaffirm the death of the myth as to make a statement on filmmaking. His unadorned style and naturalistic *mise-en-scène* removed the sleek veneer of the fairy tale and revealed the socialist pastorale for what it was – ordinary life. The picture is not pretty but is life-affirming. Out of Asya's labor a new woman and child are born, out of the farmers' stories of war and labor camps a common human bond is born, and out of the labor of the fields, a connection with the beautiful Russian land and the roots of life itself.

The clash with Goskino did not disrupt Konchalovsky's career. Although hampered in his artistic development, he was still among the best directors of his generation. He went on to make four more films in the Soviet Union, and after moving to Hollywood he adapted to the Western way and was able to continue with creative filmmaking. But *Asya Klyachina* has remained so far his unsurpassed masterpiece.[17]

The year 1987 saw the release of a significant number of "captive beauties" from Goskino's vault. *The Beginning of an Unknown Era* (1967) was another one of them. Originally it was conceived as a four-episode album to commemorate the fiftieth anniversary of the Revolution, but only three episodes were shot, and only two have survived the twenty-year ordeal. No negative of the original picture has been preserved. Only a print of Andrei Smirnov's episode, *Angel*, and the late Larisa Shepitko's *Homeland of Electricity* was found at the time of release. The missing episode was filmed by another promising young director Genrikh Gabai, who later emigrated. Goskino's disapproval of the film, besides marking a painful setback in the directors' careers, had tragic consequences for the Moscow Experimental Studio that produced it. The studio was closed, and a successful experiment came to an end.[18]

Leaving aside all lamentations on bureaucratic insensitivity to art, it is easy to see why Goskino would not agree with the film's interpretation of the genesis of the Soviet state. The two extant episodes do not focus on the heroics of the revolutionary uprising, but on its aftermath, on the plight of the people and the devastation of the land during the Civil War. Furthermore, *Angel* was based on a story by Yuri Olesha, and *Homeland*, on a story by Andrei Platonov, two writers of the 1920s who had just begun to be rescued from three decades of neglect and abuse, but were only partly rehabilitated.

Angel does not attempt to reproduce the metaphorical language of Olesha. Smirnov, similarly to Konchalovsky, experimented with the aesthetics of a "new" realism. A Soviet critic described this style effectively in a recent article: "The world of the film is solidly concrete: sand, clay, a sledge-hammer making kindling wood out of old-regime chairs with bronze ornaments, soldier caps used to pour milk in, and then brought to the mouth to release an inebriating stream that runs along the shiny gutter of the cracked cap's visor. Things, here, are so tactile that they look like pop-art objects glued to the screen . . . They mean what they mean: they are deliberately antimetaphoric."[19]

The film tells the story of a group of people thrown together by the confusion ensuing from the destruction of a railroad line. The disparate group – including a commissar, a Red Army soldier, a peasant man, an intellectual, a deserter, a pregnant woman, and a teenage girl – walks aimlessly through the ravaged countryside, sharing their misery. Distinctions of hierarchy, political color, gender, and class lose all meaning in the midst of the cataclysm that erased accepted social concepts and moral values. The drama begins when the group is captured by a band of outlaws. The confrontation between chieftain Angel and the commissar is the clash between two irreconcilable ideologies, and two true believers in their own absolute ideas. In the end, the commissar is executed by the dark angel of death, but the ending is ambiguous, leaving no clear victor or victim. The focus switches to the rest of the group that, released from captivity, resumes its long, hard journey toward an uncertain future – but a future, nevertheless.[20]

Homeland of Electricity is the story of a Russian village struck with famine in the terrible year 1921, and rescued by a *komsomolets* – a youthful member of the Young Communist League. On the surface, the story supports the official ideology: the party provides the people with guidance and technology to help them out of their misery, and leads them toward a bright future.

But the messianic theme in Shepitko's film is not based on historical materialism. Rather, it has mystical overtones. "The boy-*komsomolets* appeared to the people in a halo of diffused light to announce the new gospel."[21] As the evocative imagery suggests, the savior who brings electricity to the countryside may be the carrier of a different kind of light, the spiritual enlightenment generated by suffering. Fascination with suffering, expiation, and redemption, supported with the iconography of the Russian Orthodox Church transposed into compelling cinematic images is the hallmark of Shepitko's opus. As a result of her maximalist belief, her films, although visually striking, are often marred by the director's tendency to slip into preaching. This is particularly unfortunate in *Homeland*, because the preaching tone is totally absent in Platonov's text.

Shepitko inherited from her teacher, Alexander Dovzhenko, a keen sensibility for lyrical canvases of nature and people in harmonious symbiosis, but on that pagan landscape she superimposed her Christian vision. The equation of the journey of life with the Way of the Cross underlies all of Shepitko's films and becomes explicit in her last completed work, *The Ascent* (1977).[22] As she progressed from film to film, it became increasingly clear that the focus of her inquiry was death – though not as the negation of life, but as a trying passage to a superior existence. There was, perhaps, something clairvoyant in this attitude, as has been noted: "Shepitko's work is disturbing and, with each passing film, it becomes more disturbing, rather than affirming. Or, if there is affirmation, it is of a strange, macabre sort – the eeriness with which her work points with increasing urgency and seeming acceptance, to the death that befell her accidentally."[23]

A victim of later repression, *The Errors of Youth* was shelved in 1978, when its director Boris Frumin left the Soviet Union to settle in New York. Only in 1989, was Frumin able to return to Leningrad to restore the film, which was released that year.[24] Besides punishment for emigration, the censors objected to the overall philosophy of life expressed by the protagonist, Dmitry Guryanov (the actor who played that role, Stanislav Zhdanko, was dead by the time of the film's restoration). The narrative follows Dmitry in his restless search for a perfect life. He is affected by the "unbearable lightness of being" syndrome, which compels him to destroy whatever he has achieved in order to start it again, and again. His "errors" unfortunately lead him to an alienated existence, to the loss of moral parameters. Life itself loses meaning, and the future looks like a dead end.

At the turn of the decade, *The Swimmer* (1981), by the Georgian director Irakli Kvirikadze, was also put on the shelf. It was released in a cut version in 1984, and finally re-released in its original form in 1988. During the years of the film's captivity, Kvirikadze used to travel to cine clubs around the country with the only film print in his possession, and set up screenings for social groups. The film is a tragicomic saga of a family of swimmers, who distinguish themselves in the sport, but get into trouble with Stalin's police. An omnipresent feeling of fear and suspicion poisons the light side of life. The director makes a connection between entertainment and terror, when children drop a little bust of Stalin in a fishtank for fun, and the next day their father is arrested. The film's style may also have been objectionable. Shot in sepia color, with a stylized *mise-en-scène*, and a period musical track, the picture has the flavor of an old chronicle, removed from the real course of history.

A true discovery were the documentaries of the then still obscure Armenian director, Artavazd Peleshian. His first film, *The Beginning* (1967), was another movie made for the fiftieth anniversary of the October Revolution, and promptly shelved. Ian Christie called Peleshian the "inheritor of the mantle of Dziga Vertov, prophet of the 'cine-eye' and pioneer of Soviet propaganda newsreels."[25] Indeed, in this film and the few others that followed – *We* (1969), *The Seasons* (1975), *Our Century* (1982) – the director displays a peculiar talent for the "poetic documentary," a genre that Vertov initiated in the early 1920s, and brought to perfection over fifteen years of intensive work, before being ostracized for his "formalism." Like Vertov, Peleshian relies on imaginative camera work and striking editing techniques to create a poetic world out of naked reality. The result is not a sugary coating of reality, but a text that transcends iconic representation and conveys more than the event itself; it conveys its essence. In *The Beginning*, Peleshian "cuts together familiar and unfamiliar footage of troops, horsemen, trains, and planes with rhythmic virtuosity to make the Revolution seem an irresistible force of nature."[26] There were no objectionable themes in Peleshian's documentaries, except for an expression of Armenian nationalism in *We*. But the unconventional form, that raised doubts more than affirming beliefs, was the likely cause of his undoing by the cinema authorities.

Tolomush Okeev of Kirghizfilm experienced some difficulties with his picture, *The Sky of Our Childhood* (1967), in the course of an otherwise very successful career.[27] *Sky*, released in 1986, treated a theme that was too much ahead of its time. It sounded an alarming note about the ruthless handling of folk tradition and rituals in the name of progress. The elegiac tone lamenting the violation of his national culture was sustained by breathtaking shots of the Kirghizian peaks in their natural splendor. Ecology and ethnic sensibilities were not suitable subjects for discussion in those years. But, in spite of official disapproval, Okeev never abandoned these themes, and eventually he developed them to their fullest in *The Snow Leopard* (1985).

Similar is the case with Kal'e Kiisk of Tallinfilm. His long and distinguished career had only one black spot when one of his films fell under the axe of Goskino.[28] *Madness* (1969) was banned until 1986, supposedly because of its transparent political allusions. The action takes place in Nazi-occupied Estonia, and suggests a parallel between the German invader and the current Soviet master.

Adonis XIV by Bako Sadykov, was completed in 1977, but released only in 1986. Its political subtext did not elude the censor. The film may be labeled a *sui generis* docudrama, but it is really a metaphorical tale. The title role is played by a star of the animal farm, a beautiful white goat with an extraordinary "talent" for acting. The tale's implications are sinister, as the action proceeds from a pastoral idyll to the slaughterhouse. Adonis is raised to be a slave, and later used by a manipulative master to lead the herd to self-destruction. He himself will eventually be liquidated.

Other fine films of the 1970s, recently released, *Trial on the Road* by Alexei German, *Theme* by Gleb Panfilov, and *Rasputin* by Elem Klimov, were discussed in a previous chapter. And so were Andrei Tarkovsky's Soviet films. But a discussion of the two films Tarkovsky made abroad is in order here. *Nostalghia* (1983) and *The Sacrifice* (1986) are now considered children of glasnost in the Soviet Union, inasmuch as they were bought and shown soon after the restructuring of the cinema administration.

The Tarkovsky phenomenon

Tarkovsky said that his principal objective in making *Nostalghia* was "the portrayal of someone in a state of profound alienation from the world and himself, unable to find a balance between reality and the harmony for which he longs, in a state of nostalgia provoked not only by his remoteness from his country but also by a global yearning for the wholeness of existence."[29] The poet Gorchakov is in Italy to research the life of an eighteenth-century Russian composer, Pavel

Sosnovsky, who born a serf was sent to Italy by the master to develop his musical talent. Sosnovsky spent several years there, distinguished himself in the field, but could not get over the nostalgia for his native land. He eventually went back to Russia, and soon after his return he hanged himself. Gorchakov, like his predecessor finds himself at a crossroad of two civilizations, unable to reconcile their opposite values. He wavers between his translator–guide, Eugenia, a Renaissance portrait of feminine beauty, and his Russian wife, an earthly symbol of motherhood and the motherland. This state of confusion and alienation results in a creative dead end. Gorchakov, unable to work, goes through a period of deep spiritual crisis, to which he eventually finds a solution with the help of the madman Domenico.

The film's main structural element is once again the journey, as it was in *Stalker*. The action is supposed to be a trip through Italy, but it develops for the most part in a small town where Gorchakov feels trapped, unable to proceed. The narrative structure turns from a dynamic form into a static one, signifying a halting of the quest, a moment of stagnation. *Nostalghia* has a rich subtext drawn from literature and painting. The central metaphor of the voyage to salvation alludes (very appropriately given the setting) to Dante's *Divine Comedy*, while the painterly landscapes and some characters' portraits are inspired by the iconography of the Italian Renaissance. Eugenia's figure – her head and garb – is the incarnation of a Botticellian woman. This image of the ideal Beauty through which man would reach his spiritual fulfillment had its origins in the medieval figure of the "woman-angel," such as Beatrice in the *Divine Comedy*. Suffused with an aura of religious mysticism, she was the guide to salvation. However, Eugenia's role as a guide is ironic. In Tarkovsky's film she is a travesty of the "woman-angel," her exterior appearance being an empty shell around a dead soul. The twisting of this role serves Tarkovsky well in his denunciation of a materialistic society whose spiritual values and national heritage have degenerated into fashion. Eugenia, therefore, is not the one that can lead Gorchakov to the celestial summit. It is the madman, the visionary Domenico who shows Gorchakov the way.[30] Domenico believed that salvation could be attained by carrying a lighted candle across the therapeutic waters of the pool of St. Catherine, but he was prevented from accomplishing this task by the "sane" people who unfailingly came to his rescue.

Tarkovsky has often maintained that he did not use images symbolically, because every natural image is rich enough in meaning without endowing it with symbolic references. But the natural elements have always played an important role in Tarkovsky's poetic universe, and if not endowed with symbolic significance they are nevertheless pregnant with emotional suggestions. Fire destroys, but at the same time is emblematic of purification and spiritual rebirth. Earth is benign in nourishing the human being, but it also connotes the opposite pole of spiritual elevation. Air is the element that embodies mankind's aspirations to rise to the ethereal sphere, but it is an alien physical space where the human being does not belong. Water is especially omnipresent in Tarkovsky's films, both as an image of birth and regeneration and as an image of stagnation and corruption.

In order to reconcile his divided self and reach the ultimate state of harmony, Gorchakov, like an archetypal hero, has to go through the test of water and fire. He takes Domenico's legacy upon himself and begins the crossing of the pool. At that time the water had been drained to clean the pool, but it is nevertheless conspicuous for its absence. It takes Gorchakov three attempts before he succeeds in getting the lighted candle to the opposite side. The camera follows him back and forth on one long continuous shot, one of those rare shots where cinematic time equals real time. The shot tangibly conveys to the viewer the agony of the enterprise, whose completion coincides with Gorchakov's death and final liberation. The hero's sacrifice is mirrored by Domenico's final solution. While Gorchakov fulfills his mission quietly and dies in isolation, Domenico immolates himself on Capitol Square in Rome in front of a cynical audience. As his body is consumed by flame, Beethoven's "Hymn to Joy" underscores the macabre burlesque of the *mise-en-scène*.

When Tarkovsky made *The Sacrifice* he probably had a foreboding that this was going to be his last film. He abandoned all ambiguity and addressed directly the main issues that had always been at the core of his work. As the title implies, Alexander, the film's protagonist, offers himself to God in order to save mankind, and in particular his beloved son Little Man, from the impending catastrophe of the nuclear holocaust. However, the true nature of the disaster that threatens mankind is purposely blurred. The action shifts from the plane of objective reality to the plane of psychological reality, placing the issue of a doomed humanity into the framework of Alexander's perception. Thus, images of nuclear annihilation acquire a metaphorical meaning – the connotation of an Apocalypse about to befall a society devoid of spirituality, separated from God and from Nature. Alexander is spurred to perform the sacrifice by the eccentric

THE SACRIFICE

A Film by Andrei Tarkovskij

15   *The Sacrifice* (1986) directed by Andrei Tarkovsky

postman Otto, and draws the strength to carry it out from the "witch" Maria.[31] But the other characters perceive Alexander's action – the burning of his home – as a sign of folly. Tarkovsky does not force the viewer to take sides. The last sequence, combining elements of tragedy and farce, consists mainly of long shots, which distance the viewer from the protagonist and prevent any emotional identification. The viewer remains an observer, invited to meditate rather than participate.

Shot in Sweden with Swedish, English, Icelandic, and French actors, *The Sacrifice* is, in Tarkovsky's words, "a Russian film." Indeed, the film combines the tormented spirituality of Dostoevsky's characters with the Chekhovian atmosphere of a doomed civilization. But other names come to mind as well, first among them Ingmar Bergman who gave a perfect cinematic form to his elegiac meditations on ethics, and Akira Kurosawa who was able to achieve the maximum of expressiveness through the simplest of means. These two directors are among the few that Tarkovsky admired. Ultimately, though, *The Sacrifice* is Tarkovsky's own creation, the summation of his troubled journey through art and life, the culmination of his ascetic vision and moral commitment.

In his aesthetic credo, Tarkovsky moved away from Eisenstein's concept of cinema as montage – a principle that stresses the dialectics of life and history, and therefore a progression in time – and instead focused on life in its synchronic dimension. While rejecting Eisenstein's principles of film form, he often declared his aesthetic kinship with the master of poetic cinema, Alexander Dovzhenko. Tarkovsky's films are spatial representations of life sculpted in time – as the title of his book, *Sculpting in Time*, states.

To sculpt in time is for Tarkovsky a means to give corporeal weight to the spiritual substance. As the French critic Barthelemy Amengual noted: "The materialism of Byzantine art, which provided a palpable body to the immateriality of the divine by inscribing it in gold, enamel, colored glass, and precious stones . . . finds an equivalent in the duration of Tarkovsky's shots, a duration that acquires an almost material weight. The icon transposes the spiritual into physical space; Tarkovsky transposes it into physical time."[32] But if time gives the image the corporeal weight that makes it perceptible, the visual compositional elements confer to the image its ambiguity – that ambiguity which affords a glance beyond the representation of the image itself into the world of things unseen. The conclusion of *Andrei Rublev* showed how an abstract concept becomes matter. The quest for harmony and perfection that has tormented the artist throughout the film, and which is still unresolved at the end, suddenly explodes in the epilogue in a true epiphany of mystical splendor. Rublev's icons appear on the screen. The transition from black and white to dazzling color, through the image of red burning coals, intensifies the emotional transition from the world of darkness to the realm of light. The icon here fulfills its intrinsic function, that of expressing the spiritual caught in a material object, and represents the utmost manifestation of harmony, a perfect synthesis of spirit and matter.

Tarkovsky's cinematic icons, without being sacred objects, are nevertheless meant to integrate irreconcilable opposites. The concluding shot of *Nostalghia* is a good example. A backward tracking shot gradually reveals a Russian landscape – a dacha in a meadow, trees, a small pond, and Gorchakov sitting by the pond with his dog. The dominant lines are horizontal. As the camera moves further back, we see in the background the walls of an Italian cathedral that shoot up to the sky by the dynamism of their vertical lines. We have the juxtaposition of two opposite elements, not only on the graphic level but on the conceptual level as well. The *mise-en-scène*, however, does not suggest conflict, rather it suggests integration. On the graphic level the solemn structure of the ancient cathedral surrounds the pastoral scene with the effect of a curved line – the integrating figure of the circle. On the conceptual level, the composition suggests a surrealist landscape, where a small fragment of rural Russia fits perfectly inside the nave of a majestic Italian cathedral – the hero's subconscious reconciliation of two worlds.

The main theme of the film – the search for harmony and balance, for integration and wholeness – materializes in this concluding vision, in this fragment of sculpted time. The shot is long enough to become noticeable by its length. It exceeds conventional duration, with the effect that time itself becomes a significant structural element. Furthermore, it is not a frozen frame. While the *mise-en-scène* is perfectly still, the camera keeps running – stressing the time element. And suddenly, snow starts falling down upon the Russian landscape through the cathedral's ceiling, suggesting both divine blessing and a congealed state of harmony. The artist has attained the absolute. He has created eternal life existing simultaneously inside and outside of time.

Tarkovsky, however, was not satisfied with *Nostalghia*'s concluding shot. He thought it was too mannered, a "literary metaphor." In his words: "It is a constructed image that smacks of literariness: a model of the hero's mental state . . . All the same, even if the scene lacks cinematic purity, I trust that it is free of vulgar symbolism."[33] At that time, Tarkovsky was aiming at a truly "ascetic style," similar to that genre of Japanese poetry, the haiku, that possesses "discipline of mind" and "nobility of imagination."[34] He wrote: "Haiku cultivates its images in such a way that they mean nothing beyond themselves, and at the same time express so much that it is not possible to catch their final meaning."[35]

Tarkovsky attained this style fully in *The Sacrifice*. With the whole film underscored by the Japanese motif, visually (camera work, *mise-en-scène*, and small details such as Alexander's kimono), aurally (the Japanese flute on the soundtrack), and thematically (the nuclear explosion), the final shot can be read as an example of a cinematic haiku. The Japanese stylistic ascetism, however, is coupled with Tarkovsky's deeply rooted Christian philosophy. Four horizontal planes – the grass, the beach, the lake, the sky – four strips of color intersected by the black vertical line of the Tree of Life that fastens them together like a clasp. The tree's bare branches extend gracefully and hesitantly in two opposite directions, creating the effect of a flat figure, like a Japanese ideogram, or a cross. Little Man lies on the ground, his head against the trunk, his body forming a perfect square angle with the tree. Images like this "express so much that it is not possible to catch their final meaning." And, certainly, it is not possible to put it into words. But the viewer intuitively connects that final image to the film's opening shot of Leonardo's painting "The Adoration of the Magi," where the human being kneels in awe in front of the manifestation of the divine, and offers his "sacrifice" to God. The camera underlines the elevation of the human soul in the offering act by moving up slowly along the trunk of a tree figuring in the painting. The same uplifting movement along the Tree of Life underscores Little Man's final and poignant query after his father's sacrifice – "In the beginning was the Word. Why is that Papa?" – and concludes the film on a note of hope in a new genesis.

In January 1987 major Soviet newspapers such as *Pravda, Literary Gazette,* and *Soviet Culture* carried obituaries in memory of Andrei Tarkovsky. This was the first sign of his political and artistic rehabilitation, soon to be followed by an array of articles, memoirs, opinions, and belated film reviews. In the next two years, the magazine *Soviet Screen* published several illustrated stories on Tarkovsky. And the other major film journal, *Film Art*, amply commemorated the artist and the man. Moreover, a publication of the All-Union Research Institute of Film Art included two papers under a common heading: "The Phenomenon of Andrei Tarkovsky."[36] On the occasion of the XX All-Union Film Festival, in May 1987, the first retrospective of Tarkovsky's films appeared on the Soviet screen. All his films were shown, except *The Sacrifice* which the organizing committee was not able to secure for that event. The festival bulletin, *Sputnik kinofestivalia*, carried a review of *Nostalghia*, a première for the Soviet audience. The review's author, the leading critic Neya Zorkaya, in the previous decade had defied the official silence surrounding Tarkovsky's works with an article in praise of *Mirror*.[37] *Nostalghia* was later shown on national television (December 26, 1989).

The heir of Tarkovsky

Together with a display of sincere enthusiasm, the Tarkovsky celebration has also shown a disturbing side. A Swedish-made documentary on Tarkovsky was released in the West,[38] but another documentary on the Soviet film artist, *Moscow Elegy*, made in his homeland to celebrate his birthday (April 4, 1988), was seemingly blocked by the Filmmakers Union after a presentation at the House of Cinema. The situation is ironical. While Tarkovsky's films have become almost an object of cult among artists and intellectuals, and his memory is revered, another director was being subjected to the same treatment that once drove Tarkovsky into exile. Even more ironical is the fact that the director of *Moscow Elegy*, Alexander Sokurov, is considered Tarkovsky's spiritual and artistic heir. Tarkovsky himself implicitly confirmed this in one of his last interviews: "You see, in Leningrad there is a young director, a cinematic genius. His name is Alexander Sokurov."[39] When asked about the controversy surrounding the Tarkovsky documentary, Sokurov explained: "This situation . . . is nothing new. I was notified that the commission for the legacy of Tarkovsky actively objected to the film. The nature of the objection is not clear to me. Even more so, because I am supposed to be a member of that commission myself. I'll tell you bluntly, Tarkovsky has become an *object*. Reminiscences of him, opinions about him must be cleared with some group or another. I disturbed the *status quo*, allowing myself to approach the material from an individual point of view. I was told that I do not have a right to such a point of view, to such an intonation. Unfortunately, I had to grab the film and run away from Moscow."[40] And what was the film like? "We wanted to convey an impression of infinite sadness and love for a real human being. Chronologically, this movie is about the years of Tarkovsky's absence from the Soviet Union, and, in a sense, about the causes of this tragedy. In the film there are many Italian, Swedish, and French materials. There are also episodes of Tarkovsky's funeral, and images of the places where he lived in Moscow. One of the themes of the film is what he left behind. Furthermore, the film says that many Soviet colleagues passionately envied his talent."[41] Perhaps the last component was responsible for Sokurov's troubles with this film. With his typical disdain for the institutions, Sokurov dismissed the whole incident: "We did not make this film for the Moscow House of Cinema and for the professional audience enmeshed in inner squabbles. This film was made for the mass audience. I want everybody to see it."[42]

Like all artists of genius, Sokurov had to struggle from the very beginning. In 1978, when he was still a student at VGIK, he completed the film *A Man's Lonely Voice*. It was an immediate sensation among Sokurov's young colleagues, who recognized him as the true voice of their generation. But the custodians of tradition and mediocrity found the film unsuitable and did not grant it a release. It finally came out in 1987, together with the other unearthed masterpieces.

The works of Andrei Platonov proved to be an inspiration for the 1970s generation. *A Man's Lonely Voice* is based on another one of Platonov's stories, "The River Potudan'." The action takes place in the aftermath of the Civil War. A young fellow, Nikita, after serving in the Red Army comes back to his hometown and marries a woman of a higher class. The mismatched couple cannot overcome their differences. The marriage is doomed not so much because of the class gap that the Civil War had not bridged, but mainly because of Nikita's mental state of shock and confusion that led him to becoming impotent. Having gone through the horrors of a fratricidal war as a naive, immature youth, he did not have a chance to grow and make sense of the events. He was swept into the whirlwind of history without having reached an understanding of himself as an individual and of his relationship to the collective destiny of society. In order to find himself, he leaves home and goes through hell again, but this time it is a hell of his own choice, a self-imposed expiation path that will finally reveal to him the meaning of existence. The setting Sokurov chose, after Platonov, for Nikita's spiritual regeneration is the "materialistic hell" of the NEP days, which in the 1920s was treated as a symbol of corruption and perdition by many artists and intellectuals. Nikita works as a hired hand in a market place, exploited by a vulgar lady merchant who sells entrails. He is housed in an underground hole unfit for human living, and even spends a night in a garbage dump. Gory details of slaughtered animals and bloody carcasses give a tangible dimension to his ordeal. It is one of Sokurov's characteristics to anchor his symbolism in the concreteness of the material world. As a Soviet critic observed: "The market scene

. . . is a true discovery of our cinema . . . The whole scene, by the way it is shot, suggests that this is another reality, an inverted one – the flip side of the ur-reality, the true one. The market for Nikita is the circle of torments, the circle of hell."[43]

Sokurov's film was seen, by the privileged few, as a turning point in the stagnating cinema of the 1970s because of the new rapport it established with history. Trained as an historian before entering the film institute, Sokurov brought back to Soviet cinema the epic spirit of the 1920s. Although often compared to Tarkovsky, Sokurov is far from Tarkovsky's lyricism and baroque eclecticism. His conception of history is broader and, in this sense, closer to Eisenstein's "poetic cine-epos." And his style, too, goes back to that time. Many features of Sokurov's films can be found among the artists of the early avant-garde. He himself mentioned Eisenstein's *Strike* and the works of Kozintsev as a source of inspiration; others noted affinities with the prose of not only Platonov, but Babel, Vsevolod Ivanov, and Pilnyak, and with the canvases of Petrov-Vodkin and Filonov.[44] Like the writers of the 1920s, Sokurov avoids psychological characterization, and places his heroes in a detailed *mise-en-scène* which expresses indirectly their state of mind. Action and dialogue are reduced to a minimum. The image speaks for itself. Similarly, the use of slow motion and long takes serves the same purpose as the devices of *"zatrudneniie"* – slowing down of the narrative – that were recognized by the Formalist theoreticians as a hallmark of the literature of those years.[45]

The sense of history in Sokurov's films is enhanced by the use of newsreel footage inserted in the narrative, or by the narrative itself, shot in a documentary style with non-professional actors. The documentary as a genre, in fact, has played a big role in Sokurov's career and filled his creative space in the long period he was unable to get major projects approved. The fact that he was able to work in the cinema at all, after he left VGIK without graduating, was due to the patronage of those who believed in his talent. Tarkovsky helped him land a job at Lenfilm, having recognized in the young filmmaker his heir to "the concept of art as a spiritual mission."[46] Sokurov did not disappoint his mentor; when glasnost gave him a public voice, he even went too far, turning his profession of faith into a display of Russian "cultural chauvinism."[47] But back in the years of struggle, he was able to express his art only through documentaries, made at Leningrad Documentary Film Studio, under the patronage of the studio's director, V. Kuzin, and the chief literary editor, G. Pozdnyakova.[48] He made five and a half documentaries, unusual in form and conception, that had to wait until 1987 to see the light of day.

The Allies (original title: And Nothing More) is dedicated to the events that reshaped the international map in World War II. The materials come from archive footage, but the director manipulates the chronicle by means of associative montage and puts the focus on the individuals who made history, and those who payed the price. Elegy is a meditation on the figure of a great artist, the opera singer Fyodor Shalyapin. Loved, almost worshiped by his own people, he chose to leave Russia in 1922 to seek a better living in Paris. Does the Artist have a right to betray the love of the People? This is the question Sokurov asks through a delicately woven elegiac poem that starts with the recent interment of Shalyapin's remains in the Moscow Novodeviche cemetery, proceeds with a restrained and yet probing portrait of Shalyapin's three daughters – three foreign ladies visiting their father's house in Leningrad, now a museum – and ends with newsreel images of the Russia Shalyapin abandoned. His magnificent voice resounding over the destitute masses, penetrating into the live social ferment, magically restores for a moment the link that was broken in the course of history. The Evening Sacrifice (original title: The Salute) comments indirectly on the celebration of an unspecified national holiday. The celebration remains offscreen. The film starts when a military salute signals the end of the day, and the people begin to disperse. The title comes from the aria sung by the Bulgarian bass Boris Khristov, which toward the end fills up the screen and cleanses it of all other noises and sounds – the salvos of the artillery and the buzzing of the festive crowd. The camera captures the mood of the young people going home along Leningrad's majestic Nevsky Prospect, they are estranged, disengaged. These scenes "somehow anticipated the emotional depth and scope of the inquiry into youth problems by Yuris Podnieks in Is It Easy To Be Young?"[49] The same suggestive and meditative style gives the other documentaries their peculiar fascinating power – Alto Sonata, on Shostakovich's life, and Patience, Labor, on the hard work and pain associated with the elation of sport competitions and victories. In 1988, Sokurov returned to a documentary he made ten years before, Maria, and added a second part to it. The new footage is intended to be a sad epilogue. While in the first part Maria, a farmer woman, is alive and with her presence and work inspires the best feelings in those who surround her, the second part is about the void she left. Without her the village is a squalid place, and her family is split over a bitter dispute between her husband and daughter. Sokurov's attraction to the documentary genre has not died out, not even after he started working on features on a regular basis. His documentary, *Soviet Elegy* (1990) is a portrait of the charismatic leader Boris Yeltsin. But, as the title suggests (one more "elegy"), the mood is not triumphal. The initial sequence is a long excursion through overgrown cemeteries and dilapidated tombstones. The general impression is of "something in between a trash bin and a poor children's sandbox."[50] This is contrasted with a new, splendid, manicured, and very official cemetery. Together these are "images of a nation-cemetery with an oasis for the chosen ones."[51] Yeltsin is then portrayed on a restful afternoon in his dacha, in the days after his "defeat" at the XIX Party Conference, where he pleaded to no avail to be rehabilitated. There are no words on the soundtrack. Yeltsin just sits there, in a quiet and meditative mood, but the camera brings to the fore his indomitable spirit, a trait that had not yet surfaced in the public arena.

Perestroika and glasnost have opened the vault of a hidden treasure. Although in the inner circles it has always been known that the best productions of the past thirty years were lying on the shelves of Goskino, the general public for the first time had a glimpse of those captive beauties. The main bulk of films released were the victims of Brezhnevism, the non-conformist films produced between the late 1960s and the early 1980s. The year 1967 was particularly harsh on creative filmmaking, as this brief survey showed. Perhaps, since that was the fiftieth anniversary of the Revolution the state committee expected even more orthodox themes and imagery.

But besides these relatively recent films, older pictures were also rescued from oblivion. Among them, rare masterpieces of the 1930s, such as *A Stern Youth* (1936, by Abram Room, from a script by Yuri Olesha), *Lieutenant Kizhe* (1934, by Alexander Feinzimmer, from a script by Yuri Tynyanov), and *Happiness* (1935, by Alexander Medvedkin), which represented an eccentric trend outside of mainstream productions subservient to Socialist Realist dictates. Moreover, the State Film Archive (Gosfilmofond), for the first time made available to the public its invaluable collection of pre-revolutionary Russian films. A program of more than fifty titles, 1908 to 1919, toured European capitals in the fall of 1989, revealing the wealth of the old capitalist film studios and the talent of forgotten directors. Among them, Evgeny Bauer certainly deserves a prominent place in the history of world cinema. These initiatives made it possible not only to fill in the blanks of film production under the totalitarian rule, but also to restore the missing link between the Russian and the Soviet cinema.[52]

6   Exorcizing the past

Rewriting history

The filmmakers' search for the historical causes of today's problems paralleled and often anticipated the same process in the political sphere. As is often the case in the USSR, cinema ran ahead of the events. Soon after the XXVII Party Congress, while politicians and economists were more involved in discussion than in action, documentarists from all over the country set out to fill in the "blank spots" in the history books. One year later they were able to show an impressive array of films investigating dark areas of past history and exposing current problems, often providing a cause-and-effect link.[1]

Of all places, the industrial town of Sverdlovsk in the Urals became a center for the production and exhibition of new documentaries, and in the spring of 1988 hosted the first national festival. The films exhibited there were then included in several programs within the USSR and abroad.[2] In July 1988, on the eve of the XIX Party Conference, a program of more than eighty documentary films was organized by the FU and Goskino and shown at two major Moscow theaters, "Oktiabr" and "Rossia." The title, "The Unknown Cinema: New Geography, New Protagonists, New Discoveries of the Past," referred to the fact that Soviet documentary film has generally been neglected as a genre, and shunned by an audience that perceived it as "boring." With few exceptions, this was in all likelihood an accurate perception up to the time of glasnost. Since then, things have changed. The title of the program also pointed out the "newness" of the current documentary film, made mostly in small studios in the provinces, by young filmmakers at the beginning of their career, and covering (rather uncovering) the unknown past.

These filmmakers were not the only ones to focus on historical truth. They were part of the general trend aimed at filling in the "blanks" in the history books, which involves writers, journalists, educators, and historians up to the highest echelons of the Academy

138

of Sciences. Rolan Bykov, then a secretary of the Filmmakers Union and a prominent film director–actor, said in an interview: "Documentary film made such a jump ahead that it will take five to ten years for feature films to catch up with it."[3] In fact, nowadays the documentary film parallels and even rivals the literary *publitsistika* – a prose genre charged with sharp sociopolitical criticism, be it journalism or fiction – that since the beginning of glasnost has amazed, delighted, and inflamed an increasingly alert readership. The next step would be to refine aesthetic form and techniques which in the rush for truth have been neglected.[4]

Notwithstanding the good will of the film establishment, however, distribution and exhibition of documentaries are far from optimal, as in most other countries. Out of some one hundred movie theaters in Moscow only one, and a poorly equipped one, is devoted to the regular showing of documentaries. Exceptions occur, like the showings mentioned above, or the showings that follow the release of particularly significant films, such as *More Light* (1988) and, more recently, *This Is No Way To Live* (1990). But these are, as said, exceptions. The truth is that these films are poorly booked, receive no publicity, and when bought for broadcast on television are given unpopular time slots. This is no longer a result of political repression. "We are not talking about forbidden films," complains a reporter, "these films are actually recommended for public viewing . . . simply there are no viable distribution channels."[5] A film scholar reports the following true anecdote: A little girl believes that God does not exist, because "otherwise they would have already shown him on TV." "The kid is right," comments the scholar, "at least with regard to documentary films, if they are not shown on TV they do not exist."[6] And yet, they do. And, notwithstanding the adverse mechanics that affect the distribution system in general, information is in the public domain and, no matter how, it does get to the audiences.

A documentary that was given star billing when it hit the commercial screens in February 1988 was *More Light*, by Marina Babak. Made to celebrate the seventieth anniversary of the October Revolution, the film is a survey of seven decades of Soviet history revised according to Gorbachev's vision – reaffirmation of Lenin's legacy, denunciation of Stalinism and Brezhnevism, rehabilitation of Bukharin and his economic policies, praise of Khrushchev's honesty, and a general attempt to fill in the blanks with hard facts. The narrator is the stage and movie actor Mikhail Ulyanov, a personal friend of Gorbachev's, who played a major role, in real life, at the Party

Conference as one of the most vocal sustainers of the General Secretary's program. Ulyanov starts his commentary with a clear statement of intent: "Everyone is sick of the silence. We are going to try to talk about the past with more honesty, more light." The first image to fill the screen, in extreme close-up, is an unusual portrait of Lenin, painted in 1934 by the modernist artist Petrov-Vodkin. This portrait, called "Meditation," has rarely been shown. It was given very low marks because of the lack of confidence and optimism in the leader's stance. But what was a flaw yesterday is an asset today. A Soviet film reviewer noticed: "Lenin's stare is apprehensive. Looking into the future he seems to ask the question: How did we live all these years? This shot provides the main structural element of the film, its very conceptual nucleus."[7]

Indeed, after the opening, images rarely ever seen before on the Soviet screen start rolling in one after another: the first Bolshevik government – Bukharin, Trotsky, Kamenev, Stalin; the prosperous years of NEP that for the Soviet economy meant "the sound of Russian rubles, real money";[8] the abuses of collectivization; the desecration of churches; the decimation of the military; the purges; scenes of destruction and misery in World War II as a consequence of a weakened army; sinister figures of the 1940s – Beria, Lysenko; positive figures of the 1960s – Khrushchev; *defitsity* (lack of consumer goods) and the Potemkin facade in the stagnation period; Brezhnev's delusions of grandeur; and finally the Chernobyl disaster. There are also images of achievements, of course, to balance the picture. And the movie ends with a celebration of folkish glasnost – rock music, people's diplomacy, and peace movements. But the emphasis is on the mistakes. As Ulyanov says: "We are a gifted people, but something has held us back." Conspicuous for its absence is the image of Gorbachev himself, as well as those of Andropov and Chernenko. Their names are not even mentioned.

For all its good intentions, however, *More Light* failed to satisfy demanding audiences. Yuri Afanasev, political leader and the outspoken rector of the Historical Archives Institute, criticized the film for placing the blame on leaders only, exonerating society. The result, he said, is "a film that lies," because all those failures "cannot only be the fault of just a few people."[9] *More Light* is emblematic of the early phase of glasnost, when the denunciation of some leaders and events was meant to improve the system, not to shake its foundation. In reality, it opened a Pandora's box that could not be resealed. The process of revelation got out of hand, acquiring a life of its own.

At first Stalin was flatly exposed as a demonic figure responsible for all past and present evils; then the responsibility was partly shifted to the people who, whether passively or blindly, accepted and perpetuated the injustices of the system; and finally the inquiry went on to point a finger at the very principles of Marxism–Leninism.

Today, as the Communist Party seems to have lost its leading position, old myths are debunked one after another. Even Lenin is being stripped of his sacred halo, and the historical continuities between Lenin and Stalin have been pointed out in the press and in films.[10] There have been some proposals to remove Lenin's body from his mausoleum and inter him next to Stalin, where he belongs. The most provocative call came from Mark Zakharov, the progressive director of the Leninsky Komsomol Theater, who had staged plays featuring Lenin in a less than official light, even before perestroika. Zakharov appeared on the late night show, "Vzglyad" (April 21, 1989), and made the following statement: "No matter how much we hate a person, no matter how much we love him, we do not have the right to deprive a person of burial." Zakharov maintained that the embalmed corpse had turned Lenin into a tourist attraction.[11] The idea was immediately denounced as blasphemous by some members of the Central Committee, but in the popular imagination it gave birth to the latest joke on the subject: in tune with the era of the joint venture, the government should sell the corpse to an American entrepreneur for a fairground show.

"There are no more taboos for 'the man with the movie camera' . . . a body of information that was unthinkable before has now reached the viewer," noted a Soviet journalist as early as 1988.[12] At that time the absence of censorship was already a common practice but not a legal reality. Nevertheless, the documentarists were pushing the limits of the permissible. In the summer of 1988, an explosive documentary was shown on national television, *Risk-2*, by directors Dimitri Barshchevsky and Natalya Violina. The film equated Stalin with Hitler and Mao Tse-tung and denounced their common criminal behavior.

By looking back at the past, the documentarists try to explain the present. The common question, central to most films is: what was the cause of the present collapse of our economy, the loss of spiritual values, the lack of moral principles and civic pride, and what are the prospects for our youth in a society that has lost a clear direction? These questions cannot be easily answered, but at least they set the ground for an honest evaluation of the current situation. Mainstream

documentaries present today's problems as a direct consequence of
two periods of Soviet history: the Stalinist years that first created a
myth and then crushed it under a wave of terror, leaving the people
with shattered dreams and shattered lives; and the Brezhnev period,
that filled that void with the image of a materialistic utopia, attainable
through cynicism, unscrupulousness, and superficial conformism.
Only a few among the hundreds of significant documentaries dealing
with past history can be noted here, but they are a representative
sample. *And the Past Seems But a Dream* (1987), by Sergei Miroshnichenko, is about the brutal resettlement of whole groups of the
population in the 1930s. *The Trial* (1988), by Igor Belyaev, takes a
frank look at past mistakes and poses a question about the future of
the nation. Bukharin's wife, Nadezhda Larina, reveals for the first
time her husband's "Testament." The film was so probing that even
in the era of glasnost it was released with great difficulty and only
after an eight-month struggle. The administration was overly
cautious in releasing a film made for television (and, therefore, for an
audience of millions) which included a political document by a former
"enemy of the people." The documentary has two parts: Part I is a
chronicle of the events of the 1930s and 1940s. Part II is today's
reaction to them, a look at the future of the country conditioned by its
past.

Solovki Power (1988), by Marina Goldovskaya, stands out for the
depth and length of the investigation into one of the deadliest and
best organized islands of the Gulag. The Solovki camp became a
territorial power in itself, with its internal "laws," social structures,
commanding hierarchy. The surviving victims of the Solovki system
provide a poignant testimony to the horrors they suffered, and an
overdue memorial to those who perished. Academician Dmitri
Likhachev, who spent time at the camp, is among those interviewed,
together with other well known figures and simple folks. On a less
tragic note, *Black Square* (1988), by Yosif Pasternak refers to the title of
the famous canvas by Kazimir Malevich (1915), but deals with a more
recent past – the Khrushchev and Brezhnev period. It focuses on the
fate of the "unofficial" painters forced to work in the underground.
Khrushchev's castigation of the avant-garde artists at the infamous
exhibition at the Manege Hall (1963) is given a farcical slant, although
the director uses only original footage. More dramatic are the
reminiscences of the exhibition in Izmailovsky Park (1976), when
paintings were smashed by bulldozers. *Wood-Goblin* (1987), by Boris
Kustov, is the story of a World War II veteran who has lived in

isolation in the woods for fifteen years, during the Brezhnev period, in order to preserve his dignity in a struggle for justice against Party bureaucrats. The implication of this film is that the Stalinist legacy survived after the famous secret speech of Khrushchev at the XX Party Congress, and resurfaced with renewed vigor in the 1970s. The film presents another innocent victim of the system, no longer executed as in the old days, but politically and professionally assassinated by false charges and vicious allegations. Another such character is the central figure of the film *The Tailor* (1988), by Vladislav Mirzoyan. From the perspective of the era of glasnost the years of the Brezhnev administration are seen as a return to the Stalinist mentality without the excesses of fanatic dogmatism, but with the same distortions of basic morality, now under a mask of bigotry and respectable conformism.

Some documentaries on military figures are particularly effective in conveying the depth of the country's malaise in the Stalinist years. *Marshal Blücher* (1988), by Vladimir Eisner, is one of them. Biographical details about the man allow us to perceive more vividly the absurdity of the facts presented. Vasily Blücher had been a Bolshevik since 1916. He was a Red Army commander during the Civil War, commander of the Far Eastern Army during the hostilities in China (1929), a member of the Central Committee in 1934, and became a marshall in 1935. He earned a whole collection of medals and decorations. But the focus of the film is not on his distinguished career, rather on an episode inconsistent with a life marked by great courage and integrity. In 1937, Blücher participated in the martial court that sentenced to death the best army commanders, before being himself liquidated by Stalin's butchers. The question the film poses is: why? And not only why did Blücher take part in that sinister game, but, and more important, why did everybody else, the average citizen, participate in a collective delusion. *The Story of Marshal Konev* (1988), by L. Danilov, and *Marshal Rokossovsky, Life and Time* (1988), by Boris Golovnya, were characterized by the Soviet press as the first documents on screen of "the repressions of 1937–39, which destroyed the flower of the Red Army of Workers and Peasants." These facts, a Soviet reviewer says, are treated "openly and sharply, without ambiguity and omissions, and, most important, with convincing evidence from fully investigated facts, documents, and genuine testimony of the time."[13]

Two gems of the new documentary wave are the films by Semyon Aranovich *The Personal Files of Anna Akhmatova* and *I Served in Stalin's*

Guard, both released in 1989. The path to the completion of the Akhmatova film was long and painful, it was almost the fulfillment of a dream for the director, who fought the administration for twenty years. Akhmatova's life is reconstructed on the background of a totalitarian society, weaving the relationship between the poet and history. At the risk of being arrested, Aranovich filmed Akhmatova's funeral, in 1966, capturing the collective grief of the intelligentsia. Unique images of Yosif Brodsky among the mourners are included in the documentary. Other pinnacles of the artistic world appear in rare archival footage – Tsvetaeva, Mayakovsky, Blok, Gumilev, Mandelstam, Pasternak, and Solzhenitsyn – alternating with sinister and at times funny portraits of the leaders, from Nikolay II to Brezhnev. Out of the poetic montage, Akhmatova emerges as a towering figure, whose voice and soul preserved the spiritual dimension of the national culture in an epoch of moral barbarism. The second film is a veritable flip side of the coin, focusing on the figure of Major Rybin, one of the many officers, now retired, who once served in Stalin's secret police. The film's authors portray the former bodyguard in his present capacities, as an accordion teacher to a children's class, and do not interfere with Rybin's memories, giving him complete freedom of expression. Many intellectuals appreciated the ironical approach to the topic, but worried that unsophisticated viewers may take Rybin's words at face value, as if it were the film's point of view. Rybin's "recollections" of Stalin border on the legendary, close in literary style and flavor to the medieval *vitae* of orthodox saints:

He was strict, certainly, but just, simple, and good. Loved his wife and after her death he did not remarry and was not interested in women in general. Loved children . . . He did not disdain the simple people, and when a worker was having a bath in his personal bathhouse the Master, together with Kirov, would stand in the street and wait . . . He was a close friend of Kirov. He worried a lot about him . . . And when it was raining and he passed in his car by a trolley stop, he would get out of the car, and order the driver to take those drenched people wherever they wanted to go. That's the way he was. Unassuming. All he left in his savings book was four rubles and a few kopeks.[14]

A documentary, called *Is Stalin With Us?* (1989) by T. Shakhverdiev, comments sadly on the fact that the legend dies hard. It focuses on the contemporary scene, and introduces the viewer to a group of staunch Stalinists which includes a public prosecutor from Kharkov, a foreman from a Tbilisi factory, a taxi driver also from Tbilisi, and a Moscow schoolmistress. While there is no sure way to measure the number of nostalgic followers, the director tries to measure the intensity of their feelings. The film presents their conversations and monologues without verbal commentary, leaving it to the camera to give words and actions the proper emphasis. A few fragments are offered here in that same spirit, although without the benefit of the camera work. The schoolmistress: "My family is this one man, for whom I live . . . Every year I go to the places connected with his life, to see those houses that he might have seen, to walk the streets he might have walked. This is a thread that ties me with the man that is now gone . . . He is my happiness. I love Stalin." The taxi driver: "He will live in my heart forever . . . If tomorrow they'll put me against a wall to be shot, I will still shout, 'Long live Stalin!', like those innocent prisoners did in 1937." The factory foreman: "If the masses followed Stalin, and respected and loved him, it means that he was right in his great task." He also comments on the present situation in a typical Stalinist idiom: "The enemies of perestroika are those who disfigure the Soviet reality. Those who let the minds of the youth be governed by Western pornography, by the Western way of life, by Western ideology. Because Western ideology is attractive. This is the danger!" As for the taxi driver, he has just one thing to say about perestroika: "Stalin, in his whole life, only once uttered the word 'perestroika.' And the people, without flinching, obeyed! That was it! And now, take the newspapers: 'Perestroika!' . . . the magazines: 'Perestroika!' . . . 'Perestroika!' . . . 'Perestroika!' Well, it means that the people don't get the message."[15]

Another indicator of the people's feelings toward the "Father of the peoples" is the mail received by newspapers and journals. Many readers feel like the protagonists of the film. But they are outnumbered by those who call Stalin a "bloody czar of socialism," and a "dictator, executioner, and murderer" who can only live "in the hearts of toadies and today's Berias."[16] An investigative documentary on a significant episode of Stalinist history was started in the spring of 1989 virtually on public demand. The journal *Ogonek* (No. 26, 1987) had printed the story, well known in the West but unknown at home, of the open letter to Stalin by the dissident Fyodor Raskolnikov (pseudonym of F. Ilin). In his 1938 letter, he provided an insightful analysis of "the mad politics of the oriental despot," and his name became anathema.[17] The film, titled *Crime Without Punishment*, is based on the script by I. Margolina and V. Korotich, the editor-in-chief of *Ogonek*, and is directed by Mark Lyakhovetsky. The director noted that today one can already see a trivialization of the theme of

Stalin. "Every single frame of documentary footage that includes Stalin has been transferred on videotape, they are even shown as an illustration for rock groups' compositions. Those years are losing their tragic dimension in the mass consciousness. We may be unable to come to a conclusion of that bloody, frightening theme."[18] Because of this situation, Lyakhovetsky thinks that the objective assessment his film affords is very much needed.

Debunking the myth

Feature films, too, showed an urgency to inquire into the past and come to grips with its problematic legacy. *My Friend Ivan Lapshin*, made in 1983 by Alexei German, was released in 1985 after a two-year skirmish with Goskino. The dispute was due in part to the fact that it dealt with a very sensitive period of Soviet history – the 1930s, the years of forced collectivization, famine, the purges. Although this background is absent from the film, the realistic portrayal of ordinary life in those days, so different from the propagandistic films of the period about the marvels of industrialization, was in itself unaccept-

16 *My Friend Ivan Lapshin* (1983/rel. 1985) directed by Alexei German

17 *My Friend Ivan Lapshin* (1983/rel. 1985) directed by Alexei German

able. To make matters worse, the film was the creation of a very original talent, which automatically made the censors uncomfortable. The ambiguity of the multilayered text and the lack of clear narrative closures looked like an ideological trap to the official scanning eye, a visual quagmire that might harbor insidious meanings.

Like *Trial On the Road*, this film is based on a story by the director's father, Yuri German. The action takes place in a northern provincial town, and is related by a narrator who "witnessed" the events as a child. The main plot hinges on the struggle of the head of a small police unit, the officer Ivan Lapshin, against a gang of bloodthirsty criminals who terrorize the local population. But this movie is more than a simple detective story. In fact its slow-paced rhythm and fragmentary structure deny the conventions of the genre. Rather, the film is the evocation of a forgotten past – a past marked, on the one hand, by brutality, lawlessness, prostitution, and the hardships of communal apartments, and on the other, by lofty as well as naive ideals. The grim reality of life in the provincial town is juxtaposed to the idealized world of a play which is being staged in the local theater. In the play, criminals can be reformed through labor, and prostitutes can be redeemed through love and compassion.[19] Lapshin knows that in real life criminals are often shot in cold blood (as he eventually does with the gang's chief), and love is an elusive dream (the actress of the local theater rejects him for a friend of his). And yet, as a simple man with a basic faith in the human being, Lapshin accepts the illusion of the theater as the depiction of the ideal toward which he is striving. The motif of illusory reality runs through the film as a reminder of the Stalinist myth that was being built in the 1930s. By juxtaposing these two planes, German succeeds in removing all naiveté from his film while preserving the substance of the ideal.

When the film was broadcast on television in early 1986 it became the subject of heated debate among the public. The film was at once exciting and disturbing. It offered a glimpse of an historical period that had been proscribed until then. But the portrait of that period was very personal, and left many viewers uncertain about the intentions of the director. What was his point of view? Why did he choose a police officer as the hero? What was he really saying about the Stalinist years, besides the fact that life was hard and drab in the provinces? The confusion was reinforced by the subjective camera and the post-modernist montage, virtually new in Soviet cinema.[20] It was too early for the general audience to believe what they were seeing on the big screen, in the open. Later, it became obvious that German's hero, Ivan Lapshin, was presented as a victim of the system – a true believer in the communist ideals, doomed to perish, strangled by the machine that he helped to build. His fate was similar to that of many others – Kirov, for example, whose portrait opens the retrospective core of the film and sheds a mournful shadow on the whole narrative. The year 1935, right after the Leningrad party chief was assassinated, was the last moment before the beginning of the great terror, a moment when it was still possible to nurture the illusion of a future, perfect world. German intended to pay a tribute to a generation that believed in the Stalinist myth and perished with it. He said in an interview: "The story I am telling is about the real life of these people, their faith, their melancholy, the fact that they go straight ahead toward communism without understanding that the road is long and dangerous. Maybe these people included my father and my mother."[21]

Ivan Lapshin has also troubled some Western critics, who perceived a certain nostalgia for those years. Indeed, there is a nostalgic aura, deliberately conveyed through the film's structural and stylistic devices. But it is not the longing for the Stalin regime, rather it is nostalgia for a lost dream. With this film German acknowledges the loss of innocence typical of his generation and looks back at the early 1930s and the naive heros of his childhood with tenderness and fondness. In the course of the film, Stalin is only alluded to indirectly, by slogans and citations, but a portrait, showing the generalissimo grinning under his mustache, appears at the very end, as a counterpoint to the portrait of Kirov. Embellished with red flags and ribbons, it hangs on the steel chest of a streetcar headed for the land of utopia. Given the context, this was an ironical representation of the leader, meant to raise doubts rather than affirm beliefs. It was also clear from the narrative structure, that linked past and present, that the consequences of Stalinism were pervasive in today's society.

Other films continued the debunking of the myths of the past, some by oblique allusions, some with tragic realism, some as devastating parodies. But none reached the level of cinematic sophistication displayed by German. His film, to this day, remains the best product of the glasnost wave.[22]

The following two films, like *Ivan Lapshin*, do not portray directly historical figures and events, but present a fictional narrative on a real background. *Mirror for the Hero* (1988), by Vladimir Khotinenko, follows the lives of ordinary people, their trials and simple joys "in a day like any other during the time of the cult,"[23] in a miners' town, and at the same time conveys the illusory atmosphere of the period. Cleverly, the film links past and present by means of a fantastic device. The hero, as if by magic, finds himself back in his native town – and back in time, in the year 1949, when he existed only in his mother's womb. He meets his pregnant mother who addresses him politely, like a stranger. He observes the life of his parents shaped by collective songs, marching tunes, and radio propaganda, and is tortured by the impossibility of warning them about future consequences, or changing the course of events in any way. Back into the present time, he is able to develop a more compassionate relation with his father, and to "forgive" him for the mistakes of the past. The film was intended to appease the people of that generation, who felt personally attacked by so many films critical of the period of their youth, and holding them responsible for the tragic events of those years.

A similar purpose seems to have inspired *Tomorrow There Was War* (1987), by Yuri Kara. This was the director's first film, started in 1984 as his diploma work, and later turned into a feature-length movie. It is based on a short novel by B. Vasilev, that focuses on a group of high-school students at the end of the 1930s, and the implied tragedy of that generation. Those teenagers had not only to endure the atmosphere of suspicion and repression of the time of the purges in their daily lives, but were facing the cataclysm of World War II without even knowing it.

The odd grammar of the title conveys both the teenagers' placement in time (before the war) and the director's point of view (after the war). Kara himself commented on the main idea of the film: "I wanted to talk about the generation of the 1930s–1940s, that unfortunately cannot talk about itself from the screen. Some were killed, others still live with the fear which they carried on from the time of the cult, and which does not allow them to speak up openly . . . Now, when many have lost their pride in the flag, in the national emblem, and the national anthem, we tried to understand the people of that remote time, for whom this pride was the substance of their personality."[24]

The lives of the teenagers, their parents, and teachers are portrayed in a romantic, retro style with no pretense to documentary accuracy. Rather than a chronicle, the film is a condensed sample of the collective mood of a generation, conveyed through a few key characters and episodes. The most dramatic episode deals with the beautiful and sensitive Vika, the daughter of an "enemy of the people," who, ostracized and expelled from the Komsomol, ends up committing suicide.

While in the roles of the adults Kara cast actors of tested experience – Vera Alentova as the evil teacher Valendra, and Yuri Zamansky as Vika's father, a gentle intellectual victim of the repression – he chose young people just out of the actors' school to play the roles of the teenagers. Among them was Natalya Negoda, who soon after this first film acquired international fame as "little Vera."

In *The Cold Summer of '53* (1988), by Alexander Proshkin, the action is more directly linked with the crimes of Stalinism, and focuses on a specific episode in a small village. In the wake of Stalin's death, a general amnesty opened the gates of the concentration camps, freeing political prisoners and criminals alike. The story highlights the heroism of two political exiles who had been living in a small village in northern Russia. When the folk are terrorized by a gang of criminals, the former exiles single-handedly organize the village defense. Echoes of *The Magnificent Seven*, and in turn *The Seven Samurai*, are undeniable; the fast pace, dynamic editing, emotional camera work,

18   *The Cold Summer of '53* (1988) directed by Alexander Proshkin

and harrowing musical track, so atypical for a Soviet movie, cast a dramatic episode of national history into the mold of the western. The genre was certainly responsible for the popular success of the film, but the subject matter and its implications provided it with sub-stance.[25] The larger picture of official criminality is implied. Labor camps and mock trials are directly discussed. There is no explicit reference to the present, but there is a projection of the perpetuation of the Big Lie into the future, when at the end of the film the son of one of the political exiles who died in the fighting is reluctant to accept the truth about his father and prefers to ignore the tragedy that befell his family, afraid to lose "respectability."

While *Cold Summer* relies on action, another recent film, *Our Armored Train* (1989), by Mikhail Ptashuk, is a psychological drama. It is the tragic story of a former camp supervisor, Nikolay Kuznetsov, haunted by the memories of the past. It is now the year 1966, and his ex-colleagues either adapted to the new times, or live in isolation, full of nostalgia and spite. But he cannot do either; he is still convinced of being an "honest man," of having performed a good and necessary job, and expects society to acknowledge his service to the country. Instead, society rejects him – not necessarily because of his values, but because of the defiant, embarrassing, way he upholds them. His "idealism," his "style" are simply no longer in fashion in the

Brezhnev era, an era of complacent silence, not of soul-searching. Finally he has no other way out of his dilemma but suicide. His nostalgic friends, however, endure, like dormant viruses in society's body. This has been called a film about "corpse poison" – a poison whose "terrible action" continues long after the corpse has been buried. Significantly, one of the main characters says: "We are now retired, but tomorrow if the enemies of the people or the cosmopolitans reappear we'll be ready . . . Our armored train is on the side track, waiting. We are this armored train."[26] The character's speech is full of pathos, and conjures up the image of a phantom train bursting out of a cloud of steam in all its patriotic splendor. But often the dialogue is too long and pedantic, and it is only saved by superb acting. Notable are the performances of Mikhail Ulyanov, Alexei Petrenko, and A. Filippenko, as the Gulag colleagues, and of V. Gostyukhin as the tragic hero.

As a Soviet reviewer noted, "the film's authors are already debunking the new stereotype of the 'Stalinist' that we have created. The figure of Kuznetsov is much more complex."[27] Indeed, the film discourages the facile assumption that all criminals are alike – even the infamous butchers of the Gulag camps – and suggests that in some of them there is still a human being with his inner drama. In fact, it takes just a turn of the tables for the criminal to become a victim of the society he had once victimized.

Defense Counsel Sedov (1989) is a film of great significance, artistic as well as political. This black-and-white short (only 48 mins.), by director Evgeny Tsimbal and screenwriter Maria Zvereva, is bound to become a classic. At the height of the Stalinist terror, a Moscow lawyer, counsel Sedov, takes upon himself the task of defending four "enemies of the people," four agronomists accused of sabotage and already sentenced to death. He travels to a provincial town, hoping to convince the local procurator to reopen the case on the base of new evidence. Alas, he is fighting against a monolith of bureaucratic indifference and fear. There is no correlation between justice and law. The legal system is a machine for processing papers and human lives alike, speedily and efficiently. In a gesture that may cost him his life, Sedov, usually a quiet, unassuming, ordinary citizen, decides to appeal to the highest authorities. Up to this point the story is told in a documentary-like style, focusing on realistic details of the *mise-en-scène* and on the characters' psychology. From this point on, the narrative takes an ironic turn, and ends with a chilling twist. A hero in spite of himself, Sedov expects the worst (and the viewer with

him). But it turns out that, in the tragicomedy of errors which
unfolded in the political arena, the General Procurator (maybe, Stalin
himself?) decided to be magnanimous: the prisoners are freed and
rehabilitated, and Sedov is awarded a medal for his patriotic work.
But the ten provincial officials "unmasked" by Sedov are arrested and
killed. During a pompous show of totalitarian folly, a veritable theater
of the absurd, Sedov is crushed by the realization that he has been
used to bring new victims to the butcher shop. The announcement
sounds to his ears like his own death sentence. Then, the action
switches to newsreel footage, and the viewer sees Anastas Mikoyan[28]
delivering a venomous speech about saboteurs, traitors, Trotskyites,
and foreign agents at the twentieth anniversary celebration of the
security organs, held at the Bolshoi Theater. The theater is festooned
with self-congratulatory slogans and filled to capacity with a jubilant
crowd. Thus, the story of defense counsel Sedov acquires a ring of
truth.

The film, *Freeze, Die, Resurrect* (1989), by Vitaly Kanevsky, offers an
unusual point of view of the Gulag. The title alludes to a children's
game, and the action revolves around the life of two pre-teen friends,
Valerka and Galya. The two children live in a mining town inside the
camp system, where the demarcation between prison and freedom is
almost non-existent. Even outside the "zone," people live in barracks
and are subjected to lawlessness and tyrannical rule. Valerka and
Galya manage to enjoy life as best they can, they develop a strong
interdependence, and are obviously in love without yet knowing it.
But complications arise. Valerka has to leave, he gets as far as
Vladivostok, where he falls victim of a criminal band. Galya comes to
his rescue, but on the way home they are seized by the bandits. The
adventure plot gives the film a commercial advantage, but it does not
distract from the central idea. The director is able to recreate the
atmosphere of the time with regard to the effect it had on the children. The subhuman life of the hellish town is a poorly disguised
metaphor for the general living conditions in the country, and points
to the fact that a whole generation has been deprived of its childhood.
The film was recognized in several international festivals, including
Cannes.
   A rare exception in the midst of gloom and tragedy is a comedy
from Gruziafilm, by Nana Djordjadze, one of the younger representatives of the small pool of women directors. Her film, *Robinsoniade, or
My English Grandfather* (1986), won the Golden Camera Award at the

19 *Freeze, Die, Resurrect* (1989) directed by Vitaly Kanevsky

Cannes Festival. It is both a political satire and a romantic comedy –
the story of a British engineer who comes to Soviet Georgia in the
1920s to help with the construction of a telegraph line. He gets
involved with the sister of the local Party chief, which leads to a series
of comic situations that eventually come to a tragic end.

The seven heads of the dragon

While these films focus on the background and give the victims of
power center stage, other films switch to power itself and focus on a
central figure emblematic of political evil. The first and foremost film
in this category is *Repentance* (1984/1986), by Tengiz Abuladze, a production of Gruziafilm – the Georgian film studio. The fact that it was
possible at all to get this film past preliminary censorship (script
approval, for example) and into production was due in part to the
personal support of the then Georgia Party Secretary, Eduard
Shevarnadze, and in part to the geographical location. Georgia was
far removed from the center and enjoyed a certain degree of autonomy, thanks to the official policy of support for ethnic cultures.
According to this policy, Georgian television could use a three-hour

20   *Repentance* (1984/rel. 1986) directed by Tengiz Abuladze

period daily for local broadcasting, unsupervised by the central
Gosteleradio administration. Hence, *Repentance* was made for Georgian television, but it was not aired before its release two years after
completion. Nobody suspected at that time that the film was on its
way to becoming an international hit, and a real turning point in the
history of Soviet cinema. The circumstances of its making testify to
the talent, inventiveness, and expediency of the Georgian filmmakers
who are regarded as being among the best in the Soviet Union.

Repentance is an extended metaphor for the endurance of the Stalinist legacy. It is a "difficult" film with a complex structure, and one
must give Abuladze credit for sacrificing clarity, and possibly losing
some audiences, in order to remain faithful to his artistic commitment. The way the narrative is constructed is disorienting because of
time discontinuity and unclear transitions between reality, dream,
memories, and fantasy. The film has a circular structure. It begins and
ends at the same place and at the same time – at the moment when
the heroine of the story, Keti Barateli, learns about the death of the
tyrant and dictator, Varlam Aravidze, who had destroyed her family

when she was a child. What constitutes the body of the story between the prologue and the epilogue takes place in Keti's mind and includes her repeated attempts at exhuming Varlam's body, her trial, and her memories of childhood. It also includes her perception of Varlam's descendants – his son and heir to power, Abel (played by the same actor, Avtondil Makharadze, in a masterful performance), and his rebellious grandson, Tornike. The narrative structure is further complicated by the fact that this long dream sequence includes in turn other dreams (rather, nightmares) by different characters, so that the viewer is faced with a construction *en abîme* (a dream, within a dream, within a dream . . .).[29] All this creates the effect of a "tragic phantasmagoria," as Abuladze himself put it. The director's intent, however, was not to lead the viewer away from reality. On the contrary, the "phantasmagoria" was supposed to reveal the truth about an epoch, that by its official mendacity, institutionalized hypocrisy, delusions of grandeur, secret trials, and absurd executions now appears to be more "phantasmagoric" than any fiction.[30]

Abuladze created a surrealist tale of horror and set it in an imaginary time and place, so that from its abstraction from history it may be endowed with a universal significance. But no matter how generalized the characters and the locale are, the symbolism of the film cuts very close to the bone for a Soviet viewer. This is what the poet Robert Rozhdestvensky said about *Repentance*: "And so, 'Once upon a time . . . ' No, no more make believe and pretending that nobody understands and remembers anything! Yes, all this happened in our country! Our country, mine and yours . . . But the lessons of the past, even the most difficult and painful ones, do not disappear. It is necessary to learn them, to get to know their full extent. Otherwise, what kind of lessons are they?"[31]

The film is dominated by the grotesque figure of Varlam, the incarnation of the quintessential dictator. He is a composite caricature of Stalin, Hitler, and Mussolini, and an allusion to the cinematic "great dictator," Charlie Chaplin. To a Soviet audience he is also the effigy of Lavrenti Beria, who headed Stalin's secret police. But besides obvious references to historical leaders of opposite political color and identical totalitarian inclination, Varlam is also portrayed as a demonic figure. A religious thread runs through the film, as in Abuladze's previous pictures, *The Prayer* (1969) and *The Tree of Desire* (1978), which together with *Repentance* are regarded as a trilogy. Varlam's satanic nature is brought to the fore by opposition to the character of the painter Sandro, Keti's father. Through a skillful handling of image associations, Sandro comes across as a Christ figure, a champion of spiritual values and a victim of senseless repression. One cannot miss the symbolism of Sandro's death. He is shown hanging by his wrists, wearing a white loincloth, and the moment of his passing is underscored by a thunderous explosion (later, the viewer learns that the explosion had demolished an ancient church, on Varlam's orders). Similarly, Varlam is shown in the underground, skinning and eating a fish in a profane rite of Communion – a veritable Black Mass. Abuladze does not utilize this opposition merely to create an abstract, cosmic confrontation between good and evil. His aim seems to be more focused. The director touches on the "dictator syndrome," the pathological urge to be not so much feared as admired, loved, worshiped. In other words, to become God. And who if not Satan can best embody that urge? Like Satan, Varlam is a great actor. He appears in many guises and with many faces, and he always presents himself in the best light. But as the narrative progresses from farce to tragedy, Varlam's face consolidates into the mask of criminal folly.

Evil is insidious, the film warns, and perpetuates itself through the generations. Significantly, Varlam's corpse keeps reappearing as long as Abel justifies his father's crimes. The Soviet generation of the 1960s, who enjoyed an early cultural "thaw," certainly remembers the poem by Evgeny Evtushenko "The Heirs of Stalin," that presented the same grotesque image of the vampire-like dictator laughing in his coffin. "I find Abel even more dangerous than Varlam," said Abuladze. "While Varlam is consistent and, to some extent, predictable, Abel is absolutely unpredictable. He is a man of double consciousness, unable to tell good from evil."[32] *Repentance* not only explores the past but it also relates the past to the present and warns that the legacy of Varlam is still alive and has to be confronted in order to be exorcized. In a dramatic finale Abel's son, disgusted with hypocrisy and injustice, commits suicide, and his tragedy prompts Abel to unearth Varlam's body and throw it over a cliff. Now the viewer, having been delivered from evil, can sigh with relief . . . except that all this was a daydream – a fantasy spun in the mind of the film's heroine.

The epilogue brings the action back to a full circle. Keti comes back to reality when an old woman stops by the kitchen window and asks her whether this is the road that leads to the church. Keti sadly admits: "No, this is Varlam Road." The church that was blown up earlier in the film was a deliberate reminder of the beautiful church of

Christ the Savior, destroyed by Stalin in 1934 in order to build a huge monument to Lenin but whose site is now a swimming pool. In the film this historical episode becomes a metaphor for the loss of spiritual life, resulting in the lack of moral stamina. Keti, while picturing herself as a heroine willing to undergo trial for an act of civic courage, in real life makes a quiet living baking cakes out of her kitchen. She builds elaborate churches of sugar and honey, designed as kitschy curiosities for fashionable tables, but is unable, or unwilling, to put her life on the line in order to rebuild the spiritual church. The implication is obvious and disturbing: she is a victim, and nevertheless, like Abel, she shares responsibility for the perpetuation of Varlam's legacy. Therefore, the "repentance" implied in the title is purely speculative. The film does not end with a catharsis. Rather, it offers the viewers an open ending, and suggests that it is up to them to perform the exorcism.

Repentance became an instant sensation in the Moscow intellectual circles and at international festivals. But what was a merit for the critics looked like a flaw to young Soviet audiences. The magazine *Soviet Screen* was flooded with letters protesting Abuladze's "difficult form," that in many cases was perceived as another cover-up. "Who is Varlam Aravidze?", writes a group of Moscow students. "A composite image of all tyrants from Nero to our day? But then he is lacking concrete social roots . . . What gave birth to Varlam? We do not find an answer to this question in the film and therefore the tyrant comes across as an attribute of fate . . . This approach certainly does not respond to the present demand for historical truth." And another reader offers a suggestion of what is needed: "Today we need investigative films, film-analyses without allusions and symbols. We need the naked, unadorned truth, where Stalin is shown without the mask of a demigod . . . The problem of the 'cult of personality' is so big that it cannot be resolved through the language of Aesop."[33]

A monster similar to Varlam is the protagonist of the film *To Kill the Dragon* (1988). Based on a play by Evgeny Shvarts, directed by Mark Zakharov, and starring celebrities such as Oleg Yankovsky and Evgeny Leonov, the film was full of promise when it came out. But, aesthetically, it fell flat on its face notwithstanding the co-production deal with West Germany that provided state of the art technology and quality film stock.[34] It is worth discussing it, however, for its thematic similarities with *Repentance*. The core of this tale, set in a Gothic town, is the confrontation of Lancelot – a distant relative of *the* Lancelot –

with the dragon – a symbol of tyranny and dictatorship. The monster appears in many forms: as the dragon itself, as an innocent looking young man in a white suit, as a blood-thirsty samurai, and as an officer in a Nazi-like uniform. As expected, Lancelot wins the duel, fighting against all odds. But as soon as he leaves town, headed for future deeds, the local Bürgermeister picks up the dragon's legacy and turns into the next tyrant. The power of the dragon to resurrect himself is suggested by an ominous metaphor. As the last sequence unfolds, Lancelot meets a group of children frolicking after a dragon kite, on an unbounded snowy expanse. One adult leads the group – the dragon himself, now in the plain clothes of a schoolteacher.

In the same vein, *The Wife of the Kerosine Seller* (1989) evokes the hallucinatory atmosphere of provincial Russia under the rule of Stalin's devilish cohort. The setting is Kaliningrad, in the winter of 1953. The actor Alexander Kaidanovsky, who is best known for his role as the "stalker" in Tarkovsky's film of that name, here performs as director and screenwriter. A certain Tarkovskian mannerism is obvious in the elaborate style and imagery, but the central theme belongs to the glasnost trend. Because of the main action, *Kerosine Seller* can be called a psychological detective, but the historical and philosophical implications woven into the narrative far exceed the borders of the genre. The male lead, stage actor Andrei Baluyev, plays the roles of two twin brothers, Sergei and Pavel Udaltsov, representing two poles of the human personality – the despot and the victim, or, in Biblical terms, Cain and Abel.

Sergei, a Party official and the president of the city's executive committee, is also a mafioso chief who is being investigated for his involvement with the local racket by a detective on special assignment from Moscow. Pavel, on the other hand, has become a social pariah, having sunk to the level of a kerosine seller from the height of a prestigious position as a surgeon. The motivation for such a change of fortune was a faulty blood transfusion that caused the death of a young patient. It was Sergei, then a simple physician, who supplied a bag of blood of the wrong type, out of jealousy for his brother's career. The brothers were also in love with the same woman, who later became the wife of the kerosine seller. This pivotal episode serves as the basic metaphor for the whole film. Besides alluding to the Cain and Abel story, the blood transfusion has a more topical significance. It has been suggested that it stands for the substitution of the patient's soul with an alien one.[35] The identity of blood and soul is a visual leitmotif that casts on both despots and victims a crimson tinge the color of the communist flag. The draining of the soul under the official squeeze is graphically suggested in a flashback showing Sergei as a young *komsomolets* being awarded a medal at an official ceremony. He stands with a hand on his heart, close to the medal that has just been pinned to the white shirt, and suddenly the heart starts bleeding, staining the immaculate shirt. The red medal seems to expand on Sergei's chest, blending with the color of the gushing blood. The systematic dehumanization of the individual is conveyed by an optical effect that suggests a multiplication of the same ritual. Behind Sergei, in the background, is a huge canvas in the pompous style of Socialist Realism's celebratory paintings, reproducing the same awarding ceremony in minute detail. Within the painting there is another identical one, and so on. An ominous mirror construction.

"My two heros are certainly different people," explained Baluyev, "but they are connected by one thing: they lived in an unnatural time, when normal human relations were impossible, and equally impossible was to live as a whole individual."[36] In the film, Pavel Udaltsov is the chosen victim, the "agnus dei" destined to atone for the sins of a soulless society, and in particular for the sins of his brother. However, his actions are naive and inconclusive, stressing the defeat of the positive force in a world without God. Sergei, crushed under the weight of his own crimes, has a nervous breakdown and commits suicide. The detective, in the end, having gathered the evidence of Sergei's crimes, decides to cover them up with an elusive, deceitful report, sealing with that act his own fall into the hell of the dead souls.

Although carrying a universal message, *Kerosine Seller* is not a film for the masses. Its polished artistic form lacks emotional appeal, it is somehow narcissistic in its aesthetics, and requires a skillful reading in order to deconstruct the text. This was also the prevalent opinion among the Soviet reviewers: "If you decide not to be lazy and solve its rebuses, which look like mosaic ornaments, perfect in composition and color, then, from all those clever intricacies, all those painterly interlacements charged with meaning, you can extract the plot and the central idea."[37]

A film by Abdrashitov and Mindadze, *The Servant* (1989) stands on a higher artistic level, without reaching the summit of the best films of this famous pair. It, too, features a central character emblematic of the

Stalinist power, who leaves behind a trail smelling of sulphur. The story is based on the Mephistopheles theme. A high-ranking, all-powerful bureaucrat, Andrei Gudionov, possesses an uncanny ability to subjugate human beings to his will. His driver, Pavel Klyuev, falls under the spell and, while acquiring talent and riches, he loses his soul. Inspired by the demonic power, Klyuev becomes a famous orchestra conductor and enjoys the mansion and the woman the Master "donated" to him. But his relation to music and family is devoid of emotions, as graphically shown in a violent scene in which he rapes his wife. His state of mind here is complex, he turns against Maria (the symbolic Russian name for the soul), once the embodiment of the feminine ideal of beauty and purity, turned *petite bourgeoise* under the influence of Gudionov. But, in reality, Pavel acts out of contempt for himself. As Maria puts it, he has now become a "jackal." When the Master comes back after an absence of twenty years to exact the price, which in this case is the life of one of his old enemies, the Servant complies without a specific order. He just senses the overpowering will of the demonic creature.

A Soviet reviewer gives an even more disturbing perspective: "Klyuev is a slave not by force or psychological pressure, but by his inner need."[38] As in *Repentance*, the viewer is once again faced with the issue of the perpetuation of the evil spell from generation to generation. Gudionov, as shown in several scenes, is able to make people dance to his own tune, literally. He exercises this power on an entire soccer team, turning them into dancing marionettes. He does the same with Pavel, more focusedly, in a seducing *tête-à-tête* dancing session, guiding him through each step; and twenty years later, he repeats the same ritual with Pavel's son, only to a more contemporary rhythm. Those who are familiar with Slavic folk tales know that the power to make people dance to an obsessive rhythm belongs to the devil. The same motif recurs once again at the very end of the film, in a flashback. The Master is departing from his hometown, having been promoted to an important post in the capital. He leaves Pavel behind on the evening of his first triumphal concert, together with Maria. They run after the train, faster and faster, in a desperate effort to keep up with the Master, and their legs seem to acquire a life of their own, hitting the ground at a frenetic, mechanical pace.

The tendency toward the fantastic, that has become a trend in contemporary Soviet cinema, appeared in the works of Abrashitov and Mindadze already with the film *The Train Stopped*, which established their superior talent back in the Brezhnev period. Later, the fantastic dimension came to full fruition in *Parade of Planets*, their unsurpassed masterpiece, and colored their subsequent films, *Plyum-bum* and *The Servant*. In the latter, they opted for a poetic style, disrupting the natural narrative sequence with numerous flashbacks, and loading the visual track with extensive metaphors. At times the metaphors are too obvious. For example, when Pavel is inspired to conduct a choir the first time, almost in a trance, he has a bloody mark on his forehead, the result of a "fall"; or when Gudionov uses a secret passage that connects Pavel's house to the garden, appearing and disappearing through the underground; or, at the beach, when Pavel carries Gudionov on his back, another typical element of the folk tale, where the devil rides his victims. And so on. But the film is rescued by an overall effect of sorcery due to the superb cinematography of Denis Yestigneev and the masterful performances of Oleg Borisov as Gudionov and Iuri Belyaev as Klyuev. The music adds to the magical atmosphere, and at the same time serves as a unifying element by providing leitmotifs that link together crucial sequences. The score consists of the original music of Vladimir Dashkevich and the "Miserere," a chant of repentance performed by Klyuev's choir.

Prishvin's Paper Eyes (1989), by Valery Ogorodnikov, is a manifold text that, once more, links past and present by retrospecting on the Stalin period. The script, by Irakli Kvirikadze had to wait six years to be accepted for production. The central character, Pavel Prishvin, is a TV director–actor of the Gorbachev generation. He is engaged in shooting a movie set in 1949, where he plays a captain of the MGB (the former KGB). While shooting, he is also involved in researching a TV news unit established in that year. Why the intriguing title? It seems to refer to a suggestion from one television viewer in those early years: the fact that the anchors often lower their eyes to read the text is annoying, better glue paper eyes on their eyelids and let them read to their hearts' content.[39] In Ogorodnikov's film this metaphor introduces the theme of double vision, or of mystification of reality, and the film's complex structure reinforces the central idea. Prishvin's vision of the world shifts from one narrative context to another – the film he is shooting, the world of the old news reporters he is interviewing, the newsreel footage he weaves into the film, his nightmarish fantasies, and the contemporary reality that bears the marks of those days – leaving it to the viewer to fill the logical gaps between episodes.

Stalin pertains to all these narrative layers, and his representation varies according to Prishvin's perception, constantly shifting from

21 *Prishvin's Paper Eyes* (1989) directed by Valery Ogorodnikov

one level of reality to another. In the film within the film, Stalin is implied in the character of the MGB captain, a symbol of the arbitrariness of power. In the retro world pertaining to the reminiscences of the old reporters, the figure of film director Khrustalev serves as a sort of positive hero, Stalin's foil, and a symbolic victim. As a result of a personal vendetta triggered by a love affair, he ends up "crucified" in the snow. In the documentary footage, Stalin appears in person, and so do Hitler and Mussolini. By phantasmagoric montage, the historical footage is given a surrealist twist; the three personalities merge into one single representation of totalitarianism. Mussolini delivers Stalin's speeches, and thousands of Nazi youths salute the generalissimo who waves benevolently at the crowd. To add to the film's surrealism, segments from classic feature films are inserted in the newsreels. Images of Stalin atop the mausoleum are juxtaposed with Eisenstein's "Odessa steps" scene from *Battleship Potemkin* (1925) suggesting by analogical montage Stalin's responsibility for the massacre of the people. In the representation of Prishvin's nightmares, the phantasmagoria stoops to the level of kitsch. Here an actor gives a parodic impersonation of Stalin. Moreover, grotesque effigies of the dictator – his head blown up to gigantic proportions – haunt Prish-vin's subconscious, suggesting his helplessness in coping with the legacy of the tyrant.

The hypnotizing effect Stalin had on the people and, at the same time, the people's responsibility for having contributed to the creation of a monster, are emphasized in the film. Images of an adoring crowd parading in front of the leader, their eyes transfixed on the figure of the political idol recur in the newsreel footage. The consequences of the cult of personality are hinted at in the closing sequences. A huge statue of Stalin is dragged along a street by a truck, pulled by its feet. The street is empty, but strange figures appear on the balconies and at the windows. These are people crucified to a broomstick, stuck in the sleeves of their coats. The image refers to one specific episode of the retro movie Prishvin is making, but in the general context is emblematic of a self-crucifixion that resides in the individual, inherited from the ideology of dictatorship. And, finally, Stalin's effigy disappears from sight. The huge statue is carried away by a helicopter, flying over the city of Leningrad. It is an obvious quotation from Fellini's *La Dolce Vita* (1959) – the flying Christ over the roofs of Rome. But all similarities end right there. The substance of this scene is peculiarly Soviet. As Stalin fades out nothing is left, not even Prishvin with his sincere but helpless attempt at exorcizing the demon. The screen is filled with emptiness, with the snowy whiteness of the northern Russian landscape.[40]

Yuri Kara gave Stalin a big role in his film, *The Feast of Balthazar, or A Night With Stalin* (1989). Like Kara's previous film, this is based on a work by Fazil Iskander – the chapter from the novel, *Sandro of Chegem*, that was cut out by the censor in the novel's first edition. The film was meant to be a popular thriller with box-office potential. The story is told by Sandro, a member of an Abkhazian music and dance ensemble which is hired to entertain Stalin's entourage during a banquet. It is the ominous year 1935, and the setting is a resort in Abkhazia where the generalissimo is taking a vacation. Kara said that he wanted to convey the atmosphere of a "feast during the plague."[41] Stalin appears in a private milieu, as opposed to his canonical representation in official capacities. The focus is on the dictator at home, although "home" here is fit for royalty.

The feast takes place in a sumptuous hall with marble columns and gilded trim. The banquet table is decorated with crystal and flowers. Stalin sits in the middle, flanked by his comrades – Beria, Voroshilov,

Kalinin, Lakoba – and a few other intimates. There are even a couple of ladies. The atmosphere is deceitfully relaxed. But one can sense a tremendous tension under the surface, the tension typical of the gathering of "a gang of bandits," as a reviewer put it.[42] Stalin presides over the party like an Oriental despot, demanding humiliating acts of subservience from his associates, and bestowing his largess on the musicians. Several episodes reveal a grotesque side to what looks "normal." The drunk monarch smokes his pipe and pets a furry little creature in his lap. At first sight, it looks like a kitten. But one soon realizes that it is rather some sort of a hairy pig (maybe, a baby boar), like the ones that lay on the table, roasted and spiced for the feasters' delight. Another small but telling episode shows Stalin in the act of squashing a wasp with his fork, conveying a sense of "carnivorous satisfaction" while pronouncing its death sentence: "It did not know that my main advantage is patience."[43] Still another funny but chilling moment shows Lakoba shooting an egg that sits on the head of the cook.

The banquet is seen as though through a grey filter that removes the action from the viewer and gives characters and objects a ghost-like tinge. These are specters from the past, insidiously coming back into our time and space. And they are even more frightening for looking so harmless in their "homey" image. At the same time, these are also parodies of the extinct leaders, cartoon figures, meant to trigger laughter together with fear. And yet, in the role of Stalin, Kara cast Alexei Petrenko, an actor with great dramatic skills, because he wanted to endow the character with psychological depth. Notwithstanding the parody, Kara wanted to project the soul of a man who clearly understood the mass psychology and turned it to his advantage. As Iskander pointed out, Stalin, like the archetypal Antichrist of Russian literature – the Grand Inquisitor – understood the desire of the masses "to see in their leader the manifestation of the unholy trinity: miracle, mystery, and authority."[44] The choice of the actor is also significant for the cinematic image he projects, which is deliberately unrealistic and has more to do with the fabrication of the Stalin myth in the celebratory films of Mikhail Chiaureli (*The Vow*, 1946, and *The Fall of Berlin*, 1950) than with Stalin himself. While historical reality tells us that the dictator was short, pock-marked, and had a wilted arm, Petrenko lends the character an over-six-foot figure and handsome features. The pun here is not so much on Stalin as on the audience, that in the cult years deceived itself into "seeing" a larger-than-life hero on the screen as well as in life.

The film has been accused of commercialism because of its obvious symbolism geared to the masses. But some critics do not regard this necessarily as a fault. Higher art can be enlightening and uplifting, but often it does not reach those who are meant to be uplifted, because the metaphorical level of reality it presents does not have logical connections with the reality of everyday life. *Balthazar*, on the other hand, is for everybody, because by naming names it refers to the physical reality, "it unites us not through enlightenment or inspiration, but through our historical kinship, life experiences, and misfortunes."[45]

The past has been dug out and presented from every possible angle and in many different forms. Documentaries have brought to the screen faces that were excised from the collective picture of national history, have acquainted the new generations with tragic facts that they largely ignored, and have vindicated those who lived through the totalitarian era and had to suppress their knowledge and their feelings. Feature films have treated the same materials in an aesthetic form, steering emotions and conjuring up visual associations. Different groups of viewers reacted in different ways to the revelations of the past, from the radical youth demanding ever more direct information to the nostalgic Stalinists mourning the passing of a glorious dream. The process was intended to exorcize the demon of despotism entrenched in the institutions as well as in the people's consciousness. The shock therapy was painful and not completely successful. But it was necessary to prepare the ground for a new democratic order under the rule of law.

7   Facing the present

Society under the "kino-eye"

As compelling as it is, the investigation of the past is actually only a stepping stone into the analysis of the alarming present. Filmmakers are looking at past history in order to find the root of the disease that is eating away the best part of the country, its natural wealth, economic resources, and human potential. In this area, too, documentaries have played a major role. Whether shown separately, or grouped in programs that juxtapose historical revelations with reports from the contemporary chronicle, the glasnost documentary pictures have shown the world a face of the Soviet Union that was ignored at home and largely unknown abroad.[1]

Homecoming (1987), by Tatyana Chubakova, portrays stories about the war in Afghanistan as told by Soviet soldiers back home from the battlefield. There are two useful comparisons the viewer can make watching this film. One is with the traditional Soviet war movie. Celebration of heros, military actions, stress on sacrifice and a sense of mission, praise for the government policies give way here to a sense of futility. The camera observes with mute astonishment the devastating results of the Afghan war on the maimed bodies and souls of its veterans, mostly young fellows in their twenties who struggle to find a niche for themselves in an indifferent society. The second comparison is with the many films on the veterans of the Viet Nam War. The same questions are posed: Why? For what? Where are we going from here? The film *Pain* (1988), by S. Luk'ianchikov, treats the same theme, through the testimonies of a soldier who lost an arm in action, mothers and widows of young men that did not return, a country priest who performs the funeral rites, and the writer Ales Adamovich. The film is lengthy and static, and the testimonies have different degrees of impact, from the highly emotional speech of the soldier – "Now they say that war was a senseless adventure, but we have put our lives on the line. And who am I? A hero? . . . "[2] – to the humble sermon of the country priest – "Do not kill" – to Adamovich's philosophical meditations. But they are unified by an overall sense of mourning and "pain."

As one war ended, another violent conflict arose within the Soviet Union, among nationalities and ethnic groups. An episode of the first major clash between Armenians and Azerbaijanis over the disputed territory of Nagorno–Karabakh was captured by the documentary *Theater Square* (1988), by Grigor Arutunyan. The filmmaker did not record bloody pogroms and combat scenes, he focused on a marginal but significant event, a hunger strike staged in Erevan by hundreds of citizens. The following year, more dramatic footage was shot in Tbilisi, during the repression by Soviet troops of a Georgian national-ist rally. But it was never turned into a movie for distribution, and circulated only as amateur video. Another catastrophe of massive proportions is lamented in *Chernobyl: Chronicle of Difficult Weeks* (1988), by the late Vladimir Shevchenko. As far as form is concerned, this picture is on the traditional side and it could benefit from some editing cuts. But many sequences are striking, and the circumstances of the making of the film speak of great courage and dedication. Particularly powerful is the aerial shot from the helicopter that takes the crew to the disaster zone. The landscape does not look at all unusual except for the fact that it is "dead." The zone is deserted and still, shot in a sepia color, and direct sound recording picks up the crackling noise of nuclear radiation, popping up here and there, like an ironic deathly giggling in an unnatural silent environment. Shev-chenko and his crew were the first in the disaster zone and closely followed the struggle of the rescue workers for more than three months. As a consequence, Shevchenko died of radiation one year later, without seeing the release of his film that was being held up for revisions. The camera used for the shooting had to be buried because it could not be decontaminated.

The destruction of the ecology as a consequence of technological progress has become a matter of concern in recent times around the globe. In the Soviet Union ecological problems have been glossed over for years, and only now they are being exposed in poignant press reports and documentary films. "For a long time we lived with the delusion that ecological problems were caused only by the capital-ist system," wrote a member of the Institute of Biophysics of the Academy of Sciences, "but the policy of 'new thinking' made us reconsider that view. These problems are universal problems . . . The films dealing with this topic confirm this."[3] *Against the Current* (1988), by Dmitri Delov, is one such film. It shows how the citizens of the small town of Kirishi finally organized a protest movement against a major synthetic protein plant that was poisoning the air and the water. Children as well as adults were affected by respiratory diseases and skin rashes. Their protest rallies, however, did not accomplish much. They were called extremists and "greenies," and the factory director responsible for injuring the public health became a government minister. *Scenes at a Fountain* (1986), by Igor Gonopolsky, depicts another ecological disaster that required labor and pain and even cost a human life. While the citizens' struggle against the protein plant has the flavor of a slice-of-life drama, this one has the scope of an epic deed. The film shows the titanic struggle of a firemen's squad to cap a column of fire, 600 feet high, that developed at a natural gas well near the Caspian Sea and burned for more than one year.

Besides forests threatened by acid rain, waters poisoned by industrial wastes, and animal species on their way to extinction because of the tampering with the environment, another topic emerged in the documentaries of glasnost: the disintegration of the socialist society accompanied by an alarming spread of social ills. *The Limit* (1988), by Tatyana Skabard, is a gripping portrait of the devastating effects of alcoholism on women. This portrait was particularly horrifying to a Soviet audience because alcohol abuse had usually been associated with men, with the woman playing the role of the caretaker and nurse. The film shows a young mother in a correctional institute admitting that she tried to kill her baby daughter in a fit of rage. Children abandoned by their mothers end up in orphanages. In the film a young boy, shaken by the disintegration of the family, nurtures the thought of killing his mother when he becomes an adult. Women are also the subject of *Tomorrow Is a Holiday* (1987), by Sergei Bukovsky. It shows the dehumanizing world of industrial alienation with some touches of black humor. At the poultry factory, the women workers treat the chickens with the same callous cruelty they themselves experience in their daily lives. Live chickens are stuffed in metal containers with business-like indifference, just as the women are lodged in cramped dormitories not fit for human living. Ironically, the last sequence shows a holiday celebration, where the effigy of the dove of peace, floating in the sky as the ideal of social and political behavior, is juxtaposed to the factory's emblem – a hyperbolic puppet chicken on a skewer. In *The BAM Zone: Permanent Residents* (1987), director Mikhail Pavlov denounces the disruption of lives and families caused by the misman-agement of the "great construction projects." Ten years after the completion of the Siberian railroad, the Baikal–Amur Mainline, the workers' families who were temporarily resettled on the construction site are still living there in barracks. There are no sanitary facilities. There are no streets, only narrow walkboards laid on the mud. In the village, idyllically named Star Place (Zvezdnoe), "even the cemetery is, so to speak, temporary."[4] The dead can be reassured, however, that they are not going to be disturbed too soon.

When the first alarming news about AIDS made its appearance in the Western world, the Soviet Union promptly denied being afflicted by the new plague. Later, when evidence of AIDS cases became known, the government blamed the CIA for devising a plot to spread the virus. Now a Soviet documentary tells it how it is. *The Risk Group* (1987), by A. Nikishin, was commissioned by the state-owned enter-prise Videofilm, and shot on tape. It is available in video-salons and it is meant to inform and educate a vast public. The film is a frank discussion of the dangers of AIDS in the Soviet Union, and of the groups that are most at risk – prostitutes, homosexuals, drug addicts – supported with government data and statistics. The emotional scenes, however, are those with the most impact. The viewer's heart goes out to the pathetic lady of the night, interviewed at a police station, plainly stating without pride or shame that over a year she had approximately two thousand customers. Conversely, the viewer gets chilly shivers hearing of a letter sent to the Central Television Studio by a group of sixteen medical students. These young people who are being trained to alleviate human suffering threatened to deny medical care to drug addicts, prostitutes, and homosexuals. "Let these representatives of the risk group die of AIDS," the letter continues, "and the rest of mankind will start a new, wonderful life."[5] What the letter fails to indicate, however, is the fact that more people get infected with the AIDS virus in Soviet hospitals than in society at large. So poor are the sanitary conditions that the same needle is routinely used for several patients without proper sterilization.

The exposés of social ills that flooded the silver and the blue screens in the past three years climaxed in the latest film of Stanislav Gov-orukhin, *This Is No Way To Live* (1990). The film was hailed by both the public and the press as a sensational event. Devoid of rhetoric or tendentiousness, and frightening in its honesty, Govorukhin's film involves the viewer in a collective lament over the degradation of life in a society on the brink of moral and material collapse. The commentary points out a main paradox: "A vast country. A vast and rich country. Forests, waters, fish, fur, 50 percent of the world's black soil, colossal mineral resources, oil, gas, gold . . . and appalling poverty, shameful and humiliating poverty denigrating human dignity."[6] Crosscutting between the vastness and beauty of the Russian land and the misery of urban and rural life, Govorukhin stresses his point. Prostitution, vagrancy, rackets, and blackmarketeering are shown to grow more and more conspicuous as fixtures of the cityscape. Queues, too, are becoming longer and more numerous while supplies are dwindling. In the countryside, the situation is even worse. Those who can, leave the land that has become sterile after decades of collectivization. A touching scene shows Govorukhin interviewing three old women left behind in an abandoned village with no other food but potatoes. They are philosophical about it, but express a strong desire for a bar of soap. The nearest shop is miles away, and therefore inaccessible to them without transportation. But even if the old women were able to reach it, their wish would not come true. The next scene shows us the rural store with semi-empty shelves. This is "How the System Mocks the People," as the title of that section informs us.

A more blatant illustration of the same point involves a tour of the Exhibition of Economic Achievements, the pompous ensemble of ornate pavilions, built under Stalin in the 1930s to cover up the poverty of the country with a facade of false grandeur. An abrupt cut brings us to an elegant street in a West German city. Pointing at the scintillating shops, Govorukhin comments: "These are real economic achievements, and they are available to the people." The Soviet masses have never been affluent, but nowadays they are losing even what was once taken for granted. Vodka, for example. One episode shows a winding line of workers in a provincial town. So disproportionate is the demand that access to the store is regulated by policemen, patrolling the queue and letting customers in two at a time. In view of the campaign to fight alcoholism, this may even look like a positive measure. But this is not the point for the film's author. As the commentary says: "Leaving nothing but vodka for the people, training them for years to drink heavily to forget their misery, to stop thinking, seeing, or hearing anything, and then organizing the distribution of two bottles per person in the most humiliating and outrageous form . . . Aren't they making the people behave like savages, criminal and barbarous savages themselves?" To reinforce the idea, a brief sequence shows us a training school for police dogs. And Govorukhin comments: "How do you make a dog vicious? Keep him on a chain, starve him, and goad him."

The results of making the people vicious are shown at the very beginning of the film. This section is about crime. It includes interviews with criminals and police, and gory images of the victims. Horrid photographs of female corpses from the police files are juxtaposed to close-up shots of their rapists and murderers. These are faces that have lost all sparks of humanity and look at the camera with brutish obtuseness. Next is a chilling episode involving three teenagers, that bears witness to the spreading of mindless violence among the youth. After an accident while driving a stolen ambulance, the one of the three fellows who escaped uninjured set fire to the vehicle. He was eager to cover up the crime and did not give a thought about his two buddies trapped in the flames.

A look at the police and their ways of coping with rampant criminality provides some comic relief in an otherwise horrifying picture. The targets are police ineptitude and the lack of modern equipment. Moscow Keystone cops are compared to a couple of New York officers, including a tough policewoman, whom Govorukhin interviewed during a visit to the US. The New York cops are shown handling guns and manacles with a juggler's dexterity, while their Soviet counterparts get entangled in their own cumbersome gear. This is laughter through tears, of course, like other comparisons with the Western way of life.

Crime is at first treated as a social plague. But, as the theme unfolds, the scope of the investigation broadens to show that the root of all crimes is the big Crime the country's leaders have perpetrated against the people over seven decades of communist rule. In Govorukhin's words: "Monstrous atrocities were committed in this country: genocide, mass killings, man-made famine which exterminated millions, the destruction of economy and culture."

But even these charges pale in comparison to what Govorukhin calls "the regime's most atrocious crime." The author refers to "the creation of a new human type," the result of "seventy years of faulty genetic evolution." One sequence highlights the early phase of the mutation of the human being into "homo sovieticus," by showing children at a pioneer camp named after the boy-hero Pavlik Morozov. In the early Stalinist days, when the Bolshevik government waged an aggressive grain requisition campaign and agitated the masses against affluent peasants (the *kulaks*), Pavlik Morozov denounced his father to the authorities and had him arrested. Young Pavlik was then killed by relatives. Canonized and elevated to the summit of the communist Elysium, the murdered boy was held up as an example of loyalty to the state for all schoolchildren, throughout the Stalinist times and beyond. Only in 1989, an official resolution revoked Pavlik's hero status, and his numerous portraits and monuments became another casualty of perestroika. Govorukhin's camera records with an ironic eye a rally of young pioneers around a neglected, and by now irrelevant, statue of Pavlik. Then, with a sweeping movement, it brings us to a thicket by the camp border and focuses on a discarded and mutilated statue of Lenin. Govorukhin looks at the pathetic effigy of the leader, grins at the viewer, and opens up his arms in a hopeless gesture, underscoring the absurdity of a dogma that kept the nation enslaved for the best part of the century.

Since the mid-1950s and Khrushchev's denunciation of Stalin, it has been convenient to blame the late dictator for all past and present evils. The process of de-Stalinization, discouraged in the Brezhnev years, was then revived and intensified with the onset of glasnost. But in Govorukhin's film, there is not a single image of Stalin. The author deliberately ignores him and focuses directly on Lenin, shifting the viewer's attention to the very first link of the historical chain. Jump-cuts to monuments and portraits of Lenin occur at strategic points throughout the film to bring across the message, at times in ironical counterpoint, at times with tragic pathos. The first "faulty gene" in the evolution of the Soviet people was implanted by the founder of the Bolshevik state. The results of the hereditary process, as shown in the film, are chilling. One Soviet reviewer, with a typical Russian bent for atonement and expiation, observed: "Of course, we all know how we live. Of course, we understand that we must not live like this . . . But it is the first time that we have been shown what an inhuman limit we have approached . . . We are captive of the criminality we produced and are still living with, with little hope of ridding ourselves of it."[7]

Perhaps there is a risk that a foreign audience would inadvertently read the film too literally where the theory of "faulty genetic evolution" is concerned. While the metaphor is useful to convey the idea that certain psychological patterns are ingrained in the national consciousness because of ideological brainwashing, it would be preposterous to believe that all Soviet citizens today are "biologically" predisposed to crime. But the fact that there are filmmakers able to produce this kind of documentary, and viewers able to be moved by them testifies to the weakness of that "mutation theory." And, for all its bleakness, Govorukhin's vision is not without hope. Rather, in the tradition of the Russian Orthodox religion that is making a comeback into cultural life, it is a moment of self-flagellation that may precede redemption.

The first public screening of *This Is No Way To Live* took place on May 4, at the House of Cinema in Moscow, for the exponents of the film world. Subsequently, it was shown to the representatives of the People's Congress of the USSR, the delegates to the Congress of the Russian Republic, and the members of the Moscow City Council. In early June, it opened at the movie theater "Rossia," in Moscow. Govorukhin, interviewed by the newspaper *Soviet Culture*, said that he tried to find the clearest form and the simplest words for his film, so that it would be understood by all the people. But he added that he conceived the film primarily as "a letter to the Supreme Soviet." "I wanted to explain something to our government," he said. "I tried to put together a number of mosaic pieces and present a comprehensive picture of our life." And what was the reaction? Among the delegates to the Congress of the Russian Republic, the film generated a polarization. "The leftists went more to the left, the rightists went more to the right, and the center (which decides everything) moved slightly to the left. This is very significant, it means we achieved our goal," Govorukhin commented. Criticism, of course, poured in from the right wing, which denounced the film as an inflammatory call to violence. The director dismissed the uproar: "We cannot reeducate the staunch dogmatists who brought the country to this deplorable state. And we don't need to. We need only to vote them out."[8]

Govorukhin is used to criticism, not only from the conservative bureaucracy but from intellectual circles as well. In pre-perestroika times, his adventure movies were considered "commercial," and looked down upon by the sustainers of pristine art and moral ideals.[9] But with the liberalization of the arts and the implementation of economic reforms, the film industry changed. The realities of a free-market system nowadays require a pragmatic approach that often verges on cynicism; and while business is booming, creativity and moral commitment suffer. This was a turning point that changed Govorukhin's course. He told a Soviet colleague: "Making commercial films today is unpardonable. Today one must help one's country to survive."[10] He devoted himself to *publitsistika*, and his articles, critical of the present state of affairs and investigating the causes of the disease started appearing in journals and newspapers. His harsh analyses made him extremely popular with the readers and established his reputation as honest and bold. But within the Film-makers Union, although many respect him, very few like him. He is viewed as proud, aloof, and vocal in his criticism of the film industry's internal politics.

And yet, even those who dislike Govorukhin's personality had to admit that in *This Is No Way To Live* there is no trace of aloofness, or of grand moral stand. Govorukhin has stepped across the dividing line between author and public, and put himself into the cauldron of suffering humanity. At the same time, he has assumed his share of responsibility for the big Crime of which everyone is ultimately guilty. "There is not a single bright, 'enlightening' frame or episode in the film, there is only total 'darkness,'" wrote a prominent critic. "And yet, no one turns away from the screen, no one leaves the theater (where could one run to? there is no running from oneself!), and no one accuses the author of delving into misery. Do you know why? Because of the pain and compassion that fill up the screen."[11] The film is not moralistic. It does not provide an alternative for a better way to live. But, by stirring the emotions, it challenges the viewer to live differently.

A large number of documentaries has been devoted to the problems of youth.[12] The first to break the ice on this front was the Latvian picture, *Is It Easy to Be Young?* (1986), by Yuris Podnieks, which collected rave reviews as well as irate criticism, and served as the prototype for many films to follow.[13] It also had a great deal of resonance abroad, where the fact that it had been released was seen as concrete evidence that glasnost was "for real." The question mark in the title was a requirement of Goskino, to soften the blow of a flat statement. But the answer the film provides is unequivocally nega-tive. This documentary presents a compassionate but disturbing pic-ture of alienated and disaffected youth. Hard rock, punk attire, heavy metal, drugs, mystical flights into the world of Hare Krishna – Soviet teenagers have definitely caught up with the West. However, the causes of the phenomenon are domestic, as a candid review of the film suggests: "What they say from the screen is: 'You made us the way we are with your duplicity, your lies' . . . Let us recall one of the many tragedies in *Repentance*. One, but perhaps the most severe . . . Varlam's grandson putting a bullet through his heart."[14] It is all the parents' fault, the film suggests. And a young viewer reinforces this opinion:

Our generation grew up in an atmosphere of pompous ceremonies, at the sound of prerecorded ovations and "Hurrah!" shouts . . . Many of those words which we heard from childhood . . . became a habit . . . lost their meaning, and their utterance became a ritual. We were obedient and observed the rituals . . . did our homework without asking about its purpose, its meaning . . . We lost our illusions incredibly fast, and at 17–18 years of age we feel completely powerless. What can we change? We cannot escape those decades . . . That's the way they have shaped us.[15]

The film *Confession. Chronicle of Alienation* (1988), by Georgi Gavrilov, focuses on one exponent of the youth counterculture who slipped into a severe and prolonged drug addiction. Independent filmmakers lived for two years with the protagonist, eighteen-year-old Lyosha, and recorded on film long conversations, drug injections, life in the underground with Sveta, a girlfriend and drug companion, and the pain and abjection of a broken life. Eventually, Mosfilm agreed to provide the crew with postproduction facilities and give the finished product its imprimatur. Lyosha comes across as an educated, well-mannered youth from the upper-middle class, who chose to escape from an artificial social milieu, filled with "Persian rugs and caged parrots," into a world of artificial dreams. His "confession" is open, factual, interspersed with occasional humor, and fatalistic. The point of view of the director, who deliberately stages every scene of Lyosha's "performance," is that the cause of this human tragedy lies in the family history: the grandfather was a general who served for some time as a Gulag camp commander and by that sinful action marked the destiny of his progeny. But other characters in the film have a simpler explanation. Lyosha's mother, eager to defend the family's honor, thinks that the boy's problems stemmed from his long hair, and complains about Lyosha's stubbornness that prevented him from getting a job and living like everybody else. An older woman in the street makes the same point, expressing the social outrage at those who defy conventions: "Scoundrel, d'you know what you look like? Like a porcupine. Are you a civilized being, or what? Get a wash, here take twenty kopeks . . I would pass a law to forbid long hair . . . Catch that scum, and shave them . . . You must be sent to work. You should be building our metro, and there, on the construction site, they'll show you about 'freedom'." After all, there seems to be some connection between the Stalinist general and the reaction to long hair. And the unfortunate Lyosha descended into the underground – not of the Moscow metro, but of a narcotic hell.[16]

Society's repression of free spirits is also the subject of *Story of a Story* (1988), by B. Sadykov. A grade-school child who addressed his teachers with unusual questions is sent to the psychiatrist for evaluation. The film questions whether it is not the school that needs to be evaluated. Likewise, in *And What If . . .* (1988), by O. Lebedev, a group of teenagers who want to create a museum of Bulgakov memorabilia clashes with the absurdist bureaucracy of the Komsomol clerks. While in these films, the topic is treated with a sense of humor, in a satirical vein, elsewhere it attains the deep pathos of tragedy.

In *The Final Verdict* (1987), by Hertz Frank, society legally "kills" a young human being who went astray. The director follows the journey of a twenty-four-year-old murderer, from the moment of his arrest, through the police investigation, the trial, and the many months the inmate spent on death row before being executed. He also provides documentary materials to illustrate the young man's background, childhood, family relations, girlfriend – a normal middle-class environment that provided financial support but lacked emotional ties, love, and moral guidance. Revealing is the interview with the mother, who bitterly complains about her divorced husband, and refuses to visit her son because he "has disgraced her." The skillful camera work and montage techniques turn a potentially dry account into a psychological drama *à la* Dostoevsky. In the opening sequences there is even a brief but deliberate reference to the novel *Crime and Punishment*. As a consequence, the image of the handsome criminal who murdered a woman in cold blood because of a dispute over an illegal money deal merges in the viewer's mind with the tragic figure of a modern Raskolnikov. Through extreme close-ups and long takes the viewer gets to know the character very intimately, and witnesses his transformation from a cynical blackmarketeer to a spiritually reborn human being. In the end, his execution has a more shocking effect on the viewer than the crime he had originally committed. A Soviet commentator summarized the underlying idea of the film: "Premeditated murder is a first-degree crime. But the death penalty is always a premeditated murder. It does not remove the crime from the criminal, it places it on us."[17]

Society is also shown to mistreat its more vulnerable members in more subtle ways. The film *Are You Going to the Ball?* (1987), by

Nadezhda Khvorova, deals with the severe, even cruel, training of very young girl gymnasts who dream of becoming an Olga Korbut or a Liudmila Turishcheva. The two stars are interviewed in their mature years, leading a comfortable and respectable life. But for every two stars who attained honors and fame there are dozens of broken lives. A former trainee who did not make it to stardom, now in her thirties, makes a poignant case: "It seems to me that I lost my health with gymnastics . . . Everything aches . . . My time is over." The physician of the training center gives his diagnosis: "First of all, the spinal column in these young children will undergo a permanent change. Their growth may be stopped."[18] The film's point is clear: parents, teachers, and the state pursue gold medals in international competitions at the expense of their children's health and happiness.

To cope with the loss of values in today's society, young people in Kazan seek the support of street gangs. The film *And What About You Guys?* (1987), by V. Kuzmina, illustrates a situation where each grouping becomes a close fraternity pitted against society and against each other. Bloody fights between rival gangs, and internal vendettas claim numerous young lives – "more than those that were lost in Afghanistan," says the commentary. Other youngsters of a different persuasion organize a group of vigilantes, called "Cascade," to clean up the city. They wear paramilitary uniforms, engage in karate training, and march under banners and insignia. The film shows that the group, whether governed by a street code or by militaristic rules, provides the young people with a sense of belonging, protection, and purpose – in this case, mainly mindless violence. An extreme manifestation of this syndrome is offered in the film *This Is How We Live* (1987), by Vladimir Oseledchik. A group of homegrown Nazis with swastikas on their sleeves express their disillusionment with "the communists and their lousy humanism." The young spokesman who introduces the viewer to the neo-fascist program talks in naive and confused terms, but with great aplomb, about an ideal society to be achieved through sterilization and selection, coupling beautiful women with outstanding athletes. The adults' reaction in the film is one of tolerance, treating these fantasies as teenage bravado, and at the same time of *mea culpa*, acknowledging their generation's responsibility. A schoolteacher comments: "This is their gag reflex to our adult hypocrisy."[19]

The most visible, exuberant, and charismatic expression of the youth counterculture is rock music, as in the rest of the world. In the Soviet Union, it has a special national flavor. For two decades rock bands existed mainly in the underground, as a manifestation of a youth counterculture rejecting the regimentation of life and leisure by the Young Communist League. At first they were highly influenced by the music that had become the rage in the West, especially by the Beatles. They sang in English and imitated Western models. But already in the early 1970s a search for ethnic roots began, marked by experimentation with folk instruments and tunes. By the end of the decade, Russian lyrics replaced the English idiom and "Sovrock" was born. At the dawning of glasnost, the rock scene was sophisticated and diversified, featuring punks, heavy metal, rappers, and break dancers.[20] Thanks to the new wave of permissiveness, Soviet rock musicians are now rocking the boat of official ideology and prudish morals. Raucous voices, obsessive rhythms, and irreverent lyrics gush out of concert halls, discos, youth clubs, stadiums, radio, and TV.

This irrepressible flood that electrifies the youth and frightens the guardians of conservative thought has also become an important ingredient of documentaries and feature films. In *Dialogues* (1987), by Nikolai Obukhovich, the viewer is introduced to the crazy world of "Pop-mechanics," a special form of rock performance invented by Sergei Kuryokhin. The film shows a sample of what Kuryokhin called "musical idiotism," which consists in a mix of rock, classical bel canto, sots-art, jazz, mass culture, and vintage pop songs.[21] The happening takes place in an abandoned Leningrad palace, and includes barking dogs and singing birds. Kuryokhin has also written a number of original scores for recent films. Among them, *It* (1989) where music plays an important role in the satirical approach to the historical materials. The documentary, *Rock* (1987), by Alexei Uchitel, focuses on the sources and roots of the new musical wave, as well as on its leaders and idols. The film features Yuri Shevchuk, the leader of "DDT," whose vocal manner is close to that of Vladimir Vysotsky, the rebel of the 1960s; Boris Grebenshchikov, the magnetic and sophisticated star of "Aquarium"; and the late Viktor Tsoy, from "Kino," who became a movie star shortly before his death. This "Leningrader" with Asian features has now become a legend. In retrospective, what Tsoy said in *Rock* sounds sadly prophetic: "Rock is not a hobby, it's a way of life. Today I would be ready to sacrifice everything for it."[22]

The documentaries of glasnost have little to offer on the bright side. However, two of them stand out as a sun ray in the dark. *Early on*

Sunday (1987), by Murat Mamedov, is a loving portrait of a group of seventy-year-old peasant women, who on a winter morning go to the forest to chop firewood. They work hard for several hours, carrying huge logs to the sleigh on their own shoulders, without losing their sense of humor and their good disposition to life. Then they sit around the fire to eat a meager lunch of bread and boiled eggs, all the time talking about past and present hardships in their lives without a trace of self-pity. From perestroika they do not expect anything; they do not understand the concept that for them remains an empty word. Life has taught them to be self-reliant. And they carry on, alone, with dignity and simplicity. "There is something epic, even legendary, in this film," comments a Soviet reviewer, "these are peasant women untouched by time, and unbroken by destiny."[23]

The other uplifting picture is *The Temple* (1987), by Vladimir Dyakonov. Made for the celebration of the millennium of the Christianization of Russia, the film is a good omen for the next millennium. With the new law on religious freedom, that took effect on September 26, 1990, and the church properties returned to the Patriarchate, the Soviet government has opened the door to a revival of church activities long suppressed. But even in the dark years, the film shows, the church continued its mission. The sumptuous cathedrals and the little medieval churches that survived the Bolsheviks' dynamite, and have since figured on Intourist itineraries, have a place in this documentary. But the focus is on the people who devoted their lives to an ideal of mystical beauty and human compassion. Among them, the seventy-year-old father Nikolay, who lives in solitude on the island of Zalita in Lake Chudskoe, and is happy to survive on bread and tea; or the young monk Zenon, an icon painter of the Danilov Monastery, who conveys through this ancient art a sense of serenity and appeasement of the soul; or the humble sisters of the Pyukhtitsky Assumption Nunnery – one of very few convents operating in the Soviet Union – nuns of all ages, united in prayer and labor. The film presents the picture of a spiritual oasis in a society in turmoil. One must note, however, that the Orthodox Church as an institution has been over the centuries a symbol of authoritarian rule. And only two years after this film was made there were already signs of a leaning in that direction, with the church authorities aligned with the conservative side of the political spectrum.

Where fiction meets reality: youth counterculture

Feature films of the past three years reflect the same concerns expressed by the documentarists with regard to the present social conditions. Film after film deal with the prevalent mood of alienation, estrangement, and disaffection that is particularly disturbing among teenagers. One of the first pictures to present the problem in a gentle but outspoken way was *The Messenger* (1987), by Karen Shakhnazarov, about a high-school graduate who works as a messenger boy in an editorial office. The director had previously used musical genres as a central metaphor for his films, jazz (*Jazzman*) and tap dancing (*Winter Evening in Gagry*). Break dance has the same function in this film. Shakhnazarov, sympathizing with the young protagonist and his friends, draws a parallel between the illogicality, absurdity, and spontaneity of break dance and the state of mind of today's teenagers. The deep-set antagonism to the values of the parents' generation is expressed in the hero's normal life through mute, hostile passivity, but in the streets and courtyards it explodes into wild rhythms and free acrobatics. The hero's frustration with the hypocrisy and conformism of the surrounding world also finds an outlet in his fantasies, which materialize into visions of exotic warriors hunting leopards in the desert. These visions occur on the occasion of his frequent excursions to a deserted quarry, beyond the city limits, and remind us of another maladjusted teenager of an earlier era in Kira Muratova's *Long Farewells*.

The film is basically a comedy, with much of the humor deriving from the discrepancy between the hero's apathetic behavior and his outrageous statements. His presence in the well-to-do family of his girlfriend sends shock waves through the routine of everyday life. But occasionally, the hero's anger is unleashed in a violent and cruel way – without stopping to be funny. Fed up with his divorced mother, weeping about her lonely life, the young man threatens to set the apartment on fire, and to underline his words lights up a pile of newspapers in the middle of the room. This is a farcical terrorist act that expresses both the hero's frustration and his impotence. The film ultimately suggests that there is no future for the messenger boy. At the end, he is drafted into the army. The last shot shows him pensively staring at a comrade who has just come back from Afghanistan, his face disfigured by an ugly scar. This was one of the first critical images of that unpopular war, which is alluded to without name. The film won the first prize at the 1987 Moscow International Film

Festival; and rightly so, because besides covering topics of social significance it provided some very entertaining comedy. The young actor, Fyodor Dunaevsky, endowed his character with endearing abrasiveness throughout the film, sustained by the unfailing performances of two veterans, Inna Churikova and Oleg Basilashvili.[24]

The film *Plyumbum, or A Dangerous Game* (1987), by Abdrashitov and Mindadze, offers a much more disturbing portrait of a fifteen-year-old. Mixing reality and metaphysics, as in most of their films, the authors probe deeply into the pathology of evil. The film's protagonist is not a realistic teenager, rather he is the incarnation of a little demon. In his spare time, this adolescent with the face of a forty-year-old midget, helps a vigilantes' organization in their fight against robbers and other outlaws, under the pseudonym of Plyumbum.[25] He becomes involved in this "dangerous game" through a sense of justice, having himself been robbed. But the game Plyumbum plays proves to be dangerous, first of all, to his spiritual well-being. His original motivation gradually turns into an obsession, and the moral idea that was the basis for his actions becomes evil. Plyumbum's mechanical pursuit of "justice," devoid of love and human compassion, leads him to arrest his father – a weekend poacher – and to cause the death of his devoted girlfriend, Sonia. There are ominous echoes of Dostoevsky's devilish characters in this film, besides the obvious reference to Pavlik Morozov, which remind the viewer that the moral foundation of ethics is not an abstract principle of justice but the human feeling of brotherly love. Abdrashitov and Mindadze did not disappoint their audiences' expectations after their masterpiece, *Parade of Planets*. In this film, too, they were able to weave surrealist associations into the fabric of a realistic milieu, through the subtle quality of images and sound. *Plyumbum* was awarded the gold medal of the Italian Senate at the 1987 Venice Film Festival for "The best film for social progress and humanism."[26]

A teenage drama in a robust realistic style was turned into a film from a successful play. *My Name is Harlequin* (1988), by Valery Rybarev, is based on the play by Yuri Shchekochikhin, *Catch no. 46, Length no. 2* (the title refers to a jeans size). The film's action hinges on the "war" between two rival groups – a street gang of working-class lads, "The Wolves," headed by Harlequin, against the city's gilded youth, headed by Inter. A dispute between Harlequin and Inter over the groupie, Lena, ignites the spark for a tragic development. Lena is raped by the rival gang before Harlequin's eyes, in a scene reminiscent of Visconti's *Rocco and His Brothers*. Simple in form and plot, the film offers, besides the rape scene, bloody fights, karate kicks, and a rock concert. All elements that contributed to its popularity. But it also reflects a real situation that is a growing concern among sociologists and educators – a mounting resentment toward youngsters of affluent social classes, that often leads to violence. The press has covered several cases involving the gang of the Lyubery, bodybuilders from the Moscow district of Lyubertsy. Hostile to foreign influences, they often travel to downtown Moscow to beat up the privileged kids who flirt with Western culture, including rockers and punks.[27]

Another horrid story of juvenile delinquents made its way to the screen from the play, *Dear Elena Sergeyevna*, by Ludmila Razumovskaya. The film by the same title was made in 1988 by Eldar Ryazanov, who on this occasion strayed from his proven path of satirical comedy. The story deals with a group of classmates who terrorize their lonely and vulnerable teacher in order to change their failing grades. The teacher is finally pushed into committing suicide, after the girl in the group gets raped by her companions.

Confused teenagers without a moral anchor are not only the prerogative of Russian society. A film made in Kazakhstan by Sergei Bodrov, *Non-professionals* (1987), follows the itinerary of three adolescents traveling with an amateur ensemble that brings pop music concerts to the rural population. The young people's journey is not motivated by idealism, not by love of performance, and not even by monetary gain. There is simply no motivation. They drift along the road as they do in life. Depending on the circumstances, they can be generous or cruel, without being aware of it. Their alienation from society is conveyed by the natural background. The vast Kazakh steppe, emphasized by an indifferent camera eye, becomes the metaphor for "a cold, hostile world, in which the heros feel like occasional guests on an alien planet."[28] Unlike in other films about youth, here the alienation of the teenagers is paralleled by the isolation of the elderly confined to an institution. When the old people are invited to sing along with the ensemble the gap that divides the two groups becomes even more apparent.

The next film by Sergei Bodrov, *S.E.R.* (1989), made at Mosfilm, won the first prize at the Montreal Film Festival. The acronym stands for "*Svoboda – Eto Rai*" (Freedom Is Paradise), which the young hero, thirteen-year-old Sasha, has adopted as his motto, and sports in the form of a tattoo. Reality clashes with Sasha's aspirations because he is an inmate in a special school for "difficult" adolescents. The film stresses how the environment breeds hatred and fear, and rather than correcting the children's behavior encourages tomorrow's potential criminals. It goes without saying, given the current trend, that some of the teachers are nostalgic Stalinists. The director also informs the viewer that the first link in the chain of Sasha's misfortunes was the unjust sentencing of his grandmother, who during a famine stole five cucumbers from a *kolkhoz* and received five years. The main plot development occurs when Sasha learns that his father is still alive and is himself serving time in a penal colony in the Arkhangelsk region. Running away from the school, the boy undertakes a long journey through Russia, full of encounters and adventures, and for a short moment is reunited with his father. Although the film is topical and touches on many of the themes of perestroika, Sasha is an old-fashioned hero, and *S.E.R.* is an old-fashioned story. Unlike other adolescents in recent films, Sasha is good, sensitive, and moved by an ideal of beauty and love. He seems to have jumped out of the films of the 1960s with all their endearing characters (*Ballad of a Soldier, Fate of a Man*, and the like), or to have crossed the border from the movies of Italian neorealism. The director clearly plays a sentimental note, and, judging by the film's popular success touches a responsive chord in the mass audience.

The film *The Arsonists* (1989), by Alexander Surin, is a sort of feminist counterpart to *S.E.R.*, because the central character is a heroine who is also trapped in a correctional school, and makes a successful escape only to die in the desert. But the tone of this film is bitter, desperate, and hopeless. Another doomed heroine is the protagonist of the film, *Little Doll* (1989), by Isaac Friedberg. Here, a fifteen-year-old gymnastics champion plunged from fame to ordinary life as a consequence of a sport injury. Embittered, she seeks a self-destructive confrontation with a young and beautiful schoolteacher who is having an affair with a student.[29]

When Bodrov started shooting *Non-professionals*, in 1985, Kazakhfilm was a small studio of minor significance. Since then, it has grown to occupy a prominent position in the configuration of the Soviet national studios, with several productions of remarkable aesthetic value. The change has been brought about by an initiative from Moscow. Sergei Bodrov was one of the first Russian directors to use the Central Asian studio for his production. At about the same time (1984), Sergei Solovev taught a course at the State Institute of Cinema (VGIK) especially designed to train Kazakh filmmakers. The class

included seven Kazakh directors, three screenwriters, two cinematographers, and two art directors. This new wave now constitutes the
backbone of the creative association "Alem" (Universe). The only
other creative association at Kazakhfilm, "Miras" (Heritage) specializes in traditional national subjects. The annual output is still
small – four feature films, four dramatic shorts, four to six animated
shorts, and thirty documentary films – but the quality of these pictures has attracted prizes and international attention.[30]

A film that generated a great deal of critical attention and popular
success firmly established Kazakhfilm studio as the center of a creative new wave. This was *The Needle* (1989), by Rashid Nugmanov.[31]
The young director completed Solovev's course at VGIK, and had
already made his mark, although only within the intellectual circles,
with his diploma work, *Ya-ha* (1986). This short was a documentary
excursion through the world of the Leningrad "bohemia," through
the attics and basements occupied by young artists, poets, and rock
musicians without a regular residence permit, and through the visual
and aural texture of an aesthetic universe alienated from society. It is
not, however, a documentary, rather it is "improvisational fiction . . .
a kaleidoscopic living diary of the underground rock scene just before
perestroika, when rock music officially 'did not exist'."[32] It has been
said that Solovev was introduced to this milieu by Nugmanov, and
from there got the idea for *Assa*. It is certain, however, that this was
the beginning of Nugmanov's friendship with Viktor Tsoy, which led
to their collaboration in *The Needle*.[33]

The plot is simple but sketchy, the narrative consisting of a series of
powerful scenes loosely connected. The hero, with the exotic name of
Moro, goes back to his hometown, Alma-Ata, to collect a debt from
his former gang, learns that his ex-girlfriend is on drugs, decides to
save her, and in the end is stabbed by the drug dealers. We know
nothing of Moro's background, nothing of his relationship with his
girlfriend, Dina, nothing of his former connections with the criminal
underworld, and little about his motivation for fighting the drug ring.
We know only about his actions, which are superb in physical swift-
ness and moral standing. There is no doubt that Moro is a positive
hero, not in the socialist sense, but in the romantic sense of the word
– free from all ties, material and psychological, a lone wanderer possessing innate dignity, honesty, an unerring sense of justice, and a
mix of knightly might and kindness. And yet, as a critic noted, "there
is a difference between traditional romanticism and the neo-
romanticism of the new wave," the neo-romantic spirit undermines

22   *The Needle* (1989) directed by Rashid Nugmanov

"the central idea of doom connected with the hero, lowering the
pathos of his deeds to triviality."[34]

Indeed, Moro is not torn between the material and the ideal
worlds, he accepts both, while maintaining his distance and total
independence. He challenges the mafia boss who provides Dina with
drugs, and exploits her sexually (played by the rock celebrity Pyotr
Mamonov of "Zvuki mu"), but he himself was once part of the underworld. Viktor Tsoy is a wonderful interpreter of the neo-romantic
spirit. He did not have to act, he just played himself. Clad in black
jeans and leather jacket, he moves with the grace of a panther, sport-
ing a slightly sardonic smile, without bitterness or scorn. His movements are equally graceful when he strikes his attackers with deadly
force, and when he unleashes his energy in a run against the natural
background of the dried-up Aral Sea. But the most obvious neo-
romantic mark occurs at the end of the film. Moro has been stabbed,
and is kneeling in the blood-stained snow. This would be the perfect
closure for a traditional romantic story, with the hero leaving this
imperfect world for the real one, after having fulfilled his mission. But
Nugmanov spoils the cathartic effects. Moro gets up and walks away,

along a snowy alley that seems to lead to infinity. Tsoy's own song, "Blood Type," comes up on the soundtrack, and on the screen the words appear: "Dedicated to Soviet TV." The romantic message is totally subverted, shifting the focus from the longing for life after death to the affirmation of life regardless of death.[35]

Audiences that look for the drama of drug addiction, or some good sex scenes, not to speak of love, will be disappointed. The film is too sophisticated for that. It offers instead an aesthetically stylized world, stunning cinematography of the natural environment, a semi-surrealist *mise-en-scène*, and the last performance of Viktor Tsoy. One year after the film's release, Tsoy died in a car accident. His death triggered a wave of desperation among his fans, such as we had not seen since the disappearance of Vladimir Vysotsky – the bard of a different era and a different generation.

Not all Kazakh films are about youth, but mention must be made here of some of them, even if this means a digression from the present topic. *The Three* (1988), by Alexander Baranov and Bakhyt Kilibaev, is a delightful portrait of three hobos alienated from Soviet society, and finding dignity in marginality; *The Last Stop* (1989), by Serik Aprymov, is a naturalistic, dark depiction of life in a god-forsaken village plagued by poverty, violence, and decay; *A Wolf Cub Among People* (1989), by Talgat Temenov, is a refreshing children's story with traits of Italian neorealism; *A Little Fish in Love* (1989), by Abai Karpikov, conveys the sleepy atmosphere of a city in a sophisticated, detached style, through the adventures of a young man in search of love; *Balcony* (1989), by Kalybek Sadykov, features unrest among the rebellious youth of the 1950s, in a nostalgic mood; *The Fall of Otrar* (1990), by Ardak Amirkurov, is set in the historical period of the Tartar–Mongol hordes, but looks at the past from a contemporary viewpoint.

A significant number of features placed rock music at center stage and endowed rock culture with a symbolic meaning. The young rebels who live on the fringes of society and criticize it through the irreverence of their songs and attire, for all their naiveté and con-fusion are often seen as a force of renewal – the barbarians of a dawning civilization. Director Valery Ogorodnikov, in his film-debut, *The Burglar* (1987), tells the story of a boy who steals a synthesizer in order to help his older brother, the leader of a rock band, and gets enmeshed with illegal traffickers. The major attraction of the film is its great charge of energy, generated by the leading vocalist of the group

"Alisa," Konstantin Kinchev (who plays the role of the older brother), as well as by an endless array of Leningrad amateur rockers. This is brought to the fore by a virtuoso mixing of sounds that creates a "unique aural world."[36] This world consists of several layers. One of them is represented by the brass band at the children's club, where little brother Semen plays the tuba, and dreams of the wild and freer milieu of the rock concerts. Two visual styles alternate as do the worlds of the two brothers, from plain reportorial to eclectic-psychedelic.

If one had to name an approximate equivalent of the kind of postmodernist kitsch that became the hallmark of David Lynch's movies in the West, one would say: *Assa*. An absurdist expression in itself, the word does not exist in the Russian (or any other) vocabulary. It is, however, the title of a film by Sergei Solovev (1988), and in the juvenile jargon means confusion, turmoil, mess. "It is a word of the Moscow–Leningrad counterculture," explains a Moscow University student. "For example, when the artist Kotyolnikov paints some crazy picture, on the canvas he writes: 'Assa ye-ye'."[37] A critic provides a succinct but accurate idea of the film: "It is a mixed text, at times confusing, that includes several lines; a love story, a detective story, an episode of Russian history that deals with the assassination of Paul I. The heroes are unusual: a "godfather" – the mafioso chief–superman Krymov – midgets, rockers, the black musician Vitya . . . Everything here is strange, uncanny, even the heros' names – Alika, Bananan – and the palm trees covered with snow in Yalta." Another critic notes that this is a text one should read not by logical connections, but by visual, and cultural "*assa*ciations."[38]

The action takes place in 1980, the final days of "the old regime," when change was around the corner but time was standing still, congealed. The Black Sea resort in the grip of a snowstorm, as seen in the opening scene, provides the first "atmospheric" metaphor. Life is dormant, stagnating in fact, but inevitably there will be spring. The plot hinges on the conflict between the forces of stagnation and the forces of renewal. Krymov, played by Stanislav Govorukhin (the director of many detective–adventure movies) comes across as a figure possessing considerable charisma and sex-appeal. He is athletic, well-read, entrepreneurial, wealthy . . . and a criminal. On the other side, are the exponents of the youth counterculture, a group of rock musicians living in the semi-underground and constantly harassed by the police. First among them is Bananan, played by the Leningrad rock star, poet, and artist Sergei Bugaev, who in real life

23 *Assa* (1988) directed by Sergei Solovev

goes under the nickname of Afrika, even though he is blond and blue-eyed. In between is the young and innocent Alika, played by the beautiful Tatyana Drubich (Solovev's wife). Her character provides for a sort of love triangle without love. In fact, in *Assa*, nothing is what it seems to be. Alika is under the spell of Krymov's commanding personality, attracted to his bedroom by the magnetic energy he projects. At the same time, she is also attracted to the cluttered room of Bananan, full of all the artifacts of "rockculture," a place for flights into a dream world. But she is neither a mafioso's moll, nor a groupie, she has no hidden motives and simply follows her own inclinations. As the plot thickens, adding to the general confusion rather than to a logical denouement, the conflict between two philosophies of life, two worlds, two epochs deepens and explodes in two acts of violence. Krymov has Bananan killed by his clansmen, and is in turn killed by Alika.

Krymov's death, and Bananan's murder, mark the end of an era and open the door to a new beginning. The connection with the course of history, the sense that the present time is on the dividing line between two historical moments, is made explicit throughout the film by the recurrent episodes at the court of Paul I. These are evoked by Krymov's reading about Paul's assassination in the book, *Between*

Two Eras (Gran'vekov) by the late Natan Eidelman, a popular historian. Clearly, Krymov senses the approach of his own demise. The story has an unhappy ending, with a couple of corpses on the scene and Alika shipped off to prison. But the movie actually ends with an uplifting epilogue. Rock songs in the course of the film were played in counterpoint to the soundless, inorganic world of the mafia business. Many favorites were performed by Bananan's band, including several Grebenshchikov hits. The musical climax is finally provided with the appearance of Viktor Tsoy on the stage of the Green Theater in Yalta's Park of Culture. The snow is gone. Thousands of little flames in the crowd glimmer in the dark and mirror the star-studded sky. Thousands of young faces lit by matches and cigarette lighters look up at the leader of "Kino," and sing along with him: "Our hearts demand change / Our eyes demand change / In our laughter and in our tears / and in the pulsation of our veins / we expect change, change."

Too much idealism, too much naiveté? Different critics held different opinions. The fact is that the complex structure of the film does not allow for clear-cut values, and therefore both hero and villain images are undermined by irony, stylization, and a subtext of self-referential allusions. For example, the casting of midgets reminds us of "Bergman's *Silence*, Bunuel's *Viridiana*, and Schloendorff's *The Tin Drum*," not to speak of Eisenstein's *Strike* and, why not, Lynch's *Twin Peaks*. This creates an intellectual playground, complete with the image of a Soviet Michael Corleone and the celebration of "juvenile leftism."[39]

And yet, regardless of the intellectual game, Solovev addresses the new avant-garde with respect. "These are not destroyers, hooligans; rather they are the guardians of art. In the difficult times, when there was much cynicism, they preserved the cultural values of the past."[40] And now? Now, they want to express their own cultural values freely and publicly. To that end, Solovev and his artistic entourage planned an unusual première for the film *Assa*, at the Moscow movie theater "Udarnik." They envisioned an "art-rock-parade," with concerts by "Aquarium," "Pop-mechanics," and "Kino"; a fashion show of futuristic wondrous attire; an art exhibition of the informal associations, "Hermitage," "Friends of V. Mayakovsky," and "Academy of All Arts." The idea was supported by Goskino, Mosfilm, and the Filmmakers Union, and Solovev received permission from the Moscow Film Distribution Bureau to use the theater. But on the eve of opening day, when the halls had been decorated at great expense in labor and money, and everything was in place, the theater manager, L. Banian, simply cancelled the show. The last resort was to turn to the executive committee of Mossovet, which declared the theater unsafe for such an event. This, they said, could jeopardize the lives of many citizens, because "Udarnik" is one of the first movie theaters built in Moscow, in the 1920s, and its structures might collapse. Solovev, however, was invited to select any other site, "a palace of culture, or sport facilities," but it was too late. The show was simply killed. The noise from the new barbarians' camp triggered the alarm bell in the chanceries of City Hall.[41]

This was Solovev's first film in the carnivalesque style of glasnost. Just before *Assa*, he had made the lyrical tale of the "friendship" between a white dove and a boy, *The White Pigeon* (1987). The film carried a positive message of peace and beauty to a cruel world marked by the scars of the past. But *Assa* was a turning point, and Solovev's poetic vein changed. His next film, *Black Rose Is a Symbol of Sorrow, Red Rose Is the Symbol of Love* (1989) was shot in the "genre of decay," but "a comic decay," because notwithstanding the horror of the recent decades, "laughter makes people part with the past."[42] Again a love triangle, farcical elements, the romance of two adolescents, Grebenshchikov and his group "Aquarium," religious rites, an eccentric dissident, and a sprinkle of political kitsch with retro flashes to the Stalin time. After *Assa* and *Black Rose*, Solovev started working on the script for a film with the provisional title, *The House Under the Starry Sky*, conceived as the last part of a "perestroika trilogy" that will be called "Three Songs of the Motherland."[43]

Other directors, however, chose a serious and direct approach to the problem of youth, sex, and drugs. The screenwriter and director Savva Kulish made it clear to the viewers that his film was intended to be a tragedy, a *Tragedy in the Rock Style* (1989). The conflict is again between two generations. More precisely, between father and son. The son is traumatized when his father is sentenced to three years for embezzlement and connections with organized crime. This leads him to drugs, and finally to suicide in a spectacular car accident. *Tragedy* was a bestseller on the film market; the distributors bet on the movie's sleek technical quality and commercial themes, and they were not disappointed. The film contained enough box-office attractions: rock music, first of all, from "Pop-mechanics" and "Brigade S"; motorcycle and car stunts; a false guru, by the name of Cassius, who turns out to be a drug dealer; a drug and sex orgy, where former innocent youth, their heads totally shaved, fall victim to Cassius' lust and greed; graphic vein puncturing, urinating, and vomiting. The father's generation takes all the blame for the tragedy that befell these children, and Kulish puts himself on the bench of the accused with a cameo appearance. Notwithstanding the display of all the paraphernalia of the "rock style," which in the director's words convey the "spirit of the time," the film is traditional in its "realistic" conception and its educational intent. Allegedly, audiences of teenagers and adults would stay over for hours after the film's screening to discuss those problems in real life.[44]

No film about adolescents and their growing pains has had such a deep and broad impact as *Little Vera* (1988), by the young couple Vasily Pichul (director) and Maria Khmelik (screenwriter). This realistic commentary on the disintegration of the social fabric, starting from within a working-class family, includes all the features of a Western-style melodrama: generation gap, alienated youth, romance, violence, alcoholism, death, drugs, attempted suicide, and sex for good measure. The latter was an absolute first on the Soviet screen, and undoubtedly contributed to the success of the film. But for all its clichés, masterfully manipulated by the authors, *Little Vera* is much more than a potboiler. Devoid of all sentimentalism, it offers the viewer the picture of a gritty reality, in a deceitfully simple and unadorned style. For the first time, the stigma of *poshlost'* (lack of spiritual values), traditionally an attribute of the petty bourgeoisie, is here placed on the working class. These are people of "little faith," as the title suggests, and they are even unaware of it.[45] They feel a void, and do not know what is missing. As the older generation fades into retirement with a baggage of bitterness and frustration for their legacy of unfulfilled lives, the children are confronted with a physical and spiritual wasteland. The many lingering pans of a decaying industrial city on the shores of a polluted harbor evoke the collapsing system of values that was artificially preserved by decades of official propaganda and indifferent conformism. The responsibility for the present situation is laid flatly at the parents' feet (the authors are in their late twenties). And the film offers no future for little Vera and her companion.

Little Vera was seen by more than 50 million viewers in the USSR in less than one year.[46] Whether the audiences were attracted by the superficial elements of the film, or whether they were able to decode its deeper layers will remain a question, but the Soviet film world

24   *Little Vera* (1988) directed by Vasily Pichul

praised the movie as an event of major significance. The new realistic code employed by the authors deals a deadly blow to the discredited conception of Socialist Realism and its utopian worldview. The film's aesthetics are ideologically subversive, and perform the same operation of demystification that was being carried out in other spheres of public life.[47]

The film, obviously, had its detractors among the conservative, puritanical segment of the population (the people who more resemble Little Vera's parents). The actress Natalya Negoda, who played the title role, came under heavy fire for indecent exposure, and the whole film was castigated for being vulgar, obscene, and a bad example for youth. The popular indignation peaked when Negoda, having attracted international attention, appeared in a photo session in *Playboy* magazine (May 1989), with the caption: "The Soviets' First Sex Star."

Negoda stayed with the same production team for her next picture, *Dark Nights in Sochi* (Pichul and Khmelik, 1989).[48] But in this tragicomedy about frustrated love Negoda plays the opposite of her previous character, bespectacled, clad in baggy clothes, and unsexy. No doubt, many fans were disappointed, and this may explain the drop in box-office success. Pichul commented: "We decided that we should show another side of [Negoda's] talent . . . this role is important for Natalya, it is more complex, more interior than Vera."[49] The narrative is also more complex than in the first film, following the lives of the two central characters in a parallel but separate development. Lena, a twenty-three-year-old student, and Stepanich, a fifty-year-old con man (played by Alexei Zharkov) meet briefly at the beginning of the movie, when Stepanich tries to dupe Lena's mother into a phony deal that involves an apartment swap. Then their stories depart and unfold into two plot lines, connected by crosscutting editing. Lena and Stepanich go through unhappy love relations, disappointments, family complications, and are finally driven to the resort town of Sochi on the Black Sea. There they meet again, and band together to find the strength to go on living. But because of a bizarre incident, they end up in a precarious situation, trapped in their hotel room with the corpse of a police officer.

Notwithstanding the lack of linearity in the film's structure, Pichul considers it "a realist film," with characters that correspond to real life in the Soviet Union today. "Stepanich is a crook," he says, "who sells thin air, dreams . . . But I don't think his character is interpreted negatively; he is a free man who earns his living the best he can. He is guilty of nothing; it's the government that's guilty; it's the absurd way Soviet society functions that produces this sort of behavior. You must understand that, at the moment, perestroika has nothing to do with our daily lives. Anyway, he is sincere, and he means to be honest in his love for Zhanna [a young woman who rejects him for his son]. As for Lena, she's an ordinary woman surrounded by many men except, of course, the one she is looking for." And why Sochi? "Sochi is every Soviet's dream, a dream of freedom and warmth," Pichul continues. "To Soviet ears, the title contains a sort of sexual invitation. But the film shows that Sochi is an illusion, yet another myth: it's just a dustbin like every other Soviet town . . . At the end of the film, the characters' situation illustrates the present situation of our society. What Lena and Stepanich are saying is that they're going to make their own way, to find their own path. Alongside them there is the dead police officer: the corpse of the state." However, the film ends with the characters in the grip of anxiety, and the sense that there is no way out.[50]

The film was officially released in November 1989, but almost immediately recalled. It was banned for obscenity because of its crude language. This was the same problem that delayed Kira Muratova's

Asthenic Syndrome. Dark Nights was eventually re-released in May 1990, at the time of the Cannes Film Festival.

This survey of films focusing on young people would not be complete without mentioning a very unusual picture, *Angel Day* (1988), by Sergei Selyanov and Nikolai Makarov. Work on the film started in 1980, as a result of a pre-perestroika private enterprise. The two directors and the screenwriter, Mikhail Konovalchuk, then students at VGIK, together with a group of colleagues and sympathizers, formed the "Society for the Production of the Film *Angel Day*," and shot the movie in three weeks, on a modest budget and with VGIK's equipment. Eight years later, Lenfilm took an interest in the picture, and invited the authors to rework the film at the studio and bring it up to professional standards. The picture was then released under the aegis of Lenfilm. Still, it remains a film for cineclubs, festivals, and cultural events.

Shot in black and white, it recounts the story of a country family as seen through the eyes of the younger son, a teenager by the strange name of Mafusail, who is considered the "village idiot." The authors exploit the effect of "estrangement," generated by the discrepancy between the visual track and the soundtrack. What the viewer sees is given a twist by Mafusail's voice-over commentary. His observations are naive, weird (he is an "idiot," after all), and often result in comical effects, but they also reveal an inner truth normally concealed to the average person. It has been noted that the name Mafusail evokes the figure of Noah's uncle, one of the "seven great sages."[51] Therefore, the young protagonist combines the clairvoyance of "Ivan the fool," from Russian folklore, and his more mystical variant of the "fool in Christ" that was central to the great novels of the nineteenth century, with the universal wisdom of a Biblical personage. His innocent outlook brings to the fore the pettiness, greed, and outright criminality of the surrounding household – an obvious microcosm for society at large. Mafusail, unlike the roaring film teenagers of the 1980s, is a happy fellow who lives in his self-contained spiritual world. This tale of an exemplary life ends with the "apotheosis of the sage on his angel day."[52] While the guests reciting abstract monologues on the meaning of life, death, and society look straight at the camera, Mafusail lies in the grass with his best friend, the goat Kuzdra, his eyes turned up to the sky.

Where fiction meets reality: social ills

The films discussed above focus on youth problems as one symptom of a widespread social disease. Other films deal with society at large, the adults' world, aiming at a range of targets. The favorite target remains the legacy of Brezhnevism, which corrodes minds and souls, promotes mediocrity, stifles talent, perpetuates hypocrisy, favors organized crime, and destroys trust and love among individuals and within the family. This legacy is particularly entrenched in the bureaucratic apparatus, which is the target of *Forgotten Melody for Flute* (1988), by Eldar Ryazanov.[53] The film was extremely topical when it came out. It offered the first criticism of perestroika on the screen, through a satire with dramatic overtones. Gone is the optimism of Ryazanov's early comedies, the belief that love conquers everything, even a bureaucrat's soul (see *An Office Romance*, 1978). Starting with the bitter laughter of *Garage* (1980), Ryazanov became progressively disenchanted and his vein took a turn toward tragedy, that peaked in *Dear Elena Sergeyevna* (1988).

Forgotten Melody is the story of a high-ranking official of the Directorate of Leisure Time, by the name of Leonid Filimonov.[54] A careerist without scruples, he has made his material comfort and professional advancement his first priorities, using the connection with his father-in-law, who is a big bureaucratic shot. After practicing this philosophy for twenty years, Leonid has become another one of the many "dead souls" who populate the most recent films, a puppet without values, feelings, and moral strength. At first glance, however, Leonid does not look like a negative character. He is handsome, educated, and gallant. He even plays the flute, occasionally, when he is in a romantic mood. In short, he is an attractive man. So much so, that the beautiful, intelligent, and independent Lida, the nurse in charge of his routine heart treatment, cannot resist his charms. But, although young, Lida is not naive. From the very beginning of their romance, she is able to see through to his real self. She is totally aware that Leonid is first of all a coward; nevertheless, she sincerely loves him, sensing his inner weakness and his need for her moral support. In the end, Leonid abandons her and goes back to his wife, in order to facilitate yet another promotion. But the story reaches its dramatic climax when Leonid suffers a heart attack on the first day in his new post, and Lida rushes to his rescue. She literally resuscitates him with the sheer power of her love. And then, Lida leaves, the camera recording from a high angle her slow walk down a deep open stairwell, suggesting a final departure. Leonid has been given the gift of a new life. Will it be again the life of a bureaucrat, or will it be the life of a man?

The question is important because, besides Leonid's personal story, the film deals with the institution he represents, the gigantic apparatus of the Soviet bureaucracy. Ryazanov's satirical eye catches the psychology of the bureaucracy as a whole, trying to negotiate the demands of perestroika. While paying lip service to the new directives, the civil servants consolidate their positions. While changing their lines and looks, they retain their inner void. While introducing new methods, they preserve the substance of the old operations. The fact that there is an entire directorate designed to organize and control the citizens' leisure time is emblematic of the real nature of the bureaucracy. As the mocking, jolly song of the opening sequence states, the main task of a good administrator is to say "no" to any proposal or initiative. This is confirmed when we first meet Leonid, at a preview of an avant-garde play staged by an amateur club. He approves the performance on the spot, because now "we don't forbid these things anymore, these are different times." But, very cynically, he turns to his aide and orders him to shut down the play, without explanation.[55] The same may happen at an art exhibition, not with bulldozers – "these are different times" – but, as one of the officials suggests, with boycott, harassment, vicious press coverage, and the like. Conversely, the bureaucrats do not know what to do with the staples of pop culture that are now out of fashion, like the preposterous Tambov choir in folkish costumes, that is sent out on an endless tour extending from the shores of the Black Sea to the Kazakh steppe. The system's main concern is self-preservation. The bureaucrats' fear of losing their jobs and privileges is conveyed through a musical digression in the vaudeville style. Leonid and his colleagues see themselves begging in the street, or handing out their hats after performing a song and dance show on a bus. The musical acts provide comic relief in an otherwise gloomy situation, and stress the belief that change is only an illusionistic game, and perestroika a meaningless word.

The authors do not provide an answer to the question mark they placed at the end of the film. Instead, they offer a rich context that stimulates creative thinking. The more sophisticated Soviet audiences and the critics, did not like the approach to the theme. The mixing of genres, that range from dramatic theater to light musical fare, was seen as a trivialization of the issue and the techniques employed as cheap tricks. But the film got high ratings in the popular polls.[56] *Forgotten Melody* includes three narrative levels: the story line, Leonid's mental visions, and the authors' musical inserts. The story line offers superb characterizations (brought to life by first-class actors – Leonid Filatov, Tatyana Dogileva, Irina Kupchenko) and a detailed portrait of Soviet social classes, from Leonid's de-luxe apartment to Lida's communal living quarters. Leonid's mental visions are an indication that his moral principle (the feeble melody for flute) is not completely dead and, who knows, may be resuscitated. Three times, Leonid envisions himself taking a course of action that would be honest, courageous, and liberating, but always falls back into the old cowardly pattern. Besides commenting on Leonid's personality, these mental flights, on a more abstract level, also comment on the narrative itself, and the endless possibilities of structuring a story in a post-modernist text: it went this way, but it could have gone that way as well. The authors' musical inserts are "attractions" (in Eisenstein's sense of the word), they undermine the pathos of the drama and broaden the range of perception. This may also explain why Leonid's vision of the outer world, when he suffers a heart attack, looks more like a fairground haunted house than a subconscious hell. There is no doubt that *Forgotten Melody* is an "eclectic" text, as some detractors labeled it.[57] The authors were certainly aware of the hybrid genre, because they themselves called it a "phantasmagoric musical tragicomedy."[58] But they used eclecticism to their advantage, creating a film that is socially significant and aesthetically articulate, as well as being greatly entertaining.

The bureaucracy is also the target of a film that made a lot of waves, *Extraordinary Occurrence at Local Headquarters* (1989), by Sergei Snezhkin, more often called simply *EO* (in Russian, *Che Pe*). The film's specific focus is the Party bureaucracy of the younger ranks – the zealous officials of the Young Communist League (Komsomol). These are people in their early thirties, who are on the brink of elevation to Party membership and regalia through the pyramidal system of *nomenklatura*. Although the occurrence recounted is "extraordinary," the style of narration is plain and realistic – but not dull. Actually, the genre is a *sui generis* detective. The mystery begins when the chairman of the Komsomol neighborhood district discovers that someone stole the Komsomol flag from his office and overthrew a bust of Lenin. The investigation seems to lead nowhere, but in the end the police track down the "criminal." This turns out to be a

25 *Extraordinary Occurrence at Local Headquarters* (1989) directed by Sergei Snezhkin

teenager, protesting the Komsomol's regimentation of youth, and the authoritarian handling of leisure and recreation. The protester used the flag to decorate his humble one-room abode, in which he lived in substandard conditions together with his mother and an invalid grandmother.

The detective line, however, is not the main point of the film. It is a narrative device that brings to the fore a bitter irony and raises the question of who are the real criminals. Throughout the film, the main focus is on the central character, the young Komsomol leader Pavel Shumilin, and his personal drama. Because of the "extraordinary occurrence" that happened in his district, he is about to lose his position – and this on the eve of his appointment to a higher post. Shumilin is a fellow afflicted by the usual symptoms associated with bureaucratic servility – callousness and hypocrisy. The camera underlines Shumilin's genealogy by catching him repeatedly against the background of a gallery of huge tableaux, portraying members of the Politburo. In a scene that has shocked many viewers, Shumilin reveals the bottom of moral abjection when he sodomizes his girlfriend on the kitchen table, forcing her face down in a cake, with a picture of Brezhnev in the background. The payoff is good for the Komsomol servants. A group of Soviet-style yuppies is shown in one of the opening sequences enjoying a sex and champagne party at an exclusive bath establishment. The steaming pool, the athletic bodies, naked or clad in white sheets, the enthusiastic ovations following Shumilin's demagogic statements – all is calculated to evoke an atmosphere of Roman decadence and debauch. Shumilin's drama has an unclimactic conclusion, as befits an anti-hero. Pushed against the wall, he decides to make a grand exit, and publicly denounces the rotten nature of the organization at a Komsomol meeting (unlike Leonid in *Forgotten Melody*, Shumilin does not dream of doing it, he does it). But the system swiftly avoids the challenge. All of a sudden, the flag is recovered, Shumilin's speech is twisted to appear as a patriotic call to righteous duty, and he gets his promotion.

Che Pe is based on a short novel by Yuri Polyakov that was first turned into a play at Oleg Tabakov's Theater Studio in Leningrad, and subsequently rewritten as a film script. After its release, the movie was boycotted by the Komsomol, and for many months did not reach the viewers. When it finally did, the audience was split between those who hailed the unmasking of an odious institution, and those who protested the film's political irreverence and explicit sex scenes.[59]

The theme of social alienation, due to the loss of a common spiritual heritage, made its way to the screen at the beginning of the 1980s, and turned into a consistent trend as the years progressed. Two excellent films on this theme, *Autumn Marathon* and *Garage*, came out exactly in 1980, symbolically marking the beginning of the decade. But before glasnost, the filmmakers had to dilute their medicine for social improvement, and administer it with subtle means. In the past two years, however, glasnost has brought about many excesses. Among them, an excess of movies that pretend to analyze the spiritual condition of contemporary society and that focus on the most negative aspects of urban life with naturalistic vengeance. Often, these pictures include a religious motif of sin-cum-retribution, or sin without repentance, the death of God, the triumph of Satan, the days of Sodom, and the like. A critic noted a list of recent titles – *Have Mercy and Forgive*, *Save and Protect*, *Save Our Souls*, *Our Father*, *May I Die, Oh Lord* . . . – and commented: "We used to march in formation. Now, we pray in formation."[60]

A film of this type, but not devoid of merit, is *Assuage My Sorrow* (1989), by Viktor Prokhorov and Alexander Alexandrov. The title refers to an inscription on an ancient icon of the Virgin Mary, which plays a central role in the story.[61] An ordinary Moscow couple is divorced and the husband, Boris, looks for new quarters. He cynically helps dislodge an old lady from the room that she had occupied for sixty years – since the time she lost the rest of her apartment to communal living. Before leaving, the old lady gives one of her possessions, the holy icon, to an occasional visitor, a pregnant teenager, hoping to trigger a spark in the girl's soul. But the spiritual legacy is lost to the younger generations. The girl has an abortion, and soon after moves in with Boris. The sex scene on their first night together ironically occurs under the uncovered icon, which to the new tenants is nothing more than an ornament on the wall.[62]

Mainstream glasnost feature films have come under fire by new wave critics, who grew impatient with the opportunistic display of current stereotypes. The writer of the following assessment interprets the sentiments of a whole generation of young intellectuals: "It is a really amazing thing this glasnost in feature films. On the mass level, it boils down to active sexualization, partial narcotization, and formal anti-Stalinization of the screen (pardon my difficult neologisms). My colleague, Andrei Dementiev, is right. Asked to describe contemporary Soviet cinema, he said: 'A naked woman sits before a portrait of Stalin and smokes marijuana.' It is as if the words: 'You may!' were pronounced. And the filmmakers, used to collective action, eagerly shouted: 'Ready!' Clichés, clichés, clichés. Here is Stalin, there a naked back, here again a needle in the vein." Our critic maintains that glasnost is being trivialized by images without substance. Too many filmmakers do not go beneath the surface. Because of fear that tomorrow freedom of expression may be taken away, everyone seems to rush to say his or her word. Now, our critic continues, "everyone has already spoken, everything has been said. We are fed up. And if you do not like to be ordered: 'You may not,' we will shout to you: 'Enough!' "[63]

A film that ended up on the young critic's blacklist is *The Husband and Daughter of Tamara Alexandrovna* (1989), by O. Narutskaya. This is a family drama recounting the complex relations between father and teenage daughter after a divorce, against the background of a Moscow cityscape painted in dark colors. The story, too, ends on a dark note – "a bloody bacchanalia"[64] – with the father beaten up in the street by three of the daughter's schoolmates before the eyes of indifferent passers-by. The father is portrayed as a nice fellow, although juvenile, an aging teenager himself. The violence, therefore, seems even more bestial, an outburst of rage against an innocent victim. What triggered it was a feeling of revenge against the daughter, who promised to entertain the boys with sex games but did not deliver. Another film with similar ingredients, which left many critics cold is *Autumn, Chertanovo . . .* (1988), by Igor Talankin. The time and place of action are stated in the title. One must clarify, however, that the time is the present time, Chertanovo is a vacation spot north of Moscow for privileged people, and the action focuses on the technocratic and intellectual elite, their love intrigues, petty squabbles, cynicism, and back-stabbing practices.[65] The film ends with another victim, not totally innocent though. Maria had been fooling around with many men, besides her two significant ones: husband Stanislav – a computer scientist, all mathematics and no feelings – and lover Fedor, a screenwriter. She is eventually raped and murdered by an unknown attacker, and Stanislav, shaken out of his emotional limbo, commits suicide. The characters' alienation and their eventual demise seem to be blamed on technological progress, which turned into a dehumanizing nightmare instead of a means to enlightenment.

The list of the films under fire is long and includes, among others, *Tragedy in Rock Style* and even *Che Pe*.[66] While sympathizing with the demands of the radical critics, it would be unfair to the filmmakers to assume that all of them are moved only by professional conformism. Regardless of the degree of artistic achievement, most of those films are motivated by a sincere desire to do something useful, to serve a just cause. Many of the protagonists of the glasnost revolution, the architects of the New Model, have been paralyzed by the danger of producing something trivial, commonplace, now that everybody was tackling the same "hot" issues. Klimov, German, Smirnov, Bykov, and even Askoldov have not been able to make any films under the new conditions. The official reason is that they were busy running the affairs of the Filmmakers Union (except for Askoldov). But German expressed a common feeling a long time ago. When asked about his next project after *Ivan Lapshin*, he said that he wanted to do something different: "I'll either go back and it'll be Chekhov, or forward."[67]

Roman Balayan did exactly that – or almost that. He based his film,

Lady Macbeth of the Mtsensk District (1989), on the nineteenth-century short novel by Nikolay Leskov. This "lady Macbeth" is the wife of a rich provincial merchant, the beautiful Katerina, who being possessed by a consuming passion for the farm hand Sergei, becomes an accomplice in the assassination of her husband. This triggers a chain reaction that results in the murder of an innocent child, the killing of Sergei's new love, and Katerina's suicide. This dark tragedy of lust and greed is not redeemed by even a speck of light. Katerina and Sergei are monsters. There is something elemental in their amorality. They seem to have been born without a sense of good and evil, of heaven and hell. Their brutish sensuality is graphically depicted in the sex scene in a barn, in which Katerina takes her pleasure in being sodomized like a cow (here there is no hint of rape, nor of "political hegemony"). The two creatures are equally impenetrable to normal human relations and to the environment. Whether engaged in an idyll in the green plains of central Russia, or marching in chains on the road to Siberia, they are emotionally insulated. Nothing seems to matter, except for sex and money.

The aberration of the human personality is contrasted by a highly aestheticized style. Everything, and everybody, is beautiful in this film. The glorious Russian countryside, the merchant home with its "discreet charm," the masters, the peasants, the victims, and even the convicts. And, above all, Katerina and Sergei, two pagan deities of a hedonistic realm. Normally, beauty is an aesthetic code that connotes spirituality, a medium from the "realia" to the "realiora." Not in this film. One must give credit to the director and the leading actors (Natalya Andreichenko and Alexander Abdulov) for successfully conveying the essence of pure materialism through images of beauty. Here, the aesthetic varnishing of the surface is deliberate and significant. It attracts attention to itself, and to the ugly abyss it covers up.

This film was able to comment on today's society in an original way, by making a detour into the past. Moreover, while the setting is Russian, the reference to "Lady Macbeth" endows the picture with a tragic significance that has universal resonance.[68] The same effect is achieved in Kira Muratova's *Change of Fortune* (1987). Based on Somerset Maugham's *The Letter*, Muratova's film is set in a British colony after World War I. The central character is another woman of instinctual behavior, Maria, who murders her lover in cold blood, buys her way out of prison, and drives her husband to suicide. But in contrast to *Lady Macbeth*, the setting is squalid, a decaying village in East Asia, with begging children and empty bazaars. Here, the environment is an objective correlative of the heroine's inner void and of society's spiritual condition. Nevertheless, in addition to the story line, Muratova offers an aestheticized version of the meeting of the two lovers at the beginning of the film, as a prologue. This is a flattering self-image of Maria, repeated from different angles, and seen through her own mind's eye. Muratova lifts the viewers to an illusory ideal summit, only to plunge them abruptly into the filthy reality.

In her latest film, *Asthenic Syndrome* (1990), Muratova brings the action back home, and without the aid of metaphors confronts the naked truth. So crude and naturalistic is her approach that the film's release was delayed for months.[69] *Asthenic Syndrome* begins with a black-and-white story of a woman under stress after the death of her husband, but not necessarily because of it. The reason is more philosophical and universal. She has been under stress all her life, because of the social and existential predicament of the human being at this stage of our civilization. And in Russia, the film suggests, one is confronted with an extreme situation. Finally, something snaps, and the woman explodes in a barrage of angry, dirty words, on a public bus. The bus is empty, and the verbal abuse is directed to the camera. This is her "asthenic syndrome." But her story was just a movie (within the movie), an introduction to the "real" picture. The "real" picture begins with the audience leaving the theater, outraged at such "trash" on the screen. Then the camera, too, moves outside and begins to record life in true colors. A series of disjointed episodes and grotesque events confirm that the entire society is afflicted by an "asthenic syndrome" of epidemic proportions. It is a violent, inhuman society on the brink of nervous collapse and, perhaps, extinction. In the final sequence, the central character rides an empty metro car, that disappears into a dark tunnel.

Screenwriter Natalya Ryazantseva, who collaborated with Kira Muratova on the film *Long Farewells*, wrote an intrepid defense of *Asthenic Syndrome*, when the film lay in limbo. Among other things, she noted: "The film deals with the human being as a biological creature in the present coil of the evolutionary spiral, perhaps on the ultimate summit of progress, whence there is no way up."[70] The film was eventually released but, as expected, it did not conquer the box office. The general public had more or less the same reaction as the audience portrayed in the film itself. But the critics, and the intellectual world at large, gave it top marks. The consensus was that the film's unrelieved pessimism is rescued by Muratova's artistic inspiration and deep compassion. A reviewer wrote: "If there is a future for us, it will emerge only through a crisis, through desperation, through a keen sense of the end, just as shown in Muratova's film."[71]

Of all the glasnost films, only a handful have made a mark in the USA, and were released commercially.[72] One that was expected to conquer the American viewer, as well as the Soviet audience, was *Taxi Blues* (1990), by Pavel Lungin. However, expectations were frustrated. According to the director, the film includes techniques and motifs of the American trend of the 1970s, such as *Taxi Driver* and *Midnight Cowboy*. Lungin found that those films were able to convey the energy charge of the big city, its madness, its "mix of cruelty and humor."[73]

Lungin's big city is unmistakably Moscow, and yet it reminds us of New York. Stripped of all embellishments, the city is offered to the viewer in its naked reality, which does not exclude the absurdist dimension of life. The cinematographer, Denis Evstigneev, rendered Lungin's vision through "images condensed to the utmost limit, and extreme expressive devices."[74] The story hinges on the love–hate relationship of two unlikely friends, Ivan Shlikov and Lyosha. Shlikov is a taxi driver, an average citizen who believes in law, order, and duty, and looks with equal suspicion at marginal elements of society and the reformist trends of perestroika. Lyosha is one of the marginals, an alcoholic saxophone player, an alienated musician, hardly able to make a living. Shlikov gets into his mind to reform Lyosha, after having picked him up at night in his taxi, and taken him home. But Lyosha turns out to be incorrigible. A comedy ensues that brings to the fore the clash of two personalities, two philosophies of life, and even two ideologies. The situations are hilarious, but there is more than comedy in the director's approach. Shlikov's conservatism, his Soviet psychology, his unshaken Marxist values are coupled with his basic honesty, sincere concern for a fellow human being, and outright love for his younger friend. The Soviet "philistine," normally an easy target of satire, in this film comes across as a live human being, caring and suffering, and gets the sympathy of the director and the viewer. "Poor devil," the director seems to say, "he worked all his life, obeyed the law, and now he is told that it was all a big lie, that he was an idiot. Of course, he is an idiot, but he has a good heart."[75] A dramatic finale takes place when Shlikov realizes that Lyosha is incapable of love and compassion, due to his ingrained cynicism. The taxi driver gets involved in a spectacular car chase, with very "American" stunts, cars crashing and burning. But Lungin's sardonic vein does not allow for a tragedy. We learn from an "afterword" that Shlikov became the director of a cooperative taxicab company and bought himself a Mercedes. As for Lyosha, he was recognized as a musical genius.

If the film's epilogue has a fairy-tale flavor, so does Lungin's personal story – although his bearded and ruddy-cheeked figure does not fit the Cinderella image. After working for many years as a screenwriter, having some of his scripts accepted only to be distorted by untalented film directors, and having dreamed of becoming a director himself, all of a sudden his dream came true through the magic wand of French producer Marin Karmitz. The film was shot in Moscow, on a French budget, and released by Lenfilm/ASK and Eurofilm/MK 2. At age forty, Lungin had never directed a movie. This was his first experience, and it won him the award for Best Director at the 1990 Cannes Film Festival.

Much of the film's success rests on Lungin's talent as screenwriter and director, and on the cinematographer's original approach. Equally important were the two marvelous interpreters of the central roles, actor Pyotr Zaichenko as the bullish taxi driver, and Pyotr Mamonov as the emarginated musician. Mamonov is a legendary figure of the pre-perestroika Leningrad rock scene and avant-garde underworld. He comes from the same cultural background that nurtured Lungin in his youth years. In *Taxi Blues*, the saxophone score is performed by Vladimir Chekasin, but Mamonov's impersonation is so skillful that many specialists thought it was for real.

Contemporary Soviet society has undergone a close scrutiny on the part of the filmmakers of glasnost. The judgement has been negative 99 percent of the time. The critics have even invented a term for the naturalistic trend focusing on problems with unrelieved gloom: *chernukha*, which means "painted in dark colors," but it also has a condescending overtone indicating poor quality and exploitation of the subject for commercial purposes. At first, the frank treatment of social ills which were kept from the news and from public discussion for decades was an ingredient for success. But as the mass media acquired an objective voice, the need for information through art became less pressing. Having satisfied their hunger for truth, the audiences found it to be too depressing, unless combined with some entertaining features. Revealing of the popular mood are the box-office hits of the past three years which conquered the masses.

Blockbusters: the triumph of cowboys, godfathers, and Cinderellas

The reason why audiences are attracted to genre films is a matter of serious study and heated debate in the Soviet Union.[76] Nobody has come up with a "scientific" explanation so far, but some filmmakers have captured the essence of the phenomenon intuitively. They were able to offer the public a combination of ingredients that struck the right chord at the right time. The Soviet film industry so far does not gauge the rate of success in terms of revenues, as does the American, but in terms of attendance. Thanks to the centralized system, it was easy to compute the number of tickets sold. Those data, however, were not released by Goskino, and only now are coming out of the archives. The data show that, while every year there are some ten movies that sell over 20 million tickets, only one or two are seen by more than 40 million. These are the blockbusters (in Russian, *"boeviki"*). The blockbusters of the last three years are a *"western,"* *The Man from Boulevard des Capucines* (1987); a thriller, *Kings of Crime* (1988); and a melodrama, *Intergirl* (1989).[77]

The Man from Boulevard des Capucines, by Alla Surikova, alludes to the location of the first establishment of the Lumière brothers in Paris. Although the film is not "facing the present," it nevertheless reflects the present predicament of the Soviet film industry, and testifies to the taste of the contemporary viewer. *Capucines* is essentially a commentary on cinema itself: its nature and values, its aesthetic function and social impact, its magic, and its commercial exploitation. But this self-reflexive discourse is cast into the mold of a classical popular genre: the American western. As a result the film met with the approval of a mass audience that was able to relate emotionally to a well-known code of stock characters, situations and settings. The film's central theme is "good" v. "bad" cinema, the setting is the Golden West at the turn of the century.

A familiar scene: a vast, arid landscape; under the scorching sun a lone stagecoach is bravely dashing across the empty plain through clouds of yellow dust; suddenly . . . the attack; it is Black Jack and his band; chase, stunts, crossfire . . . the stagecoach passengers and the driver get to their guns, the Salvation Army ladies to their first aid kits; only one passenger is unperturbed and keeps reading his book.

26   *The Man from Boulevard des Capucines* (1987) directed by Alla
Surikova

His name is Mr. First. He is dressed with extreme sobriety in a black
suit, black tie, black hat; his stance is modest, his looks serene. A
traveling salesman engaged in the fight is vexed by his behavior:
"Why don't you shoot, dammit?!" "I can't," answers First. "Why?
Did you come to these parts without a gun?!" inquires the in-
credulous salesman. "I did not come to kill," is Mr. First's unassuming answer. "Well, then they'll kill you," the salesman replies with
matter-of-fact finality. Now the fight is over and the bandits are about
to leave, loaded with the stagecoach's money; Black Jack stops by the
window and asks First: "I bet you one to ten, mister, that you're not
reading the Bible." "You're right," says First and hands his book to
Jack. A flash of the cover reveals its title: George Sadoul, *A History of
World Cinema*. Jack leafs through and observes that there are many
blank pages; "There is room for history, sir," First answers with a
smile, "Be bold, and perhaps your name too will be written on these
pages. The book awaits its heros."[78]
    What follows is the story of Mr. First's mission to reform the way of
life in the town of Santa Carolina, whose dwellers are engaged in the
usual activities that befit the conventions of the genre – drinking,
gambling, fistfighting, gunfighting, sex, prostitution, blackmailing,

and stealing. Notwithstanding opposition from a vicious pastor and a greedy saloon owner, Mr. First succeeds in his task – lo and behold! – through the magic of cinema. The cradle of the town's vice, the Furious Bison saloon, becomes the shrine for the screening of the Lumière pictures that Mr. First brought to town. Actual footage from *L'arrivée du train, Le déjeuner de Bébé,* and *L'arroseur arrosé* is presented to the delight of the spectators. But, just as the saloon's patrons have switched from whiskey to milk, the Indian chief has buried his toma-hawk, and the chorus girls have exchanged their French can-can attire for austere tartan dresses, Mr. Second comes along and, taking advantage of Mr. First's brief absence, sets up his own movie show. Once again actual footage flashes on the screen: sex, violence, and pornography from unspecified pictures in a cheap decadent style. Passions are stirred, the saloon turns again into a wild arena where whiskey fuels the fire. Big business prevails and Mr. First is forced out of town by the power of the almighty dollar. Nevertheless, he scores a victory of no small significance: he is joined in the journey by his betrothed, Miss Little, the reformed star of the variety show, and by Black Jack, who has repented and decided to devote his life to cinema. Together they "ride East, toward the rising sun, on the wings of the wind of hope."[79]

The adventure genre, the lighthanded parody, the musical acts accounted for a box-office success. People were also attracted by the actors in the leading roles. An all-time audience favorite, Andrey Mironov, won the Best Actor category in the 1987 *Soviet Screen* poll, for his performance as Mr. First. Sadly, he died while acting on stage, soon after the making of this film, and this fact may have added even more to his popularity. The actress playing Miss Little, Alexandra Aasmiae, won second place for Best Actress in the same poll.[80]

The next film by Alla Surikova is another comedy set in the past. But, notwithstanding the catchy subtitle, "A Detective Story of the Stone Age," it did not score very high on the bestseller list. *Two Arrows* (1989) is based on a well known play by Alexander Volodin, which ran into a great deal of difficulty with the authorities in the 1970s, and was performed mainly in theater studios. The comic effect in the film is achieved by filling the stone age scene with today's consumer goods. The oddity of the images provides a new angle for a critical look at contemporary society. Star names, such as Natalya Gundareva and Nikolay Karachenko (who played Black Jack in *Capu-cines*) afforded the film a modest success.

When *Kings of Crime* was completed, in 1988, director Yuri Kara decided to distribute it independently through the Gorky Studio. This infuriated distribution officials.[81] When the film appeared on the screen it earned record box-office revenues in no time. This infuriated highbrow critics. At the 1988 Odessa Festival of Popular Genre Films, *Kings of Crime* was awarded the ironical prize of the "Three Ks," which stand for "K-onjuncture," "K-ommercialism," and "K-itsch." If the three Ks are stigmas in the eyes of the defenders of art films, they are also ingredients for success. One of the film's sustainers predicted that *Kings of Crime* "will attract no less than 46 million viewers." This was the beginning of 1989. A few months later, in July, *Variety* reported a figure of 70 million.[82] No official Soviet data are available due to independent distribution. But Kara himself admitted that the film brought in considerable profit, which enabled the studio to start the production of films of many different genres and to organize publicity and promotion.[83]

Blockbuster *Kings of Crime* is the first thriller on Mafia organized crime within the Soviet Union. The genre has been a longtime favorite of the Soviet audiences who have enjoyed foreign movies, or domestically made pictures with the action usually set in the West or

27   *Kings of Crime* (1988) directed by Yuri Kara

in some Latin American country. Kara decided to give the genre a national twist, and set the action in an unspecified Soviet republic in the Caucasus, in the Brezhnev period. The literal translation of the Russian title, "Thieves Within the Law," describes the situation more accurately and hints at the political system. The whole system is corrupt. Two Mafia families confront each other in an endless spiral of violence, police and prosecutors are bought with the "godfather's" money, justice is a mockery, and innocence is trampled upon. Amid murder and racket, the beautiful and curvaceous Anna Samokhina makes her debut in the role of Margo, who as a girl was raped by a taxi driver and after a series of unfortunate circumstances is killed by her own father. The stage is strewn with dead or maimed bodies and blood flows freely. Gory details abound, like a hot iron pressed on the belly of a mafioso, or a tough guy sawing off his own hand. It is almost too much to take. And this is exactly the point that the detractors of the film seem to have missed. Violence is deliberately exaggerated, undermined by a touch of irony that invites the viewers to "play" with the conventions of the genre.[84] Similarly, the political subtext is obvious and the allusions are crude. But, so what? After all, it is a popular genre and the people like it when the filmmaker speaks "their" language.

Another director, Pyotr Todorovsky, knows how to speak to the mass audiences and get directly to their hearts. Only, he does not rely on blood and adventure, but on tears and misfortune. *Intergirl* is a contemporary melodrama in two parts, employing the Cinderella motif with a final bitter twist.[85]

Tanya Zaitseva, played by stage actress Elena Yakovleva, is a hard-currency prostitute who entertains foreign executives at an Intourist hotel in Leningrad, like scores of other young women. The business earns her very good money and enables her to afford better food, clothes, and even furs, things normally out of reach for Soviet women. Tanya has a double life, and while at night she deals with the clients, bribes the hotel staff, and often negotiates her way out of the police station, during the day she holds a job as a nurse and lives in a modest but proper apartment with her loving mother. Obviously, life is not easy, the night job is demanding, and Tanya is tired. But unlike many of her colleagues, Tanya has a stroke of luck. The prince appears (though baldish and in a grey double-breasted suit) in the person of a Swedish businessman who falls in love with Tanya and marries her. Tanya leaves for Stockholm, and settles in a capitalist

28   *Intergirl* (1989) directed by Pyotr Todorovsky

paradise filled with all those consumer goods she worked so hard to
get back in Leningrad. But do they live happily ever after? No, says
the logic of the film. This is not a fairy tale, this is "life," and life
entails contradictions and suffering. As Part II begins, tears start
flowing (both on the screen and among the audience). Tanya is consumed by nostalgia for her homeland. In retrospect, even the harsh,
dehumanizing, everyday Soviet reality that drove her to prostitution
seems preferable to the comfortable but dull life of the Swedish upper
classes. After meeting a truck driver from Leningrad, she decides to
return, and deserts her still enamored husband without a thank-you
note. But on the way to the airport, Tanya is killed in a car accident.

Todorovsky's style is pseudo-realistic, and demands to be taken at
face value. The film pretends to portray a slice of life, and an ugly one
at that. Besides prostitution, the narrative includes the underworld of
blackmarketeering and illegal currency dealing; extreme poverty and
alcoholism (that afflict Tanya's father, estranged, and now remar-
ried); base instincts (Tanya's father blackmails her); desperation and
suicide (Tanya's mother poisons herself with gas); and the lure and
disillusionment of emigration. The social issues, however, are pale

and out of focus. There is none of the naturalistic impact of the documentaries, nor of the shock effect of, say, *Asthenic Syndrome*. The problems remain in the background without acquiring any relief; they are not important in themselves but only inasmuch as they affect Tanya's life. Besides, the viewer is amply compensated with a glimpse of the hedonistic bonanza of the Intourist hotel and of the Swedish shops and stylish homes.

But the focal point of the story is the heroine and her sad destiny. It would be misleading to read the film in moralistic terms – bad girls who go astray meet with retribution. The tone of the narrative is not judgemental, it is understanding, compassionate, and mournful. This classical approach has never failed to conquer the audience's heart. It worked for the readers of "Poor Lisa," two centuries ago, and it works today for the viewers of "poor Tanya."[86] Tanya, however, is not a saintly prostitute *à la* Dostoevsky, or even a "poetic" prostitute, like Fellini's Cabiria. There is something disturbing in the present approach – the fact that prostitution has become almost a "normal" profession. Judging by the mountains of letters received by *Soviet Screen* (May, 1990, 4–5), viewers of all genders and ages identified with the plea of the unfortunate hooker. Adolescent girls dreamed to be as lucky as Tanya – Part I, only. Many loved Tanya for her homesickness, for her strong Russian roots. And virtually all admired her for defying the system and fulfilling her materialistic dreams. Critics have compared *Intergirl* to the blockbuster of 1980, *Moscow Does Not Believe in Tears*, in terms of the mythology of the fairy tale and the public's reaction. The two films tell a similar story through a similar aesthetic medium. The differences are only superficial, they have to do with the contingencies of two different epochs and the occupations of the heroines. Simply put, Cinderella–worker has become Cinderella–hooker.[87] Another sign of the present time is the pessimism of the unhappy ending that reflects the general mood of the population. After a few months' circulation, the picture was unmistakably headed for record box-office sales. A critic commented: "The value of the new cine-bestseller so far can be measured only by the amplitude of the lines that splash out like a flood in front of the stately facades of our state movie theaters."[88]

These are the new "movies for the millions." But what is new about them? They are actually built on the mythical archetypes that from time immemorial have been the skeleton of narratives not only in the Western civilization, but in most parts of the world. Soviet audiences used to flock to see Fairbanks' adventures and Pickford's sweet stories in the 1920s. Later, the "trophy movies" captured in Germany after World War II were released on the Soviet market, and a whole generation of teenagers was conquered by the charismatic Tarzan–Weissmuller. The 1970s witnessed the craze for Indian movies. As the USSR pursued a friendly foreign policy with Third World countries, Indian tales of love and death with exotic princesses, handsome warriors, dazzling palaces, and fancy gardens hit the Soviet screen and the imagination of the mass audience. The idea of creating "movies for the millions,' in the 1930s, rested on the success of foreign blockbusters. The Minister of Cinema, Boris Shumyatsky, who launched the campaign to conquer the masses with national productions, demanded features combining the entertainment quality of American film with domestic subjects and ideology. Some were successful, such as the adventure *Chapayev* and the musicals of Grigory Alexandrov.[89] The formula proved viable in the hands of skillful filmmakers and produced good results until very recently – as noted, *Moscow Does Not Believe in Tears*.

What is new in the blockbusters of the glasnost period is the absence of ideology. These films have switched from a position of subservience to government policies to social criticism and political opposition, or at least neutrality. They have also lost the foundation of dogmatic certitudes, which results in a sense of disorientation and the impossibility of a happy ending. The current mood (that can be called post-glasnost, by analogy with post-modernism) has inevitably affected the narrative form, which often seems to be burdened with contradictions, exaggerations, clichés, and self-reflexive devices. At times this treatment is deliberate and engages the viewers in a playful dialogue. At times, it is the reflection of a certain confusion in the director's mind. The viewers are not invited to "play," they are asked to identify and empathize.

8   Peering into the future

The filmmakers of glasnost have been able to restore the past and record the present, but they have been less successful in predicting the future. With the political pendulum swinging back and forth from left to right, the economic system collapsing under the pressure of half-hearted reforms, and the entire country bursting at the seams with national rebellion and popular unrest, the future looks very bleak. Most films of this period do not have a perspective, or if they do, it is a catastrophic one. After seventy years of utopian projections and bountiful economic plans without foundation, frustration, disillusionment, and even despair have set in. It is true that without a memory of the past there can be no future. And that is why the historical "blank spots" were quickly filled in. But it is equally true that without a belief in the future past and present have no meaning. Having lost faith in the ideology, with its promises of a materialistic paradise, a few filmmakers look for substitutes. Some turn to religion. But even so, they are unable to find spiritual solace at the end of the road. What they foresee are the horrors of Armageddon. Others avoid mysticism and work out a sci-fi model of a dreadful future society, flipping the utopia upside down. Still others, resort to escape into an aesthetic dimension – the dimension of the absurd, the carnival of life. In a nutshell, the glasnost films conjure up the future through the prism of carnival, dystopia, and the Apocalypse.

Carnival

Carnival has a special connotation in literary theory. It describes both a style and a strategy. The style is rich, ornate, baroque; the strategy is subversive. The term was first applied to the grotesque mode of writing, but cinema has borrowed it, together with other literary terms, definitions, and concepts.[1] In a grotesque narrative, the events are presented as being normal, and the settings suggest the ordinary world. But characters, events, and places stand in an absurd relation to each other. While the trivial is blown up to hyperbolic proportions, commonly accepted values are trivialized. Normal relations are, therefore, upset, logic is destroyed without justification, and the natural order is subverted. The effect is unsettling because it leaves the viewer without parameters for a "correct" reading of the text. It creates a semantic vacuum which challenges established worldviews. Russian literature and theater have a long and brilliant tradition of works in the grotesque mode. It was perfected by Nikolay Gogol and perpetuated through one and a half centuries, notwithstanding official frowning. For Soviet cinema, however, this mode is largely new, although there were some precedents. In the 1920s, several films were produced by the Factory of the Eccentric Actor (FEKS), headed by Grigory Kozintsev and Leonid Trauberg, and over the years there have been some isolated cases, such as Medvedkin's *Happiness* (1935) and Ryazanov's *Garage*. But a grotesque trend never got a foothold on the screen. It was regarded by the censor as irreverent, destabilizing, and therefore inadmissible for mass consumption. The official establishment that favored the comfortable, supportive mode of Socialist Realism, addressed the subversive challenge with ruthless repression. Only now, the grotesque vein has begun to find its legitimate cinematic expression.

The most conspicuous builder of the grotesque carnival on screen is director Yuri Mamin, a former student of Eldar Ryazanov. His directorial career started in the new era, in 1986, when he was jolted to fame by the satirical comedy, *Neptune Festival*. This funny short does not deal with the future, but is an interesting starting point in view of the two following films, *Fountain* (1988) and *Sideburns* (1990). Together, they complete a triptych of a sort, that shows Mamin's progressive disillusionment with the direction of the new course. In the four perestroika years, Mamin's humor moved from farce, to grotesque, to chilling sardonic laughter.

Neptune Festival is set in a remote Siberian village. The film poked fun at false patriotism, as the village folk set up an absurd competition with a group of Swedish visitors. The contest consists of plunging into an ice hole in the frozen river, with allusions to the famous battle on the ice from *Alexander Nevsky*. The nationalistic spirit of the contest is bombastically sustained by Prokofiev's score. The effect is hilarious. But Mamin's vision, from the very first film, went beyond laughter. "Such false patriotism has led to absurd situations that have

29 *Fountain* (1988) directed by Yuri Mamin

become rather common in our life and do not seem funny anymore," the director said. "Satire often borders on drama and even tragedy. But to laugh at our setbacks is a way to overcome them."[2]

This may also apply to Mamin's next film *Fountain*, like the previous one produced by Lenfilm studio, with a script by Vladimir Vardunas. But unlike *Neptune Festival*, *Fountain* does peer into the future and leaves the viewer with a disturbing feeling of impending disaster. The hero is an urban collective, the tenants of an ordinary Leningrad building. But what is ordinary in real life may look quite extraordinary in an aesthetic setting. The effect is achieved mainly by means of hyperbole. Normal situations are exaggerated to an absurd degree. The viewer, by accepting the absurd as part of the ordinary world, will eventually perceive the familiar world as being absurd. The tenement is so run down, due to years of neglect, bad administration and lack of basic maintenance supplies, that it is about to collapse. What started as a hairline crack in one of the main walls has rapidly progressed, turning into a menacing rift that runs from the foundation to the roof. The roof has already given way on one side, and the house committee is taking various measures to support it. First they try to reinforce it with placards of official slogans discarded to the attic (POWER IN THE USSR BELONGS TO THE PEOPLE, and the like). But these turn out to be too weak. Then, they find a threesome of drunkards who (peculiar Atlases!) agree to sustain the roof on their shoulders for a shot of alcohol by the hour. To complicate matters, due to a banal accident, the tenement suffers a water cutoff and a power failure. Chaos ensues, and the only way out is into the fantastic. The elevator, suddenly activated by a short circuit, shoots up . . . up and away into space, like a rocket, carrying one astonished old man who was accidentally stuck inside. The end.

Fountain's fantastic ending, however, is not an escape into fantasy. It is a confirmation that the events that unfolded throughout the film, for all their apparent normality, were no less extraordinary than the fantastic ending itself – a device Gogol used successfully in works such as *Dead Souls* and *The Overcoat*. Moreover, the character of the old man is an important ingredient of the film's dramatic strategy. A visitor from a Kazakhstan village, he is an alien in the tenement. Coming from a different culture and a non-industrial society, he is appalled by the urban way of life, and what seems normal to the building dwellers looks like an aberration to him. Although this character has a small role, it is his point of view that leads the spectator through the film and accounts for the absurdist atmosphere of the action. Within the general metaphor, there are also allusions to the irresponsible ecological exploitation of the Central Asian regions by the government, and to the eventual destruction of those cultures.

Soviet critics have noted that the tenement is an obvious visual metaphor for the country itself, in dire need of restructuring, if not already beyond repair.[3] And the problem is not only with the physical premises, they said, but with the "human factor" that inhabits them. This tenement, instead of being a catalyst of the social fabric, divides the individuals into separate units. It is a sort of Tower of Babel where people speak different languages and act at odds with one another. They insulate themselves from the tragic reality within the walls of their tiny apartments, and in those mouse holes they create their personal little worlds. One family has a flower business; they cultivate tulips under plastic sheets, in stacked wooden boxes that have taken up virtually every inch of the living space. One floor above, a World War II veteran polishes his medals to a perfect shine day after day. And the composer who lives on the top floor seeks inspiration for his next symphony by donning an Icarus costume and taking off daily for a flight over the courtyard. When disaster hits, these oblivious creatures are quite unprepared and become victims of their own doing. In the end, as civilization breaks down, the tenants of the condemned building find their own fantastic solution to an unsolvable situation. They build a bonfire and begin to dance in circle to the rhythm of primitive folk instruments. It is a sort of an ancient propitiatory rite, a leap into the irrational. It is, above all, a grotesque affirmation of life in the spirit of the carnival.[4]

Dystopia

Mamin's latest film does not qualify as carnival. Rather, it has the icy, surrealist quality of a dystopian world. Gone are the masks of the bacchanalia, swept away with machine-like efficiency by a new superior breed of vigilantes. In Soviet literature there are few models of dystopia, a vision of the future subject to strict censorship, but one stands out as a classic of the genre, on the same level as Orwell's *1984* and Huxley's *Brave New World*. This is Evgeny Zamyatin's *We*, banned when it was written (1921) and never published in the Soviet Union until 1988. In cinema, although utopia abounded, there were no examples of dystopia before the era of glasnost.[5]

Sideburns is a satire about Soviet reality of the 1990s, a warning that perestroika has already generated its myths, stereotypes, and aberrations. It is a projection into the next decade, showing the totalitarian mood and the unrelieved violence of *Clockwork Orange* memory. Beneath the surface, the film probes into the nature of dictatorship, the psychological root of power, the moral imperative, and the degeneration of the social utopia. In *Sideburns*, Mamin's satirical whip castigates Russian nationalism and the exploitation of cultural traditions for political purposes. Two groups are pitted against each other. On one side are the free-wheeling, hedonistic punks, called "Cappella," lost in an orgy of sex and sound modeled on Western clichés. These are grotesque masks that would be at home both in Fellini's *Satyricon* and in a "Pop-mechanics" happening. They are ludicrous, gross, and repulsive but, ultimately, they are harmless, like a species on its way to extinction. On the other side, are the fanatic guardians of law and order and of pristine Russian values, called ASP. The acronym stands for the name of the nineteenth-century poet Alexander Sergeevich Pushkin, a symbol of high civic ideals to every Russian. They sport a portrait of the poet on their flag, and wear frock-coats, like the contemporaries of the Decembrists, but in reality they conceal a petty dictator's soul under their sideburns, starched

30   *Sideburns* (1990) directed by Yuri Mamin

collars, and bow ties. In a revealing scene, two ASP leaders transform a bust of Lenin into a bust of Pushkin by remolding the clay. The group soon turns into a paramilitary force, skillful in deadly martial arts techniques; and, with the blessing of the authorities, it cleans up the "Cappella." ASP eventually becomes so menacing as to be a threat to the authorities themselves. In a police ambush, all ASP members and their leaders are captured and stripped of their power: their bushy sideburns are shaved together with their hair. But, like a monster with seven heads, the group rises again. This time, the skinheads are clad in yellow blouses, and shout Mayakovsky's poems. The film does not offer any alternative, only an eternal recurrence of the same totalitarian spirit under different guises and in different garb.

Sideburns may have bruised some sensibilities among right-wing cultural associations, such as the notorious "Pamyat," because a boycott was organized to block domestic circulation. This is one of the first examples of censorship by money power, rather than by Goskino's dictate. Goskino, actually, promptly released the film in the spring of 1990 and sent it to festivals abroad, with Sovexportfilm handling foreign sales.[6] At home, however, circulation was stalled. According to Mamin, a front organization by the name of "Orfei" bought the picture from Lenfilm for 2 million rubles, only to keep it in the closet. "Orfei" is not concerned about recouping the money – "a sign," said Mamin, "that they have already been paid off by some high-positioned authorities."[7]

In *Zero City* (1989), by Karen Shakhnazarov, dystopia is conveyed in the form of a personal nightmare. The action is supposedly set in our days, with a few flashbacks in the retro style. But the emphasis is on the search for a breakthrough into the future, which does not seem to exist. Without being solemn, the film raises the ontological question: do we still exist?

Zero City is a good combination of a popular genre – the thriller – with cultural clichés, political kitsch, ideological satire, and Kafkaesque surrealism. An engineer from a Moscow factory, Alexei Varakin, arrives in a provincial town on business. It is early morning and the town is deserted. Straight from the railroad station he goes to the office of his destination, and here he is greeted by a stern receptionist sitting at her typewriter with businesslike importance. A normal situation by all standards, except for one detail: the receptionist is completely naked. Neither the woman nor the young executive that brings in some papers seem to pay any attention to this fact, and before Varakin can recover from the shock he is shown into the director's office. But even the director, when "warned" about the strange occurrence, treats it with matter-of-fact indifference. The business conversation aggravates the hallucinatory atmosphere, with the director promising to refer Varakin's complaints to their chief engineer who, as it soon turns out, has been dead for two years. But this is only the beginning of Varakin's unsettling adventure. The narrative unfolds in the realm of the absurd, without however progressing, and the unhappy Muscovite eventually gets enmeshed in a plot involving murder (or was it suicide?), mistaken identity, and political intrigue. As he is forced to eat a cake in the effigy of his own head and, later, perform a dance at the local Elvis Club of rock-and-roll fans, the fear of being lost in a nightmarish world mounts together with the desperate need to escape. But there are no trains from the town's station, and the only existing highway ends abruptly in a thick wood. The hero is trapped, and not only physically. He is caught in a vicious circle of events that are beyond his understanding, and yet make perfect sense to the uncanny inhabitants of Zero City.

But what kind of city is this, after all? The viewer becomes progressively aware that this is a city without coordinates, a zero on the

31   *Zero City* (1989) directed by Karen Shakhnazarov

world map, existing only as a visual expression of Varakin's inchoate
fear. On the other hand, Varakin's predicament is absolutely real
and, what is worse, it is shared by millions of Soviet citizens. The
whole country, the film suggests, may very well end up in a big,
round zero. Significant in this respect is the sequence of Varakin's
visit to the Historical Museum. He is taken on a tour of an exhibition
that looks like something between a diorama show and a waxworks.
It is a journey through Russian–Soviet history; actually, a grotesque
parody of it. Events and figures are placed in phony contexts,
chronology is distorted by odd juxtapositions, and cheap embellish-
ments-cum-hyperbolic-ornaments degrade history to the level of a
fairground attraction. Stalin in a white uniform, surrounded by the
symbols of his empire, is now a wax mannequin in the museum, but
his ghost still lives in the soul of the town's public prosecutor,
nostalgic for the law and order of the good old days. This, however, is
not the most ominous manifestation of the ghost's survival. More
disturbing is the fact that Stalin left behind a trail of living dead – the
entire town's population is a community of puppets with dead souls.
They support perestroika and hail the latest trend of openness for the

simple reason that this gives them the freedom to inaugurate the first rock-and-roll club in town. Obviously, in Zero City history is dead, and so is the collective memory of the past. In the end, the hero is left floating in a small rowboat in the middle of a lake, shrouded in a thick fog. Because where there is no past there cannot be any future.[8]

In the film *It* (1989), by Sergei Ovcharov, history is not just a theme but the main protagonist. In his previous films, *Believe It Or Not* (1983) and *Lefty* (1987), Ovcharov worked with the material of national folklore and folk storytelling. *It* is based on the nineteenth-century satirical tale, *History of a Town* (1870), by Saltykov-Shchedrin. The novel was a survey of Russian history compressed in the microcosm of a provincial town, whose bosses and bureaucrats were poorly disguised parodies of Russian monarchs and dignitaries. Thanks to the liberal policy of Alexander II, the czar whose reforms have been compared to Gorbachev's, this biting satire was not blocked by the censor.

The film's commentary follows the literary text verbatim, but characters and events are manipulated in order to accommodate contemporary history, with a projection into the dystopia of the twenty-

32   *It* (1989) directed by Sergei Ovcharov

33   *It* (1989) directed by Sergei Ovcharov

first century. It starts from the very beginning, with the legendary Ryurik, the founder of the Russian state, and proceeds through the centuries with preposterous cameos of successive sovereigns and empresses. Up to the fatal 1917, the tone is farcical, the action is sheer buffoonery. Then, the slapstick gradually fades into the grotesque. Laughter becomes uneasy, and finally sinister. The character of Lenin fades into that of Stalin, then Beria (here there are already cinematic quotations from *Repentance*), and then Khrushchev. This line of continuity is masterfully established by actor Rolan Bykov, who plays all four roles. With the progression of the fatal chain, the mood becomes more and more pessimistic. Next comes a hybrid character, loosely associated with Brezhnev, whose mental and moral disarray is reflected in his dismembered body. Reminiscent of Méliès' old tricks, the leader's head sits on the desk all by itself, letting out an incoherent slur, or is sent to the repair shop for a quick fix. Finally, the "nice guy" takes over. Good-looking, neatly dressed, well-intentioned, tolerant, he is a liberal and a democrat. But his laissez-faire policy is ineffectual. Soon things get out of control, crime and violence cause social and political chaos. The leader, his handsome features hardened into a stone mask, turns into the enforcer of law and order who leads the country into the next century – a wasteland, ecologically devastated, populated by a regimented and dejected humanity, a surrealist brave new world.

Is this *It*? Not exactly. *It* seems to refer to a vague but terrifying menace, a curse on the Russian destiny. Whatever the title may imply, a hint is given in the last paragraph of Saltykov-Shchedrin's tale, which concludes the film: "Filled with wrath *It* dashed off, storming over the earth, rumbling, droning, and groaning . . . *It* was approaching, and as *It* got closer time came to a standstill . . . "[9]

Apocalypse

One situation that is often associated with the Apocalypse is war. Not in conventional Soviet war movies that stressed patriotism and victory, but certainly in Western films of the past two decades (Coppola's *Apocalypse Now*, for example). At the very beginning of perestroika, however, one such film appeared in the Soviet Union as well. The year 1985, the fortieth anniversary of the victory in World War II, called for an extraordinary number of war movies. Most of them were mediocre productions, others were spectacular but shallow, but one was worthy of note, *Come and See*, by Elem Klimov.[10]

This film is based on an actual event, and depicts the brutality of the Nazi invaders in the Belorussian village of Khatyn. The script is by Ales Adamovich, a vocal pacifist, and now a deputy in the People's Congress. *Come and See* was awarded the first prize at that year's Moscow International Film Festival, and has attracted millions of viewers in the Soviet Union. The sparse American audiences who saw it were profoundly disturbed; they either loved it or hated it. Indeed, this film does not allow the viewer to remain indifferent. The viewer's senses are relentlessly assaulted by the powerful camera work, combined with striking imagery, a harrowing soundtrack, and even a palpable illusion of smell. The medium itself, more than the narrative, conveys the horror of the war by taking the viewer through a painful physical experience. This is supposed to parallel the ordeal of the film's protagonist, Flyor, who is able to preserve his human dignity amid violence and destruction. But, while focusing on violence and brutality the film is intended to transcend the physical experience and raise the viewer into the realm of spiritual values. Evocative in this respect is Mozart's cathartic *Requiem*, underscoring the final camera tilt toward the sky. *Come and See* portrays the war in order to spread a peace message. In line with the Soviet policy of arms control, the film with its apocalyptic title warns the viewer about the possibility of a nuclear holocaust. Klimov himself made that connection: "After the première of the film . . . a Japanese film critic told me: 'Your Khatyn is our Hiroshima'."[11]

This theme is treated more directly in *Letters of a Dead Man* (1986), by the young director Konstantin Lopushansky. The film portrays life in an underground shelter after a nuclear explosion. The dominant brownish coloration corresponds to the somber emotional tone of the movie. The central figure, a scientist (played by Rolan Bykov) who feels he has contributed to the destruction of mankind, carries the philosophical theme throughout the film. Contrary to positivistic logic, this ex-scientist believes that although the genetic base of life has been destroyed, the human spirit will survive and be able to regenerate itself. A tenuous affirmation of hope is crystallized in the image of the Christmas tree, which the scientist builds from fragments of scrap metal for a group of traumatized children condemned to die in the nuclear winter.

By the time Lopushansky made his second film he had gained some degree of fame among an international elite of film connoisseurs. *Visitor to a Museum* (1989) won the prize for best direction at Moscow Film Festival, but like its predecessor was ignored by mass audiences. *Visitor* is a futuristic fantasy ("a realistic projection," the director argues) about the destruction of our planet.[12] While in *Letters* life came to an end because of a nuclear explosion, in this film the cause of life extinction is ecological disaster. On an earth disfigured by dead oceans, extinct animals and plants, polluted air, and exhausted soil the last survivors are hopelessly aware of their own doom. Many of them, biologically affected by the devastation of the environment, are mutating into subhuman creatures and kept in reservations carved out of industrial dumps. The horror of this underworld is not in sharp contrast with the world on the surface. Here, too, life is hellish. It is only one infernal circle higher, and already caught in a downward spiral that will precipitate it to the bottom of the abyss. Lopushansky's apocalyptic picture has an unapologetic religious underpinning. The director said that he "wanted to continue the philosophical–Christian tradition of the national culture" and address the issue of "sin and retribution." The aesthetic fabric of the film, while engaging the viewer in the free game of image association, underlines and reinforces the main idea: excessive pride in

34   *Visitor to a Museum* (1989) directed by Konstantin Lopushansky

reason led mankind away from God. The pursuit of scientific–
industrial progress without a parallel spiritual development proved to
be self-destructive. At the end of the road, when the truth becomes
apparent, it is too late to reverse the fatal course. The transient sinner,
the "visitor," ridden with guilt, can only let out a helpless and ter-
rified cry.

Apocalyptic are also two films by Alexander Sokurov, *Mournful
Indifference* (1987) and *Days of the Eclipse* (1988). *Indifference* is based on
Bernard Shaw's play, "Heartbreak House," and the impending
cataclysm here is the breaking out of World War I. Sokurov was
certainly aware of the subtitle Shaw gave his play, "A Fantasy in the
Russian Style on an English Theme," and the director endowed the
drama with the resonance of Russian echoes. One cannot avoid mentioning Chekhov. The film conveys the feeling of a doomed society
playing at being alive, rather than living a full life. Alienated from
each other and the world, the characters are "indifferent" to their
own predicament, which is resolved in a final thunderous explosion.
Sokurov's style is "modernistic," in his own words, mixing fiction
and documentary footage, and creating visual and aural paradoxes.
World War I newsreels are interwoven with the fictional action, and
Shaw himself appears next to his characters. The censors, apparently,

saw allusions to contemporary Soviet society, disguised under the cover of another time, another place, and the film was first rejected on ideological grounds. Objections were also raised because of the "difficult style," and as a result the film was edited in the underground. When it was eventually released, and presented at the Berlin Film Festival as the USSR's official entry, it found its admirers among a small number of art film lovers, but it played to semi-empty houses in the commercial theaters. Sokurov was saddened by the many letters of protest he received from the average moviegoers; in a few towns "the population demanded that the film be removed from the screen."[13]

Days of the Eclipse is the first film Sokurov was able to make without controls and regulation. A true child of glasnost, *Eclipse* has a refreshing look, both direct, like a rough documentary, and elusive, like lyrical poetry. The film is loosely based on a suspense novel, *A Billion Years Before the End of the World*, by the famous science-fiction writers, the Strugatsky Brothers, who had also inspired Tarkovsky's *Stalker*. In the film, the end of the world may be far away, but is certainly implied. It casts a metaphysical tinge on the characters and setting, notwithstanding their palpable texture. The line between matter and spirit, real and surreal, manifest and subconscious is too thin to provide a rational demarcation. Often the divide is simply erased, without warning, and the viewer is thrown into another dimension.

The film's form suits the philosophical theme. The hero, a young doctor named Dmitry Malyanov, devotes his research to proving that physical health depends on a person's spiritual well-being – in other words, on the correspondences between the body and the universe. To pursue his research, Malyanov retreats to a dusty village in Central Asia, lost in the middle of the desert, where disease abounds among the natives who live in poverty and ignorance. By his looks, Malyanov is an unlikely scholar. Played by non-professional actor Alexei Ananishnov, the hero, with longish blond hair and tight jeans would seem more at home in a rock group. But Malyanov is perfectly comfortable in the stuffy room he occupies, cut off from civilization, surrounded by loneliness, fear, and death. There is practically no action in the film, except for the hero's everyday occupations – writing, strolling in the village or in the desert, pausing to sense the mystery of nature in the sun and the sand. He also meets with a gallery of strange characters, from a young Tartar, whose family was deported there under Stalin's terror, to a "real" angel-boy from the outer world, who spends a night under his roof. There is something fatal about Malyanov; most of the people who are attracted to him end up tragically, as if they came too close to the truth. The feeling of an occult danger permeates the atmosphere, following the hero from place to place, from one encounter to another. But the threat is not so scary in its manifestations as it is in its mysterious causes. Through spectacular photography, arresting camera handling, sound mixing, and color manipulation, Sokurov gives a cinematic expression to the inexpressible. This is cinema at its best.

Sokurov's next film, *Save and Protect* (1989), if not apocalyptic, is certainly about death. Loosely based on Flaubert's novel, *Madame Bovary*, the film is not concerned with the amorous occupations of a provincial lady, but with the essence of her earthly journey toward the grave. Sokurov "shrouded the story of unhappy Emma in the funereal metaphor of the Depart, the Demise, the End."[14]

Parallel cinema

At times of transition and instability, virtually every culture produces its own avant-garde, a movement whose artistic credo is projected into the future. The glasnost era has witnessed the emergence of a new Soviet avant-garde, known as "parallel cinema." These young filmmakers, all under thirty, operate mainly outside the film industry and finance their works from private sources. The parallel films are shorts (any length between one minute and forty-seven minutes), made with primitive means and considerable skill. The most common format is 16 mm. film, but 35 mm. and video are also used occasion-ally. These outsiders, not unlike the rebellious artists of the historical Russian avant-garde (1910s–1920s), believe that they are breaking new ground. They regard their films as experimental workshops that will bring about cinema's aesthetic rejuvenation. Unusual for an avant-garde, they are not in an adversarial position *vis-à-vis* the offi-cialdom. Rather they are following a distinct but "parallel" way, keeping aloof from society and avoiding confrontation – the reason being that they think there is no culture to oppose, culture is simply dead. Like all "children," they are critical of the "fathers." "Dependence on the mass subconsciousness killed the Soviet avant-garde of the 1920s," wrote parallel critic, Sergei Dobrotvorsky. "Today's reformers are cutting off all ties with tradition, are turning to the archaic experience, and with magnificent ignorance are reinventing the language." As befits a true avant-gardist, our writer stresses the movement's messianic call. He sees the main strength of

"these uneducated, provincial dilettanti" in their new way of thinking, "which is nothing less than the long overdue encounter of the
Lumière Brothers with God."[15]

Like the rock culture, parallel cinema was born in the underground. One of the leaders, Gleb Aleinikov, wrote that at first the
underground movement wanted to represent an "alternative"
culture, opposed to the official one, but it soon came to the realization
that there was no real alternative, since "the humanistic sphere of
social life turned out to be deideologized to the point of losing the
capability to participate in the process of the formation of culture."
The task of the underground then became the formation of "a true
national culture, which would unite artists of many different orien-
tations."[16] The first experiments in parallel cinema began in 1984,
both in Moscow and Leningrad. By 1987, the underground volcano,
activated by the glasnost earthquake, erupted and spilled on the
surface its hidden treasures. Parallel cinema was confronted with two
choices: either disband, or take up a new status. "We chose the
second alternative, and started our peculiar cinepolitical activity,"
Aleinikov stated.[17] In 1988, various parallel groups united to form the
Leningrad Independent Kinoacademy, for the preparation of film
directors. Then, another similar institution appeared, the Free
Academy, that consists of the Leningrad Free University and the
Moscow Free Lyceum. These solemn names are used to disguise
rather modest operations. But the intentions behind them are serious.
These institutions represent a trend called "new culture," whose goal
is to provide "the humanistic knowledge that cannot be acquired in
our school system."[18] The parallels also have an independent
magazine, *Cine-Phantom*, with headquarters in Moscow. Its founders,
Igor and Gleb Aleinikov, have established the official birth date of
parallel cinema in 1987, when the magazine began being published in
typewritten form.[19] The magazine also sponsors festivals of parallel
cinema. The first Cine Phantom Fest took place in Moscow (November 14–21, 1987), and featured twenty film directors. The second took
place in Leningrad (March 3–5, 1989), with fifty directors. A program
of parallel films was included in the 1989 Moscow International Film
Festival, and afterwards toured abroad.

There are two distinct currents in parallel cinema, the Moscow
school, that consists mainly of the works of the Aleinikov brothers
and Pyotr Pospelov, and the Leningrad school, represented by
Evgeny Yufit, Andrei Myortvy, Evgeny Kondratyev, Oleg
Kotyolnikov, Boris Yukhananov, Vadim Drapkin, and others. The aes-

thetics of the Moscow shool have been influenced by conceptualist art. "The Muscovites concentrate on pure expressiveness, experimenting with form, searching for new language possibilities . . . Their works represent a complicated synthesis of 'direct cinema,' conceptualism, and meditation with elements of sots-art." The Leningrad aesthetics are all the opposite. "Leningraders are more inclined to use comics, *épatage*, shock therapy of the social consciousness . . . They repudiate all sense altogether, raising absurdity to a high degree of the absolute."[20] It is not by chance that this mode emerged precisely in Leningrad. Today's artists have a good model in their local culture. The roots go back to the absurdist work of the Oberiuty, who continued to operate until the mid-1930s as the last bastion of the agonizing early avant-garde.

The main trend of the Leningrad school is "necrorealism," also common to literature, painting, and pop music. It is a bizarre concept that delights in necrophilic themes and images with a superrealism of detail and an irreverent playfulness. But it has a serious purpose: to study the body after the soul has left it. The inspiration came from the official speeches and the solemn ceremonies of the Brezhnev days, from "the empty words pronounced by decorated 'zombies' on towering podiums." Therefore, "in the lower depths of unofficial culture the epos of late stagnation was born. It was heroic idiotism. A somber, tragic art, permeated with bold black humor."[21] The inventor of the term is Evgeny Yufit, who practiced this style in his films, *The Stretcher-bearers Werewolves* (1985), *The Logger* (1985), *Spring* (1987), *Suicide Boars* (1988), and others. Another exponent of necrorealism is Andrei Myortvy (pseudonym of Kurmoyartsev), whose film *Mochebuitsy-trupolovy* (1988) is already a classic. The title is untranslatable. As for the content, the editor of *Cine-Phantom* confessed: "Unfortunately, it was impossible to find any materials in our files that would offer an interpretation of the brilliant work of Andrey Myortvy . . . His great talent is still a riddle for our experts."[22] Nevertheless, these films preserve a tenuous narrative, and feature some sort of characters – though none that one would love. "These are wretched monsters, phantoms of communal flats and city garbage stocks. They are necrophiliacs and corpses. They are idiots, cretins, degenerates, curs, mongrels," says Dobrotvorsky. He also warns us not to confuse these creatures with "the zombies of commercial cinemas," because these are the representatives of a political idea. Necrorealism is "an attitude toward a distorted world," suffocated by a totalitarian system that still exists, a world of corpses without a soul, a world of walking dead.[23] Necrorealism notwithstanding, Yufit was one of the few among the "parallels" to make a film within the framework of the state industry. *Knights of the Skies* was produced by Lenfilm in 1989. This film looks like "a hooligan, combed and dressed up for a special occasion."[24]

Evgeny Kondratev is one of the most prolific authors. He started out with films that were an assault on common taste (for example: *Assa*, 1984; *Necrorealism of Yufit*, 1985; *I Forgot, the Idiot . . .* 1986–87)[25] and that later turned into polished exercises of a meditative artist, especially *Daydreams* (1988) and *Fire in Nature* (1985). His film *Lena's Men* (1989) was noted at the Leningrad festival. It is a film about love as a global phenomenon, which includes homosexual relationships. Oleg Kotyolnikov, who is a painter besides being a filmmaker, relies on the mechanical manipulation of film. He uses the old avant-garde technique of scratching into the film's emulsion and drawing directly on the photographic image. Boris Yukhananov is a stage director, a theoretician of dramatic art, and a video artist. His video works are at the same time dynamic, because of his reckless camera, and static, because he rejects the concept of montage altogether. Best known among his films is *The Mad Prince Fassbinder* (1988). Another video artist is Vadim Drapkin. His works have a lyrical bent, as the titles suggest: *Music for the Soul* (1985), *Our Dreams, or Inner Reality* (1987–89), *Music No. 4* (1989), and others. The picture would not be complete without mentioning the film group CHE–PAYEV. The name itself is intriguing, because it combines the legendary Che Guevara with another legend of Soviet history, the movie hero Chapayev. The group was organized in 1988 with the task of conducting "theoretical research in the area of contemporary cine-mythology, and also of conducting practical propaganda of the total Chepayevan idea."[26] The main figures in the group are screenwriter and theoretician Olga Lepeskova, and director Alexei Feoktistov. The group has already a long filmography. Among the titles are: *Gift to an Unknown Muscovite* (1988), *Battle for the Fleet* (1988), *Symmetrical Cinema* (1988).

In Moscow, the Aleinikov Brothers steal the show. But another Muscovite is also worthy of note. Pyotr Pospelov won the Leningrad festival with the film *Reportage from the Land of Love* (1987–88). Official critics that attended the festival praised the film for being professionally mature and at the same time refreshingly avant-garde.[27] An unofficial critic described it as "an open text, like the reality it portrays." She writes: "It is one possible variant of reality, acted out and not realized."[28] The Aleinikovs specialized in sots-art films which show a clever manipulation of the medium and the canonical themes of Soviet propaganda. In *Tractors* (1987), they make fun of the myth of collectivization and its cinematic icons, and in *Postpolitical Cinema* (1988), they splice together portraits of Lenin and Eisenstein. But in the latter, they go beyond politics and focus on insignificant episodes of everyday life, offering a glimpse of postpolitical existence as a restful pause for the exhausted viewer. Among the many films by the Aleinikovs are: *The Cruel Male Disease* (1987), *End of the Film* (1988), *Typist* (1988), and *Someone Was Here* (1989). The latter was produced by Mosfilm. This, together with other instances of participation in the frame of the official establishment, is an indication that parallel cinema is now entering a new phase, gradually shifting into the mainstream.

The question has been raised about the fact that parallel filmmakers are now taking part in television programs, write articles in official magazines, and use studios to produce their films. Gleb Aleinikov answered that this does not threaten the independence of parallel cinema, or change its nature. "Parallel cinema is no longer an underground movement," he explained. "We collaborate with the mass media because they invite us, and we are glad of the contact: it is a means to reach the audience . . . Parallel cinema does not polarize the film world, but broadens it."[29] The official film establishment, which has become more flexible in its new structures, has opened the doors to the newcomers. Unlike the movement of the 1920s, that was rejected and finally destroyed, these artists are being integrated. There is already a drain of talent away from the avant-garde into the film industry. It seems that the former underground, after coming to the surface, is determined to securely lay its steel tracks, and become officially parallel. Or, as it has been noted, parallels may even cross in contemporary geometry.[30]

Conclusion

Soviet cinema throughout its history has been a sensitive recorder of socioeconomic changes and of shifts in cultural policies. The beginning of the Gorbachev era, with its broad program of reforms, its dynamic foreign policy, its media awareness, its openness, and its sophisticated public relations, has also been the beginning of a new orientation in the cinema industry.

The first five years of glasnost have shattered old taboos; have dethroned cultural czars; have unlocked the vaults of secret archives, releasing captive masterpieces of cinematic art; have opened the Pandora's box of classified information, regaling filmmakers with a bonanza of long-awaited but troublesome subjects; and have freed the artists' creativity and unleashed their imagination. In this respect, the film industry has undergone an extraordinary renaissance, comparable in many ways to the revolutionary renewal of the early 1920s and the cultural "thaw" of the 1960s.

As in those early periods, cinema has anticipated and forecast the events that were to take place in the political arena. And once again, the creative ferment was accompanied by economic restructuring. But in this area today's filmmakers are confronted with the harsh reality of a system on the brink of collapse, and with an uncertain future. While feasting at the glasnost banquet, they are struggling with an unmanageable perestroika.

At no other time were there so many film titles ending with a question mark or suspension dots – a visible sign of anxiety and frustration. By the end of the 1980s the situation was critical. Empty shelves were attributed to speculation and political sabotage. The value of the ruble on the black market had plunged to an unprecented low. Even though the official exchange, and most prices, were kept artificially stable, inflation was rampant throughout the country. The dawning of a small-scale private enterprise system was marred by rackets and mafia-style abuses, and hindered by high taxes. The

234

values of Marxist–Leninist ethics, horrendously distorted under Stalin, and trivialized in the ensuing decades, were seen by the younger generations as meaningless jabbering. Disaffected youths were seeking alternative ways in rock music and drugs. The family, as an institution, was undermined by a rising divorce rate. Gay people and prostitutes had come out of the closet to demand a rightful place in society. AIDS was no longer exclusively a Western plague. Secessionist sentiments in the Baltic, Caucasian, and Russian republics threatened to trigger a civil war. A surge of reactionary patriotism in the central government raised the specter of a military dictatorship.

The cinema industry moved steadily from centralized control to independence and privatization. The economics of production and distribution evolved through the stage of *khozraschet* to ventures into the free-market system. Goskino lost most of its functions, and at the beginning of the 1990s there were rumors that the old monolith was going to be demolished altogether. Production of feature films doubled, and some of them attracted large crowds. But, in general, there was a decline in attendance – partly because glasnost was not a prerogative of film alone, and the public received an overdose of depressing information from the mass media; partly because of serious competition from the video business. The filmmakers' goal for the next decade is to combine entertainment and quality, to make good movies with a mass appeal. This rests on the assumption that the policy of cultural and economic liberalization will continue, notwithstanding the enormous difficulties it faces.

The history of Russia has shown a very consistent pattern of autocratic rule with recurrent episodes of revolutionary upheaval and reforms from above. The films of glasnost have underlined this fatal course casting a pessimistic outlook on the future. The end of this millennium will tell whether perestroika and glasnost were able to break the evil spell for good, or whether they flashed in the darkness bringing about a fleeting moment of enlightenment, and faded out.

Notes

Preface and acknowledgments

1 See in particular Jeffrey Brooks, *When Russia Learned to Read*. Princeton NJ: Princeton University Press, 1985; John Bushnell, *Moscow Graffiti*. New York: NYU Press, 1990; Katerina Clark, *The Soviet Novel: History as Ritual*. Chicago: University of Chicago Press, 1981; Abbot Gleason *et al.*, eds., *Bolshevik Culture: Experiment and Order in the Russian Revolution*. Bloomington, IN: Indiana University Press, 1985; Peter Kenez, *The Birth of the Propaganda State: Soviet Methods of Mass Mobilization, 1917–1929*. Cambridge: Cambridge University Press, 1985; Ellen Mickiewicz, *Split Signals: Television and Politics in the Soviet Union*. New York/Oxford: Oxford University Press, 1988; Gerald Stanton Smith, *Songs to Seven Strings: Russian Guitar Poetry and Soviet "Mass Song."* Bloomington, IN: Indiana University Press, 1984; S. Frederick Starr, *Red and Hot: The Fate of Jazz in the Soviet Union*. New York/Oxford: Oxford University Press, 1983; Richard Stites, *Soviet Popular Culture: Entertainment and Society in Russia since 1900*. Cambridge: Cambridge University Press, 1992.

Introduction

1 On early Soviet cinema see Jay Leyda, *Kino: A History of the Russian and Soviet Film*. Princeton, NJ: Princeton University Press, 1983; M. Carynnik, ed., tr., *Alexander Dovzhenko: The Poet as Filmmaker*. Cambridge, MA: MIT Press, 1973; L. H. Cohen, *The Cultural–Political Traditions and Developments of the Soviet Cinema, 1917–1972*. New York: Arno Press, 1973; S. Eisenstein, *Selected Works in English: Writings 1922–34*. ed., tr., R. Taylor. Bloomington, IN: Indiana University Press, 1987. V. Kepley, *In the Service of the State: The Cinema of Alexander Dovzhenko*. Madison, WI: University of Wisconsin Press, 1986; A. Michelson, ed., *Kino-Eye, The Writings of Dziga Vertov*. Berkeley–Los Angeles: University of California Press, 1984; V. Petric, *Constructivism in Film*. Cambridge/New York: Cambridge University Press, 1988; R. Taylor and I. Christie, eds., *The Film Factory*. Cambridge, MA: Harvard University Press, 1988; Iu. Tsivian *et al.* eds., *Silent Witnesses. Russian Films 1908–1919*. London: British Film Institute, 1989 (on prerevolutionary Russia); D. Youngblood, *Soviet Cinema in the Silent Era, 1918–35*. Ann Arbor, MI: UMI Research Press, 1985.

236

1 The waning of the Brezhnev era

1 He was promoted to marshal of the Soviet Union (among previous political leaders only Stalin had held that military rank) and chairman of the presidium. He was also awarded the Lenin prize for literature, for his memoirs and collected works, most, if not all, of them written by a ghost writer.

2 Before being called Goskino, it had several other names. See Cohen, *The Cultural–Political Traditions and Developments of the Soviet Cinema 1917–1972.* A description of Goskino and other institutions in the 1970s can be found in Val Golovskoy, *Behind the Soviet Screen* (Ann Arbor, MI: Ardis, 1986). This book covers the years 1972–1982, and does not reflect the changes that have taken place more recently in the administrative structure of the movie industry.

3 It is viable to use class terminology to describe Soviet society, if one replaces the concept of property with that of power and privilege.

4 Golovskoy, *Behind the Soviet Screen*, 59. The statistical data that follow come from this same source.

5 *ibid.*, 61.

6 The most prestigious studios of the Caucasian republics is Gruziafilm, in Georgia. An interesting case is that of the Kirgizian studio, which acquired a reputation through the works of a few talented film directors (Tolomush Okeev, Bolotbek Shamshiev), but primarily because of the studio's director, Chingiz Aitmatov, a novelist known and appreciated nationwide. Many Kirgiz films were based on his literary works. Furthermore, he produced the first films of young directors from other republics, such as Andrei Konchalovsky and Larisa Shepitko. A phenomenon of the 1980s is the emergence of Kazakhfilm studio with a new crop of very creative film artists (see chapter 7).

7 This term was used by Maya Turovskaya in "Pochemu zritel' khodit v kino," in V. Fomin ed. *Zhanry kino.* (Moscow: Iskusstvo, 1979), 138–54.

8 The subject was actually broached in an earlier film by Iulii Raizman, *Your Contemporary* (1967), which anticipated this trend.

9 Sergei Mikaelian, "Premiia," *SE*, No. 21 (1977), 21.

10 Inna Levshina, "Novogodniaia skazka El'dara Riazanova," *SE*, No. 24 (1975), 10.

11 Françoise Navailh, "La femme dans le cinéma soviétique contemporain," in Marc Ferro ed. *Film et histoire* (Paris: Editions de L'Ecole des Hautes Etudes en Sciences Sociales, 1984), 155–61.

12 *SE*, No. 5 (1977), 11.

13 Quoted in an article which castigates Riazanov's grotesque style. Andrei Zorkii, "V ocheredi za garazhi," *SE*, No. 11 (1980), 7.

14 The archetype for this motif in Soviet film history is *Member of the Government* (1940) by A. Zarkhi and I. Kheifits, a classic of Socialist Realism.

15 Jeanne Vronsky, *Young Soviet Filmmakers* (London: George Allen and Unwin Ltd., 1972), 49.

16 Alla Gerber, "Aktrisa," *SE*, No. 24 (1976), 7.

17 The subtext of *May I Have the Floor* is once again the Stalinist film *Member of the Government*. Here, however, it is used for contrast.

18 All Soviet citizens from their school years are acquainted with Sergei Esenin (1895–1925), a "peasant" poet who represents a nostalgic attachment to the land and folk traditions (his bohemian life and formalist experiments with verse were usually glossed over). The name Kim is an acronym for Communist International of Youth (Kommunisticheskii Internatsional Molodezhi). Many people born in the 1920s and 1930s were given similar names by zealous idealistic parents.

19 Here and below, Dinara Asanova, "Rezhisser predstavliaet fil'm," *SE*, No. 3 (1977), 10. Soviet children begin school at age seven.

20 Lana Gogoberidze, "Neskol'ko interv'iu," *SE*, No. 2 (1979), 16.

21 Another director, Emil Lotianu, transferred a Chekhov story into luscious images of a decaying world in his film *The Shooting Party* (1979).

22 The radical critic, Nikolai Dobroliubov (1836–1861), started this trend with his famous article, "Chto takoe oblomovshchina?"

23 Since the early 1980s, Konchalovsky has been living abroad, where he has directed a number of films. See chapter 5.

24 Most notably, *Ballad of a Soldier* (1959) and *Clear Sky* (1961) both by Grigori Chukhrai; *The Cranes Are Flying* (Mikhail Kalatozov, 1957); *Fate of A Man* (Sergei Bondarchuk, 1959); *My Name Is Ivan* (Andrei Tarkovskii, 1962).

25 Insightful observations on German's style in *Twenty Days* were published in N. Dymshits, "Pod chuzhim imenem (Metamorfozy melodramy)", in Fomin ed., *Zhanry kino*, 155–69. For a discussion of German's career, see A. Lipkov, "Proverka na dorogakh," *Novyi mir*, No. 2 (1987), 202–25.

26 On the evolution of German's cinematic language, see Giovanni Buttafava, "Alexei German, or The Form of Courage," in Lawton ed., *The Red Screen*.

27 Another significant deviation from the cliché in this film was to cast Yurii Nikulin, a former clown of the Moscow circus, in the leading role. Nikulin turned out to be an excellent interpreter of the compassionate, sensitive, intelligent Major Lopatin.

28 On the "poetic school," see Mikhail Bleiman, "Chto segodnia? Chto zavtra? 1967–1971," *O kino – Svidetel'skie pokazaniia, 1924–1971* (Moscow: Iskusstvo, 1973), 477–569; and Herbert Marshall, "The New Wave in Soviet Cinema," in Lawton ed., *The Red Screen*.

29 Very controversial has been the case of Sergei Paradzhanov, who was arrested on a charge of homosexuality and given a seven-year sentence. He was released after four years, partly because of pressure from the West. He resumed his work as a director in the early 1980s, and died in 1990.

30 Andrei Tarkovskii, "Ispoved'," *Kontinent*, No. 42 (1984), 400. On *Mirror*, see Neia Zorkaia, "Zametki k portretu Andreia Tarkovskogo," in V. Fomin ed., *Kinopanorama: sbornik statei.* (Moscow: Iskusstvo, 1977), 143–65.

31 Tarkovsky was given permission to go to Italy, in 1982, to work on the film

Nostalghia. When, in 1984, he decided to extend his stay, the Soviet authorities stripped him of his citizenship. Tarkovsky died of cancer in Paris, in December 1986. Thanks to the new policy of glasnost the major Soviet newspapers carried obituaries, and the artist was rehabilitated (see chapter 5).

32 This has been pointed out in J. Gerstenkorn and S. Strudel, "La quête et la foi où le dernier souffle de l'ésprit," in M. Estève ed., *Andrei Tarkovsky. Etudes Cinématographiques*, No. 135–38. (Paris: Minard, 1983), 75–104.

33 The writers of "village prose" include Valentin Rasputin, Vasily Belov, Viktor Astafev, and Fedor Abramov.

34 On Shepitko, see chapter 5.

35 After the death of Mikhail Suslov, in January 1982, old Communists started dying one after another, leaving a void in the top echelons which Andropov's men proceeded to fill.

36 The crackdown on Brezhnev's extended family began even before the leader's death. In January 1982, the KGB arrested a ring of diamond smugglers and black marketeers which was headed by a senior official of the Ministry of Culture, Anatoly Kolevatov, his deputy Viktor Gorsky, and Boris Buryatia (alias Boris the Gypsy), a flamboyant ex-circus performer and the lover of Brezhnev's daughter, Galina. About the years of transition, see Dusko Doder, *Shadows and Whispers* (New York: Random House, 1986).

37 Alexander Kalyagin, who played the rogue in the film, also portrayed Chichikov in a dramatization of Gogol's novel which was aired on national television close to the time of the film's release.

38 These two films are discussed in A. Plakhov, "Ne bukva, a sut'," *Ekran* (1987), 39–44. Ostrovsky's play was already put on the screen by Yakov Protazanov (*Bezpridannitsa*, 1936). The Russian title of *Ruthless Romance* is "*Zhestokii romans*," which literally means "cruel romance," and refers to a genre of urban popular music – a self-pitying ballad – that emerged *c.* 1900.

39 Examples of plays dealing with juvenile delinquency were *Dear Elena Serg-eyevna* (*Dorogaia Elena Sergeevna*) by Liudmila Razumovskaia, staged at the Lenin Komsomol Theater in Leningrad; *The Little Carriage* (*Vagonchik*) by N. Pavlova, produced at the Little Stage of the Moscow Art Theater; and *Catch no. 46, Size no. 2* (*Lovushka No. 46, rost vtoroi*) by Yuri Shchekochikin, staged at the Central Children's Theater. Both *Dear Elena* and *Catch* were then made into movies, (see chapter 7).

40 Lena's role is played by Kristina Orbakaite, the daughter of the pop superstar, Alla Pugacheva.

41 The prototype of this genre in Soviet cinema is the film *Road to Life* (1931, Nikolay Ekk). The comparison of the two films shows the change of attitude in the treatment of the same topic. In the film of the 1930s, the camp director (played by Nikolay Batalov) was a true hero, without weaknesses or hesitations, and the ending was flatly optimistic.

42 Dinara Asanova died of a heart attack in April 1985, during the shooting of

the film *The Stranger* (*Neznakomka*), which remained unfinished. She was awarded posthumously the 1985 prizes of the Council of Ministers and of the Central Committee for *Tough Kids*.

43 V. Antonova, "Zov v nochi," *IK*, No. 7 (1985), 84. This scene is another obvious allusion to *Road to Life*.

44 Other films dealing with youth were *In Broad Daylight* . . . (*Sred' bela dnia*, V. Gurianov, 1984); *The Cage for Canaries* (*Kletka dlia kanareek*, P. Chukhrai, 1984); *Overheard Conversation* (*Podslushannyi razgovor*, S. Potopalov, 1985); and the documentaries *First Sorrow* (*Pervaia bol'*, 1985), *It Is Painful to Draw Mama's Portrait* (*Mne strashno risovat' mamu*, 1985), *The Most Beautiful* (*Samaia krasivaia*, 1985), *The Kids Get Even* (*Rasplachivaiutsia deti*, 1985).

45 The title refers to Englischen Garten in Munich, where the headquarters of Radio Liberty and Radio Free Europe are located.

46 This TV series won the KGB movie award for 1984. The Soviets have numerous contests and festivals sponsored by various institutions, including the KGB.

47 In the escapist genre we should also list the "disaster movies," such as *The Crew* (1979) by Alexander Mitta, which was rated third on a list of the ten greatest box-office successes. *LG* (January 14, 1987), 8.

48 This was the second American Film Festival since 1959, when the first Soviet–American cultural agreement was signed. In those old days of the Khrushchev "thaw" the Soviet public was treated to seven American hits and Gary Cooper's live appearance. This time, the festival was privately organized and funded through donations, and included thirty movies old and new and more than twenty-five performers, producers, and directors of some standing (Cicely Tyson, Daryl Hanna, Richard Gere, Marlene Matlin, and others).

49 Here and below, Evgeniia Tirdatova, "Kogda-nibud' ia udivliu etot gorod," *SE*, No. 10 (1988), 20–21.

50 See, N. Savitskii, *Razgovor nachistotu. O fil'makh Vadima Abdrashitova i Aleksandra Mindadze* (Moscow: Soiuz Kinematografistov SSSR, 1986).

51 Besides being very successful at home, *Parade of Planets* was screened at the 1985 Venice Film Festival, and later received the first prize at the Avellino Festival. Together with *The Train Stopped*, it has been shown in the major European capitals, and was highly praised by the critics.

52 This term was first applied to Russian literature by the satirist Mikhail Saltykov-Shchedrin (1826–1889), and refers to the Greek fable writer, Aesop. An emancipated slave, Aesop could not openly challenge the establishment and had to resort to allegory or indirect statements.

2   Perestroika in the film factory

1 Gorbachev emphasized his policy on the arts in a meeting with a group of writers at the Kremlin, on June 19, 1986 (*Pravda*, June 20, 1986), 1. On cultural policies, see an editorial in *Kommunist*, No. 15 (1987), 3–14; John

Dunlop, "Soviet Cultural Politics," *Problems of Communism* (November–December 1987), 34–56; Nancy Condee and Vladimir Padunov, "The Frontiers of Soviet Culture: Reaching the Limits?" *The Harriman Institute Forum*, vol. 1, No. 5 (March 1988), 1–8; Richard Stites, "Soviet Popular Culture in the Gorbachev Era," *The Harriman Institute Forum*, vol. 2, No. 3 (March 1989), 1–8; Josephine Woll, "Glasnost and Soviet Culture," *Problems of Communism* (November–December 1989), 40–50; Jane Burbank and William G. Rosenberg, eds. *Perestroika and Soviet Culture* (*Michigan Quarterly Review*, Fall 1989). Alec Nove, *Glasnost' in Action. Cultural Renaissance in Russia*. (Boston/London: Unwin Hyman, 1989).

2 Even *Pravda* hosted the first swallows of glasnost, such as Evtushenko's poem "Don't-Rock-the-Boaters" ("Kabychegonevyshlisty," September 9, 1985).

3 Addressing the Writers Union in June 1986, Evtushenko stated: "Some of us warn that democracy allegedly leads inevitably to anarchy and the shaking of the ship of state. But it depends on who is steering the ship, and the helm is now in reliable hands. Our writers' hands must also be on this helm since, under socialist democracy, captaincy is a matter for the entire people." Quoted in Elizabeth Tucker, "A Cultural Thaw in Moscow," *The Washington Post* (November 9, 1986).

4 Besides those in the Filmmakers Union, the most radical changes have taken place in the Union of Theater Workers. Pockets of conservative resistance at first prevented significant reforms in the Writers Union, the Artists Union, and the Composers Union, although some personnel turnover occurred. But by the end of 1989, even those strongholds capitulated. See, in particular Woll, "*Glasnost and Soviet Culture*"; and John Dunlop, "*Soviet Cultural Politics*."

5 Klimov's films include: *Welcome, Unauthorized Persons Not Allowed* (1964), which already met with resistance on the part of the authorities; *Adventures of a Dentist* (1965); *Sport, Sport, Sport* (1971); *Rasputin* (1975/released 1985; *Kinoslovar'* gives 1981 as the date of release, but actually the film was not distributed until 1985); *Larisa* (1980); *Farewell* (1982); *Come and See* (1985), which had been kept from production for some ten years.

6 In July 1987, Yakovlev became a full Politburo member, in charge of ideology. From the very beginning he has been one of Gorbachev's close advisors. Yakovlev and Yu. P. Voronov, head of the Central Committee Culture Department (elected in April 1986), presided over the V Congress of the Filmmakers Union. See Julia Wishnevsky, "Former Outcast Elected Head of Cinema Worker's Union," *Radio Liberty Research Report*, 200/86 (May 21), and "Soviet Press Treatment of the Proceedings of the Congress of Cinema Workers," *RLRR*, 230/86 (June 16).

7 Sergei Bondarchuk, film actor and director, extremely popular in the 1960s. Became an important figure in the Filmmakers Union and a close associate of Goskino's chief, Filipp Ermash. He was perceived as an instrument of Goskino within the Union throughout the period of stagnation.

One of the main grudges against him arose from his harassment of Andrey Tarkovsky. The V Congress' resolutions and the transcripts of the speeches were published in *Iskusstvo kino*, No. 10 (1986), 4–125.

8 Secretariat elected at the IV Congress (May 1981): L. Kulidzhanov, Chairman (incumbent), Sh. Abbasov, A. Alov, Ya. Brentsis, I. Vereshchagin, G. Dvalishvili, G. Denisenko, M. Ershov, O. Ioshin, R. Karemiaz, V. Klabukov, B. Konoplev, V. Kostromenko, G. Mar'iamov, A. Medvedev, K. Mirmukhamedov, I. Smoktunovskii, V. Troshkin. Secretariat elected at the V Congress (May 1986): E. Klimov, Chairman, V. Abdrashitov, O. Agishev, A. Aliev, A. Batalov, M. Belikov, R. Bykov, I. Gelein, A. Gerasimov, M. Gluzkii, B. Golovnia, A. Grebnev, E. Grigor'ev, R. Grigor'eva, I. Gritsius, V. Demin, M. Zvirbulis, R. Ibragimbekov, E. Ishmukhamedov, K. Kalantar, K. Kiisk, K. Lavrent'ev, Ya. Lapshin, P. Lebedeshev, V. Lisakovich, I. Lisakovskii, V. Mel'nikov, B. Metal'nikov, K. Mukhamedzhanov, Kh. Narliev, V. Nakhabtsev, V. Nikiforov, Yu. Norshtein, T. Okeev, G. Panfilov, V. Petrov, A. Plakhov, S. Solov'ev, E. Tashkov, V. Tikhonov, M. Ul'ianov, O. Uralov, I. Kheifits, F. Khitruk, D. Khudonazarov, V. Chernykh, V. Churia, G. Chukhrai, K. Shakhnazarov, E. Shengelaia. See Moira Ratchford, "Perestroika and the Soviet Cinema," MS, Georgetown University, 1988.

9 The exception was R. Grigor'eva, a film director of the Gorky Studio and the Secretary in charge of relations with the amateur cine clubs. On the woman question, see Richard Stites, *The Women's Liberation Movement in Russia* (Princeton, NJ: Princeton University Press, 1978).

10 Nikolay Gubenko was appointed the artistic director of the famous Taganka Theater, after Yuri Lyubimov was forced into exile and his replacement, Anatoly Efros, died in 1987. Later, Yuri Lyubimov was reinstated in his old post. Gubenko's films as director include: *A Soldier Came Back From the Front* (1972), *Orphans* (1977), *From the Life of Vacationers* (1981), *Life, Tears, and Love* (1974).

11 The removal of three prominent conservative members of Goskino's Collegium, Bondarchuk, Kulidzhanov, and Rostotsky, served the same purpose. The new leadership of Goskino, as of June 1987, consisted of: A. Kamshalov (Director), N. Sizov (1st Deputy Director), Deputy Directors M. Aleksandrov, O. Yoshin, P. Kostikov, I. Mikhailenko, V. Desiaterik, S. Solomatin; other Collegium members, A. Bogomolov, G. Chukhrai, Yu. Ozerov, E. Surkov. Since then there have been changes.

12 From an interview, *SE*, No. 4 (February 1987), 2–3.

13 The Law on the Press was approved by the Supreme Soviet on June 12, 1990, and took effect on August 1, 1990. The law was based on the proposal of three legal scholars, Yuri Baturin, Vladimir Entin, and Mikhail Fedotov. It established freedom of the press, banned censorship, and allowed all formal and informal groups as well as individuals to establish newspapers, radio programs, and television channels. See *KIARS Report*, vol. vii, No. 17 (1990). See also, "Zakonoproekt o pechati i drugikh sredstvakh massovoi informatsii," *Izvestiia* (December 5, 1989), 3; "Zakon o

pechati,'' *Izvestiia* (June 21, 1990), 3; "Zakon o pechati," *Krasnaia zvezda* (June 6, 1990), 1.

14 Eduard Volodarskii (playwright–screenwriter), "I vot eto vremia prishlo . . .," *SE*, No. 17 (1989), 7.

15 Cited in Anna Lawton, "Searching for new Values," *SO* (April 25, 1989), 6.

16 Andrei Plakhov, "Dva goda zhizni," *SE*, No. 10 (1988), 10.

17 The case of Askoldov is somewhat peculiar because of the troubles he had with the Filmmakers Union and the release of the film *Commissar*, even in the glasnost period. See chapter 5.

18 On August 20, 1990, Alexander Yakovlev appeared on Soviet television to read a statement of repentance in the name of the government and to rehabilitate officially all the murdered and the exiled. Gorbachev's government returned citizenship to writers Alexander Solzhenitsyn, Vladimir Voinovich, Lev Kopelev, Vasily Aksyonov, Irina Ratushinskaya, and many others. See David Remnick, "Russian Resurrected," *WP* (August 26, 1990), C1, C4.

19 See more about it in chapter 3. Also, Viktor Demin, "Chem pomoch' Minsku?," *IB*, No. 5 (1989), 13–17; and Liudmila Saenkova, "Belorusskii kinematograf vremen 'Teatra...' i 'Boli'," *SE*, No. 4 (1989), 6–7.

20 See N. Rtishcheva, "Na polku ili k zriteliu?" *SE*, No. 7 (1989), 13.

21 Plakhov, "Dva goda zhizni," 11.

22 For a detailed discussion of pre-perestroika censorship, see Golovskoy, *Behind the Soviet Screen*, especially pp. 29–36; and Cohen, *The Cultural–Political Traditions and Developments of the Soviet Cinema 1917–1972*.

23 Sergei Lavrent'ev, "Beskonechnaia istoriia," *SE*, No. 7 (1987), 21.

24 Lavrent'ev, *ibid*.

25 Interview by Olga Nenasheva, "Pomogite, rezhut!," *SE*, No. 23 (1987), 21–22.

26 V. Chernykh, "Mozhno-to mozhno, no tol'ko nel'zia," *IK*, No. 1 (1989), 91–92.

27 O. Sukharevskaia and V. Fomin, "Slukhi v epokhu glasnosti," *IB*, No. 1–2 (1988), 15–22.

28 At the VI Plenum (January 1989), the following were nominated: A. Adamovich, M. Belikov, R. Bykov, B. Vasil'ev, A. Gel'man, V. Dostal', K. Kiisk, Yu. Klepikov, E. Klimov, V. Kuznetsov, D. Lun'kov, Kh. Narliev, L. Ozolinia, T. Okeev, A. Smirnov, P. Chkheidze, E. Shengelaia, E. Yakovlev. At the VII Plenum (March 1989), the following were elected: A. Adamovich (Moscow), M. Belikov (Kiev), B. Vasil'ev (Moscow), A. Gel'man (Moscow), K. Kiisk (Tallin), Yu. Klepikov (Leningrad), D. Lun'kov (Saratov), T. Okeev (Frunze), E. Shengelaia (Tbilisi), E. Yakovlev (Moscow). R. Bykov was later placed on the list of the Writers Union. See *IB*, No. 1 (1989), 1, and No. 3–4 (1989), 1. Also, M. Pork and V. Uskov, "Trudnye uroki demokratii," *SE*, No. 4 (1989), 2–3.

29 V. Adzhiev, "Ministry i poklonniki," *Komsomol'skaia Pravda* (July 2, 1989), 4. The author of this article quotes entire passages from Kamshalov's books, *Pravo na poisk* (Moscow: Molodaia gvardiia, 1984) and *Geroika*

podviga na ekrane (Moscow: Iskusstvo, 1986), and compares them with verbatim passages from other works. The point of the article is that nobody wants to make a fuss about it, not even the authors whose works have supposedly been stolen, because people defer to Kamshalov now that he is the Minister of Cinematography.

30 *IK*, No. 3–4 (1989), 53.

31 *IB*, No. 3 (1990), 1–8. The establishment of the FU of the RSFSR has been an issue for twenty-five years. The proposal was first made at the constituent Congress of the FU of the USSR, in November 1965, and then repeated at the III Congress (1975) and at the IV Congress (1981), but every time it was rejected.

32 *IB*, No. 3 (1990), 6–7.

33 *IB*, No. 3 (1990), 2–3.

34 Anna Lawton, "Soviet Filmmakers Create Federation While Trying to Avert Katastroika," *Variety* (June 13, 1990), 3.

35 See *IB*, No. 6 (1989), 1–3; and "Informatsiia k razmyshleniiu o s'ezde kinematografistov," *SE*, No. 15 (1989), 5. One of the most outspoken critics was film director Vadim Abdrashitov, himself a Secretary of the Union. See his article, "Samochuvstvie," *SK*, (December 12, 1989), 4. Other opinions in "Esli by mne dali dve-tri minuty," *SE*, No. 7 (1990), 2–5.

36 "Iskusstvo, kommertsiia, rynok," *Zerkalo*, (June 1990), 2.

37 The Council includes the representatives of fifteen republics, plus two representatives from the Moscow and Leningrad unions that have been granted republican status, plus one President and two Vice-Presidents.

38 From an oral interview (Moscow, June 10, 1990).

39 Vitali Zhdan has been a teacher at VGIK since 1948. He became rector in 1973, when the clampdown on the reforms of the 1960s became definitive, following the appointment of Filipp Ermash as head of Goskino (1972).

40 *IB*, No. 6 (1989), 13.

41 "*Iskusstvo kino* – organ SK SSSR," *IB*, No. 1 (1989), 3.

42 See *SF* (R), No. 7 (1990): 16–17, 26. For pre-perestroika press, see Golovskoy, *Behind the Soviet Screen*, 63–67.

3   Learning a new game: *khozraschet*

1 "K novoi modeli kinematografa," *SE*, No. 6 (1987), 2. See also *IK*, No. 4 (1987), 3–30. On the resolutions of the V Congress, see *IK*, No. 10 (1986), 121–25.

2 S. Freilikh, "Novaia model' – novoe myshleniie," *Pravda* (March 7, 1987), 3.

3 *Model' i struktura kinematografa. Osnovnye printsipy, mekhanizm* (Internal proposition of the USSR Filmmakers Union, May 1986).

4 Report from the V Plenum (November 1988), in *SE*, No. 3 (1989), 6.

5 Eduard Volodarskii, "I vot eto vremia prishlo . . .," *SE*, No. 17 (1989), 6.

6 See the statement by V. Sidorenko of Goskino, in *Tekhnika kino i televideniia*, No. 9 (September 1988). See also, Eric S. Johnson, "Khozraschet as the

Center-Piece of Reform in the Soviet Film Industry," MS, Georgetown University (1989).

7 *IB*, No. 3–4 (1989), 11–18. See also Daniil Dondurei, "Novaia model' kino: Trudnosti perekhodnogo perioda," *KZ*, No. 3 (1989), 3–13.

8 On the state of the film industry between the V Congress and the VI Congress see, *Kino mezhdu s'ezdami (Shirokim vzgliadom); Igrovoe kino mezhdu s'ezdami; Neigrovoe kino mezhdu s'ezdami; Animatsionnoe kino mezhdu s'ezdami;* all published by Soiuz kinematografistov, 1990.

9 For a survey of Mosfilm associations, see V. Vishnyakov *et al.*, "Reform of Mosfilm Studios," *SF* (E), No. 5 (1988), 6–17; B. Pinsky, "Terpeniie, ubezhdennost', trud," *SE*, No. 5 (1988), 18–19; V. Chernykh, "Kto prav pokazhet vremia," *SE*, No. 1 (1989), 28; and "Mozhno-to mozhno, no tol'ko nel'zia," *IK*, (1989), 91–92.

10 B. Pinsky, *ibid.*

11 The Kinofond Charter appeared in *IB*, No. 3–4 (1987), 51–54.

12 The film in question was *Theater in the Time of Perestroika and Glasnost*, discussed in chapter 2. See V. Demin, "Chem pomoch' Minsku?," *IB*, No. 5 (1989), 13–17; and Ludmila Saenkova, "Belorusskii kinematograf vremen 'Teatra...' i 'Boli'," *SE*, No. 4 (1989), 6–7.

13 Chernykh, "Kto prav pokazhet vremia," 91.

14 This was first discussed at the Plenum of the CP Central Committee, in April 1985, and eventually resulted in the "Law on State Enterprises" (1987). To be "self-financing" means that the state enterprises are allowed to bargain with suppliers and wholesale customers, use extra profits for wages and benefits, or suffer bankruptcy for inefficiency. See Ben Eklof, *Soviet Briefing* (Boulder, San Francisco, London: Westview Press, 1989), 89.

15 This was the father of the popular TV commentator.

16 Chukhrai made these points as early as February 1986, in an interview with film critic G. Kapralov, "Chto kormit kinostudiiu," *Pravda* (February 14, 1986), 3. The experiment was even brought up by the outgoing First Secretary, Kulidzhanov, at the V Congress of the FU, and claimed as a feather in his hat. See *SK* (May 15, 1986). Further information on ECS was provided by Paul Pozner (son of V. Pozner, Sr. and brother of V. Pozner, Jr.), in an oral interview (Moscow, July 11, 1989).

17 Interview by Viktor Matizen, *SE*, No. 3 (1990), 25. The production of ECS included *If Your Home Is Dear to You* (1967), *White Sun of the Desert* (1970), *Don't Get Mad!* (1969), *A Soldier Came Back From the Front* (1972), *Ivan Vasilevich Changes Profession* (1973), *Memory* (1971), and many others.

18 *ibid. SE*: 25.

19 *ibid. SE*: 25.

20 *ibid.* 24. Chukhrai's films include: *The Forty-First* (1956), *Ballad of a Soldier* (1959), *Clear Sky* (1961), *Once Upon a Time There Was an Old Man and an Old Woman* (1965), *Memory* (1971), *Quagmire* (1978), *Life Is Beautiful* (1980), *I Start Dreaming of You* (1985).

21 On the provisions of the Law, see Ben Eklof, *Soviet Briefing*, 89–90; and *Pravda* (June 8, 1988), 1.

22 Alexander Lipkov, "Kooperativy – komu oni meshaiut?" *SE*, No. 5 (1989), 2. See the government's position in the interview with First Deputy Chair of the USSR Council of Ministers' Bureau of Social Development, V. Lakhtin, taken by V. Mozhin, *Argumenty i fakty* (March 25–31, 1989), 4.

23 Lipkov, *ibid.*

24 *IB*, No. 3 (1990), 20.

25 From Razumovsky's report at the VI Congress of the Filmmakers Union (June 6, 1990).

26 I. Karasev, "V gorode Sochi temnye nochi," *SE*, No. 13 (1989), 20–21. Also, *Variety* (July 5–11, 1989), 76.

27 *Variety* (July 5–11, 1989), 74.

28 The AFMA companies participating in the 1989 Moscow Film Festival market were: API, Carolco, Pathé Communications, Dino De Laurentiis' Film & Television Co., New World International, Cineplex Odeon International, Trans World Entertainment's Emerald division, and Israel Shaked's Transcontinental Pictures Industries.

29 *Variety* (July 5, 1989), 78.

30 Hy Hollinger, "Mosfilm Cuts Ties with Sovexportfilm," *Variety*, (May 16, 1990), 2.

31 The irony here is that Dostal is also the Deputy Chairman of Goskino. See *Variety* (May 23, 1990), 9.

32 B. Pinsky, "Rynok," *SE*, No. 5 (1989), 19; Daniil Dondurei, "Play Acting or a School for the Future?", *SF* (E), No. 5 (1989), 16–17; "Soviet Film Distributors Get Greater Leeway," *SF* (E), No. 7 (1989), 25; Anna Lawton, "Happy Glasnost," *World & I*, vol. 4, No. 12 (December 1989), 30–43.

33 See Anna Lawton, "Hands Off Distribution, Soviet Filmers Tell State," *Variety* (June 27, 1990), 9.

34 *IB*, No. 3 (1990), 21–22. The reference is to resolution No. 1003 (November 18, 1989), signed by Nikolay Ryzhkov, called "About the perestroika of the creative, organizational, and economic activities in Soviet cinema" (O perestroike tvorcheskoi, organizatsionnoi i ekonomicheskoi deiatel'nosti v sovetskoi kinematografii).

35 See A. Lipko, "Komu-pechal', komu-liubov'," *SE*, No. 5 (1990), 22–23. *Black Rose* is discussed in chapter 6.

36 See G. Kapralov, "K ili U," *Pravda* (June 3, 1990), 3.

37 "My uidem s vysoko podniatoi golovoi," *LG*, (June 6, 1990), 8. The problem is also discussed in Deborah Young, "Anarchy Dominates USSR Film Biz," *Variety* (October 15, 1990), 66.

38 *SE*, No. 8 (1990), 31.

39 Volodarsky, "I vot eto vremia prishlo . . ." 7.

40 E. Lyndina, "Lad'ia v puti . . ." *SE*, No. 2 (1989), 6. *Kings of Crime* is discussed in chapter 8.

41 P. Shepotinnik, "With Perestroika, Without Tarkovsky," *New Orleans Review*, vol. 17, No. 1 (1990), 80. The film is discussed in chapter 6. Mistakenly, the film has been called, by the Soviet critic Alla Gerber, *One Day in the Life of Joseph Stalin*, and this title has been picked up by the Soviet

and American press. Lad'ia's managers complained about it in a letter to *SE*, No. 6 (1989), 2.

42 Lyndina, "Lad'ia v puti . . ."

43 A. Suzdalev, "A farvater eshche ne raschishchen," *SE*, No. 2 (1989), 6.

44 Volodarsky, "I vot eto vremia prishlo . . ." 7.

45 Lipkov, "Komu-pechal', komu-liubov'."

46 Daniil Dondurei, "Good-bye, Sovetskoe kino?" *SE*, No. 6 (1990), 14.

47 From Andrei Razumovsky's report at the VI Congress of the Filmmakers Union.

48 *IB*, No. 3 (1990), 20.

4 Serving the Muse or the people?

1 This quote and the following ones are from the Plenum report, in *IB*, No. 5 (1989), 1–7.

2 "Ustav kinematograficheskogo fonda SSSR," *IB*, No. 3–4 (1987), 52.

3 For an excellent survey of opinions on cinema by prominent figures in pre-revolutionary years (Gorky, Tolstoy, Stanislavsky, Meyerhold, Benois, Bely, Mayakovsky, and others), see Neia Zorkaia, *Na rubezhe stoletii* (Moscow: Nauka, 1976). See also, Anna Lawton, "'Lumière' and Darkness: The Moral Question in the Russian and Soviet Cinema," *Jahrbücher für Geschichte Osteuropas*, vol. 38 (1990): 244–54.

4 See, Richard Stites, "Soviet Popular Culture in the Gorbachev Era," *Harriman Institute Forum* (March 1989); and *Soviet Popular Culture*.

5 G. M. Lifshits *et al.*, eds., *Sotsial'naia zhizn' fil'ma. Problemy funktsionirovaniia repertuara* (Moscow: VNIIK, 1983) and *Sotsial'no-esteticheskie kharakteristiki fil'ma i prognozirovanie zritel'skoi poseshchaemosti* (Moscow: VNIIK, 1984); M. I. Zhabskii *et al.*, eds., *Metodologiia i metodika sotsiologicheskogo issledovaniia kinoauditorii* (Moscow: VNIIK, 1987). See also, *Kino i zritel'*, Vypusk 1 and 2 (Moscow: Soiuzinformkino, 1987).

6 "Chto proiskhodit s kino?" (Round Table), *LG* (August 14, 1987), 8.

7 Maya Turovskaya, "Pochemu zritel' khodit v kino," in V. Fomin ed., *Zhanry kino*, 138–74.

8 "Chto proiskhodit s kino?"

9 V. Maiasov, "Predvaritel'nye itogi," *IB*, No. 3–4 (1989), 8–9.

10 "Kakogo zritelia my zasluzhivaem," *SE*, No. 3 (1987), 3.

11 "Kogda mify stanoviatsia real'nost'iu," *SE*, No. 5 (1987), 2.

12 "Nel'zia ne dumat' ob obshchem dele, o kino, o zritele," *SE*, No. 4 (1987), 3.

13 V. Mel'nikov, "Khozraschet dolzhen byt' podlinnym, a ne bumazhnym," *IB*, No. 3–4 (1987), 18.

14 "Kino bez kino," *IK*, No. 6 (1988), 88. See also, E. Stishova, "Lavry i ternii," *Ekran* (1989), 31–36.

15 The sociologist of culture, Danil Dondurei, expresses a very pessimistic view of the decline of movie audiences in, "Good-bye, sovetskoe kino," *SE*, No. 6 (1990), 14–15.

16 *Variety* (July 5–11, 1989): 59–60; *IB*, No. 3–4 (1987), 56–62; V. M. Vil'chek *et al.*, *Fil'm v kino i na televidenii* (Moscow: VNIIK, 1987); *SE*, No. 8 (1989), 4–7; unpublished research of Moscow Scientific Research Institute of Film Art (VNIIK).

17 *Variety* (July 5–11, 1989, 60) provides figures in dollars: *Little Vera* grossed $43.3 million in three months; *Cold Summer*, $39.6 in nine months; *King Kong*, $35.4 in four months; *Short Circuit*, $28.8 in ten months. These data do not seem to be reliable, because Goskino does not release figures on revenues. Goskino's attendance data show: *Little Vera*, 54.9 million viewers in twelve months; *Cold Summer*, not available; *King Kong*, 55.1 in twelve months; *Short Circuit*, 31.7 in twelve months.

18 See in particular, E. Stishova, "Lavry i ternii," *Ekran* (1989), 31–36.

19 "Anketa kinokritikov," *IK*, No. 6 (1990), 40–41. Available data for *Repentance* show attendance in twelve months at 13,656,800 viewers (1st part), and 13,652,600 (2nd part), "Chto smotriat zriteli," *SE*, No. 4 (1989), 26.

20 "Chto smotriat zriteli," *SE*, No. 8 (1989), 19.

21 *SE*, No. 8 (1990): 2–5. The profile of the respondents has been consistent through the years. The following is a breakdown for 1989. Social groupings: (1) white-collar workers, 36.8 percent; (2) school and technical institute students, 29.4 percent; (3) university students, 16.8 percent; (4) blue-collar workers, 13.7 percent; (5) housewives, 1.8 percent; (6) retired people, 1.2 percent; (7) farmers, 0.4 percent. 65 percent are from large cities, and among them 15 percent from Moscow and Leningrad. 55 percent are women, 45 percent are men. Age: 18–20, 24.7 percent; 21–24, 24.6 percent; 14–17, 19.7 percent; 25–30, 17.2 percent; 31–40, 7.9 percent; 41–55, 3.9 percent; under 14 and over 55, 1.2 percent.

22 *SE*, No. 3 (1987), 5, and No. 22 (1987), 2–3.

23 *SE*, No. 8 (1990), 4.

24 *SE*, No. 9 (1987), 22.

25 M. Zhabskii, "Interesnoe kino . . . ?," *SE*, No. 2 (1989), 30.

26 *Variety* (July 5–11, 1989), 80. On the early phase of the video business, see Ellen Mickiewicz, *Split Signals*, 11–13.

27 The figures in this section, if not otherwise indicated, were obtained in an oral interview with Moscow film scholar Kirill Razlogov (Washington, October 21, 1990).

28 S. Kudriavtsev, "Chernyi, chastnyi, parallel'nyi," *SE*, No. 8 (1988), 2.

29 Dondurei, "Good-bye," 14.

30 Richard Taylor, "Boris Shumyatsky and the Soviet Cinema in the 1930s: Ideology as Mass Entertainment," *HJERT*, vol. 6, No. 1 (1986).

31 On pornography in the video business see, Valerie Sperling, "Explicit Sex in Video and Film in the Soviet Union" MS, Georgetown University, 1990).

32 From an oral interview (Washington, October 28, 1990).

33 All quotes from A. Lipkov, "Komu-pechal', komu-liubov'."

34 *SE*, No. 8 (1990), 22.

35 P. P. Erofeev, "Video: Pervye nabliudeniia i perspektivy razvitiia," *Fil'm v kino i na televidenii* (Moscow: VNIIK, 1987), 124. A similar situation devel-

oped in East Germany after November 1989. 4,000 to 5,000 video outlets have opened, wherever space was available, "shingles have been nailed up outside mom-and-pop stores, living rooms, basements, extra bedrooms," *Variety* (September 3, 1990), 1.

36 Here and below, from an interview taken by Aleksandr Morozov, "Kasseta na tamozhne," *SE*, No. 9 (1989), 19.

37 Clips of the film appear in the Kazakh documentary, *Bakhit: First Blood* (1990), by Bakhit Kilibaev.

38 Viktor Yasmann, "Green Light for the Video Revolution in the USSR?" *RLRR* 441/88 (September 26, 1988); S. Kudriavtsev, "Chernyi, chastnyi, parallel'nyi," *SE*, No. 8 (1988), 22; and Valerie Sperling, "Explicit Sex in Video and Film in the Soviet Union," MS, Georgetown University, 1990.

39 In 1985, the projections were much less optimistic. The plan provided for an increase to 60,000 in 1990 and 120,000 in 2000, "Kompleksnaia programma razvitiia proizvodstva tovarov narodnogo potrebleniia i sfery uslug na 1986–2000 gody," *Pravda* (October 9, 1985), 1; reported in Ellen Mickiewicz, *Split Signals*, 11. As of July 1989, there were 2 million VCRs in the Soviet Union, according to *Variety* (July 5–11, 1989): 59. A Soviet researcher, in an article published in 1987, complained of the scarcity of VCRs. According to him, the first experiments with video technology occurred already in the mid 1960s, but then the country fell behind the other nations. In 1983, the Scientific Research Institute of Film Art (VNIIK) conducted a public opinion poll on video, with a sample of 890 respondents across social status, profession, location, age, and sex. To the hypothetical question: "Would you buy a VCR, if it were available?", 70 percent answered in the affirmative. P. P. Erofeev, "Video," 110–27.

40 *SE*, No. 4 (1989), 29.

41 *SE*, No. 8 (1990), 22.

42 Outstanding films such as *My Friend Ivan Lapshin* and *Repentance* were made before 1985.

5   Off the shelf

1 Quoted in Ian Christie, "The Cinema," *Culture and the Media in the USSR Today*, J. Graffy and G. A. Hosking, eds. (New York: St. Martin's Press, 1990), 48. Originally in "Plus Sixty," *Moscow News*, No. 29 (1988): 15. *Kuban Cossacks* was once a very popular Stalinist musical, made in 1950. Yuri Lyubimov later became the director of the avant-garde Taganka Theater, emigrated in the early 1980s, and came back to Moscow and his theater in 1988. Galina Vishnevskaya fell in disgrace because she was the wife of exiled Mstislav Rostropovich. Aleksander Galich was a guitar bard who also emigrated.

2 Andrei Zorkii, "Beleet parus odinokii," *SE*, No. 8 (1987), 15.

3 Vysotsky is now openly celebrated as one of the most significant artists of recent Russian culture. An entire issue of *Sovetskii ekran* (No. 3, 1988) was dedicated to his art as stage and film actor. A number of films on his life

and career as singer–guitarist have also appeared. Among them a video, *Memories* (*Vospominanie*, 1987), a feature with documentary footage, directed by Vladimir Savel'ev for the Dovzhenko Studio in Kiev; a documentary by Aleksandr Stefanovich, *Begin at the Beginning* (1986), which features some of Vysotsky's songs and stars another then controversial musician, Andrei Makarevich of the rock group, Time Machine; and a documentary consisting of fragments of film shot and preserved over the years by Vysotsky's friends and admirers, and produced by Petr Soldatenkov for the Sverdlovsk Documentary Studio. See *SE*, No. 12 (1989), 18–19. Two lengthy profiles have appeared in *Ekran* (1988), 48–63.

4 Zorkii, "Beleet parus odinokii," 15.

5 Christie, "The Cinema," 49.

6 Zorkii, "Beleet parus odinokii," 14.

7 For a detailed account of the controversy surrounding *Commissar*, documented with transcripts of meetings and resolutions, see Elena Stishova, "Strasti po 'Komissaru'," *IK*, No. 1 (1989), 110–21; translated in *Wide Angle*, vol. 12, (1990), 62–75.

8 Askoldov was apparently advised by Alexei Romanov of Goskino that his film could be released if he removed the Holocaust reference and changed the ethnic identity of the family. See Christie, "The Cinema," 54. For the official image of female combatants in the Civil War, see Stites, *The Women's Liberation Movement in Russia*, chapters 10, 11, and 12.

9 Elena Stishova, "Kolybel'naia," *SE*, No. 21 (1987), 14–15; Maia Turovskaia, "Commissar," *SF*, No. 5 (1988), 26–27; L. Pavliuchik, "Bol'shevitskaia Madonna," *Pravda* (November 8, 1989), 3. See also Françoise Navailh, "La commissaire de Berditchev," *Pardès*, No. 8 (1988), 229–34. Some ten years earlier another film had already questioned the traditional values of the Civil War, *The Forty First*, by Grigorii Chukhrai (1957). Here, a revolutionary woman soldier falls in love with an officer of the White Army, and, although conditioned by the class struggle imperative to shoot him, she comes out of the ordeal a new woman, with an affirmation of feelings over ideology. The film did not make waves and was quietly forgotten. Later, the film *Flight* (1971) by Alov and Naumov, based on a story by Mikhail Bulgakov, treated the Whites with human sympathy. Although released, the film was subjected to harassment.

10 See note 9.

11 From a press conference transcript (San Francisco, March 21, 1988), reported in Mikhail Lemkhin, "Aleksandr Askol'dov – chelovek neotkuda," *Novoe russkoe slovo* (June 17, 1988), 14.

12 See an interview with Askoldov by Vladimir Garov, in *SF* (E), No. 2 (1989), 12–13 and 25.

13 Stishova, "Kolybel'naia," 121.

14 Iurii Bogomolov, *Andrei Mikhalkov-Konchalovskii: Tvorcheskii portret* (Moscow: Soiuzinformkino, 1990), 8. This small booklet, that includes all of Konchalovskii's works and is a total rehabilitation of the director, is published and distributed by Goskino's marketing and promotion branch.

The recommendation on page 2 reads: "These materials . . . must be widely used by the distributing organizations during meetings with the viewers in movie theaters, culture halls, and clubs. They will help in the preparation of evenings dedicated to the works of this famous film director."

15 S. Freilikh, "Vozvrashchennoe vremia," *SE*, No. 12 (1988), 18.

16 Bogomolov, *Andrei Mikhalkov-Konchalovskii*: 11.

17 Konchalovsky's films made after *Asya* are: *A Nest of Gentry* (1969), *Uncle Vanya* (1971), *A Lovers' Romance* (1974), *Siberiade* (1979). His Hollywood films are: *Maria's Lovers*, *The Runaway Train*, *Duet for One*, and *Shy People*. On *Asya*, see T. Khlopliankina, "Istoriia Asi Kliachinoi, kotoraia liubila, a potomu ne sostarilas'," *SE*, No. 15 (1988), 14–15. On Konchalovsky in Hollywood, see interview "Tam i zdes'," *SE*, No. 1 (1990), 24–25. Konchalovsky's name does not appear in the Soviet reference books published in the early 1980s, such as Drobashenko *et al.*, eds., *Sovetskoe kino, 70-ye gody* (Iskusstvo: Moscow, 1984) and Iutkevich *et al.*, eds., *Kino, entsiklopedicheskii slovar'* (Sovetskaia entsiklopediia: Moscow, 1986).

18 See chapter 3.

19 Oleg Kovalov, "Iz smiren'ia ne pishutsia stikhotvoren'ia," *SE*, No. 23 (1987), 4.

20 Smirnov had a moment of glory with his next film, *Belorussia Station* (1972), which is now a classic of contemporary Soviet cinema. But after that, *Autumn* was banned in 1975, and released in 1987; *Faith and Truth* was so badly ruined by cuts and revisions, in 1979, that it could not be rescued. Nevertheless, Smirnov remained active, writing plays and scripts, and involved in the affairs of the profession, as his appointment in 1988 to acting First Secretary of the FU shows.

21 Kovalov, 'Iz smiren'ia ne pishutsia stikhotvoren'ia," 5.

22 See chapter 1.

23 Barbara Quart, "Between Materialism and Mysticism: The Films of Larisa Shepitko," *Cineaste*, vol. xvi, (1988): 9. This article does not discuss *Homeland of Electricity*. In her brief and creative life, Shepitko made four more films: *Heat* (1963), *Wings* (1966), *You and I* (1971), *The Ascent* (1977), and just before her tragic death started working on *Farewell to Matyora*, completed in 1982 by her husband, Elem Klimov. Klimov made the short, *Larisa* (1980), in memory of his wife and colleague.

24 A report on the censorship process for this film is in Golovskoy, *Behind the Soviet Screen*, 127–29.

25 Christie, "The Cinema," 58. About Dziga Vertov, see Michelson, ed., *Kino-Eye*.

26 Christie, "The Cinema," 58.

27 Okeev's production has been copious and consistent from the 1960s to the present. In 1986, he was elected to the Filmmakers Union's Secretariat.

28 Kiisk made some twenty films and served as the First Secretary of the Estonian Filmmakers Union. He was also twice elected to the Secretariat of USSR Filmmakers Union, the last time in 1986.

29 Andrei Tarkovskii, *Sculpting in Time* (New York: Alfred A. Knopf, 1987), 204–5.

30 Domenico means "man of the Lord" in Italian.

31 A pagan sense of magic blends with Tarkovsky's religious vision. Starting with *Andrei Rublev*, the animism of the ancient Slavs and their cult of nature mingles with Christian values throughout Tarkovsky's opus.

32 "Andrei Tarkovski après sept films," in Estève ed. *Andrei Tarkovsky,* 170.

33 Tarkovskii, *Sculpting in Time,* 216.

34 *ibid.,* 107.

35 *ibid.,* 106.

36 In *SE*: Vadim Iusov, "Slovo o druge," No. 6 (1987), 14–15; Evgeniia Malysheva, "Andreiu Tarkovskomu," No. 7 (1987), 19; Iurii Bogomolov, "Logika voobrazhaemogo," No. 20 (1987), 16–18; Marianna Chugunova, "Fil'm – eto postupok," No. 7 (1988), 6–7 and 19; S. Freilikh, "Vozvrash-chennoe vremia," No. 12 (1988), 18–19; V. Shitova, "Iz zemli, vody i ognia," No. 3 (1989), 18–19. In *IK*: Two pieces by director Gleb Panfilov and actor Oleg Iankovskii, "Na pamiat' Andreia Tarkovskogo," No. 3 (1987), 113–17; from the correspondence Tarkovskii–Kozintsev, "Ia chasto dumaiu o vas," No. 6 (1987), 93–105; Leonid Batkin, "Ne boias' svoego golosa," No. 11 (1988), 77–101; Andrei Tarkovskii, "Samoe dinamicheskoe iskusstvo vysizhivaetsia godami," No. 12 (1988), 69–73; translation of Michail Leszcylowski, "Odin god s Andreem," No. 12 (1988), 74–78, orig-inally in *Sight and Sound,* vol. 56, (Fall 1987), 282–84; Dmitrii Salinskii, "Rezhisser i mif," No. 12 (1988), 79–91; L. Anninskii, "Popytka ochish-cheniia?," No. 1 (1989), 24–33. In A. A. Volkov *et al.* eds., *Khudozhestvennyi mir sovremennogo fil'ma* (Moscow: VNIIK/Goskino SSSR, 1987), see Iu. Tiurin, "Istoricheskii fil'm Andreia Tarkovskogo," 5–27; and L. Alova, "Zarubezhnaia pechat'o tvorchestve Tarkovskogo," 27–48. A whole sec-tion was dedicated to Tarkovsky, in *Ekran* (1989), 68–92. A series of articles appeared in *KZ*, No. 3 (1989), 153–91. Also, Neia Zorkaia, "Martirolog Andreia Tarkovskogo," *Ogonek*, No. 15 (April 1989), 14–17.

37 Neia Zorkaia, "*Nostal'giia* Andreia Tarkovskogo," *Sputnik kinofestivalia,* No. 1 (May 19, 1987). On *Mirror*, see "Zametki k portretu Andreia Tarkovskogo," cited in chapter 1.

38 *Directed by Andrei Tarkovsky,* written and directed by Michail Leszcylowski, presented at Cannes Film Festival May 21, 1988.

39 Boleslaw Edelhajt, "Entretien avec Andrei Tarkovski," *Cahiers du Cinema,* No. 392 (February 1987), 39. Here Tarkovsky describes the difficulties Sokurov encountered in making his film *A Man's Lonely Voice.*

40 Suzanna Al'perina and German Zaichenko, "Khudozhnikov odinokikh net" (from a conversation Sokurov had with students of Moscow State University) *SE*, No. 19 (1988), 5.

41 *ibid.*

42 *ibid.*

43 Oleg Kovalov and Andrei Plakhov, "Golos pokoleniia," *IK*, No. 8 (1987), 66. The quotation is by Kovalov; the two authors alternate in a critical

dialogue. In this article, Sokurov's handling of the deeper layers of Platonov's philosophy is contrasted with Konchalovsky's treatment of the same story, that in the Hollywood version came out with the title, *Maria's Lovers*. Konchalovsky's film is "a melodrama with elements of psychoanalysis, some titillating erotic scenes, and even horror movie effects . . . The problem is not that the action here is transposed in post World War II America. The problem is that the director deliberately left out of his artistic arsenal all that is connected with the national mentality, all the historical, traditional, moral, and spiritual concepts that he himself used to uphold," 62.

44 "Golos pokoleniia"; also, Francois Albera, "Voyage dans un cinéma en mutation," *Cahiers du cinéma*, No. 395–96 (May–June 1987), 98–105; Lev Karakhan, "Variatsiia na temu," *SE*, No. 2 (1988), 8–9.

45 See Anna Lawton, *Cinema and the Russian Avant-Garde: Aesthetics and Politics*, Occasional Paper of the Kennan Institute, No. 213 (1986).

46 Kovalov and Plakhov, "Golos pokoleniia," (Plakhov), 64.

47 Christie, "The Cinema," 56–57.

48 At Lenfilm, Sokurov was supported by the best creative minds, Yu. Ozerov, Yu. Averbakh, Yu. Klepikov, and D. Asanova.

49 Kovalov and Plakhov, "Golos pokoleniia," (Plakhov), 71.

50 Sergei Burin, "Inoe tsarstvo," *Ekran i stsena* (September 27, 1990), 4.

51 *ibid.*

52 See the very informative and substantial catalogue, Yuri Tsivian *et al.*, eds. *Silent Witnesses*.

6 Exorcizing the past

1 Sergei Muratov, "Neizvestnoe kino," *IK*, No. 12 (1988), 22–39; Vyacheslav Kondrat'ev, "Ochen' nadeyus'," *IK*, No. 1 (1989), 52–55; Felicity Barringer, "Soviet Documentaries That Face Up To Reality," *NYT* (March 29, 1989), p. C17; Karen Rosenberg, "Glasnost at the Movies," *WP* (March 26, 1989), p. G1; Anna Lawton, "Rewriting History: A New Trend in the Documentary Film," *SO* (September 29, 1988), p. 6; "Searching for New Values," *SO* (April 25, 1989), p. 6.

2 The festival included two films that were not officially released because they were blocked by the production studios: *Theater in the Time of Perestroika and Glasnost* and *Pain*, both from Belarusfil'm. Only rough prints were shown because the films were blocked before completion. About the festival, see Andrei Nuikin, "Nuzhno perebolet'," *SE*, No. 24 (1988), 3. About censorship, see chapter 2.

3 L. Bortvina, "Unhappy Love," *SR*, (July 22, 1988), 3.

4 Nuikin, "Nuzhno perebolet'," 3.

5 A. Kolbovskii, "Stanet li izvestnym 'neizvestnoe kino'?," *SE*, No. 16 (1988), 14.

6 Muratov, "Neizvestnoe kino," 39.

7 L. Karpinskii, "Svetoteni pravdy," *SE*, No. 5 (1988), 5.

8 From commentary on the soundtrack.

9 David Remnick, "Glasnost: The Movie," *WP* (February 8, 1988), B10.

10 Bruce Nelan, "Chipping Away at an Icon," *Time* (August 14, 1989), 34–35; Anna Lawton, "Happy Glasnost," *The World & I*, (December 1989), 30–43.

11 Esther B. Fein, "Bury Lenin? Russian Die-Hards Aghast," *NYT* (April 28, 1989), A10. Zakharov staged *The Dictatorship of Conscience* (*Diktatura sovesti*, 1986) by Mikhail Shatrov, where Lenin and his ideology were put on trial, but eventually acquitted. Playwright Shatrov managed to secure for himself the monopoly on the theme of Lenin, which earlier belonged to Nikolai Pogodin, a classic playwright of the Stalin era. Shatrov was able to write non-standard plays on this theme even in the pre-glasnost period. Among them, *Blue Steeds on Red Grass* (*Sinie koni na krasnoi trave*, staged 1985) and *The Peace of Brest–Litovsk* (*Brestskii mir*, staged 1988).

12 Ia. Varshavskii, "Kto protiv?", *SK*, (July 19, 1988), 5.

13 Igor Itskov, "O doblestiakh, o podvigakh, o slave . . ." *SE*, No. 9 (1988), 4.

14 This is not a direct quotation from the film, but a summary of Rybin's speech, as reported in Irina Pavlova, "Protivostoianie," *SE*, No. 12 (1989), 24.

15 Len Karpinskii, "Stalin v nas?", *SE*, No. 18 (1989), 4–5.

16 Aleksei Erokhin, "Razve delo tol'ko v Staline?" *SE*, No. 3 (1989), 14.

17 L. Alabin, "Psevdonim – Raskol'nikov," *SE*, No. 7 (1989), 15.

18 *ibid.*

19 It is easy to recognize in that provincial production the much acclaimed play *The Aristocrats* (*Aristokraty*), by Nikolai Pogodin, which premièred in 1935 at the Moscow Realistic Theater.

20 According to a Soviet scholar, "*Ivan Lapshin* on TV generated a record number of protesting letters." P. P. Erofeev, "Video," 118. See also Christie, "The Cinema," 50; and German's interview by Emmanuel Decaux and Bruno Villien, "Du côte de Guerman," *Cinematographe*, No. 124 (November 1986), 56.

21 *Catalog of the 30th International San Francisco Film Festival* (April 1987), 37; originally in an interview with V. Amiel and E. Derobert, *Positif* (December 1986). About the idealism of Ivan Lapshin, see E. Stishova, "Blizkoe pro-shloe," *Ekran* (1987), 107–12.

22 In 1987, twelve Soviet critics thought it was the best national film of all time. See the evaluation chart appended to Christie, "The Cinema," 73–75.

23 L. Ovrutskii, "Oglianis' v pechali," *SE*, No. 17 (1988), 4–5.

24 Petr Cherniaev, "Zvatra byla voina," *SE*, No. 7 (1987), 2.

25 *Cold Summer* won the popular contest of the journal *Sovetskii ekran* for the year 1988. See *SE*, No. 8 (1989), 4–7.

26 *NF*, No. 9 (1989), 6–7.

27 Natal'ia Ivanova, "Kak sudit' budem?", *SE*, No. 13 (1989), 7.

28 Anastas Mikoyan had been in charge of foreign and internal trade since 1926; since 1930 also of food industries. He became a full member of the Politburo in 1935, and a deputy prime minister in 1937.

29 See Neia Zorkaia, "Dorogoi, kotoraya vedet k Khramu," *IK*, No. 5 (1987), 33–53.

30 See interview by Alla Gerber, "Dve vstrechi s Tengizom Abuladze," *SF* (R), No. 7 (1987), 11 and 14.

31 *LG* (January 21, 1987), 8.

32 Interview by Gerber, "Dve vstrechi s Tengizom Abuladze," 11.

33 T. Khlopyankina, "Pod zvuki nabatnogo kolokola," *SE*, No. 15 (1987), 4–5.

34 Evgenii Shvarts' play *The Dragon* (1943), supposedly an allegory of Nazi evil, was first staged in 1944. It was immediately withdrawn after just one performance in Moscow and one in Leningrad. It was revived in 1962, but it was again taken out of production after a few performances. One of those was staged by Zakharov.

35 V. Mikhalkovich, "Sumbur vmesto kino?" *SE*, No. 6 (1990), 12.

36 O. Nenasheva, "Zhena kerosinshchika," *SE*, No. 7 (1989), 9.

37 A. Gerber, "Sbilis' my. Chto delat' nam," *SE*, No 15 (1989), 6.

38 Viacheslav Shmyrov, "Zagovor obrechennykh," *SE*, No. 15 (1989), 12.

39 See Mikhalkovich, "Sumbur vmesto kino?" 10.

40 See L. Anninskii, "Po ischeznovenii Stalina," *SE*, No. 4 (1990), 12–13.

41 T. Kononova, "Pir Valtazara," *SE*, No. 1 (1990), 9.

42 V. Matizen, "Piry Valtazara ili Noch' so Stalinym," *NF*, (June 1990), 6.

43 S. Rassadin, "Pakhan na otdykhe," *SE*, No. 7 (1990), 13.

44 Kononova, "Po ischeznovenii Stalina," 10.

45 Rassadin, "Pakhan na otdykhe," 13.

7   Facing the present

1 For example the programs of the Glasnost Film Festival that opened at the Smithsonian Institution on March 27, 1989, and subsequently toured the USA. Twelve programs from the festival are now available on videocassette, distributed by "The Video Project," in Oakland, California.

2 Viacheslav Kondrat'ev, "Ochen' nadeius' . . . " *IK*, No. 1 (1989), 52.

3 G. R. Ivanitskii, "V goru po kraiu propasti," *SE*, No. 24 (1988), 5.

4 From the film soundtrack, reported in Muratov, "Neizvestnoe kino," 25.

5 Feliks Andreev, "Chuma XX veka," *SE*, No. 22 (1988), 21.

6 Excerpts from the film's commentary cited in Viktor Merezhko, "The Govorukhin Effect," *Moscow News* (June 10–17, 1990), 14.

7 Viktor Merezhko, "The Govorukhin Effect."

8 "Ot glasnosti k pravde," *SK*, (6/2/90), 11.

9 Govorukhin made the following films: *The Vertical* (1967), *The Name Day* (1969), *The Life and Adventures of Robinson Crusoe* (1973), *The White Explosion* (1970), *Contraband* (1975), *The Wind of Hope* (1978), *The Rendez-Vous Is Not To Be Changed* (1979), *The Adventures of Tom Sawyer* (1981), *Ten Little Negroes* (1988). See Iutkevich *et al.*, *Kino slovar'*: 97. Recently, Govorukhin played a major role as a Soviet mafioso in the popular film *Assa* (1988), by Sergei Solovev. His ideas on commercial film are expressed in, S. Govorukhin, "Zametki retrograda," *Ekran* (1989), 134–41.

10 Viktor Merezhko, "The Govorukhin Effect."
11 Valentin Tolstykh, "Kak zhit' dal'she," *Zerkalo* (June 1990), 9.
12 On this subject, see Andrew Horton, "Nothing Worth Living For. Soviet Youth and the Documentary Movement," in Kepley ed. *Wide Angle*, vol. 12, (1990), 38–46.
13 Viewers' opinions in *SE*, No. 7 (1987), 6–7.
14 Alexander Egorov, "Eto – nashi problemy," *SE*, No. 6 (1987), 8.
15 Tatiana Maksimova, "My – vashi deti," *LG* (June 3, 1987), 8.
16 Quotations from the film as reported in Viacheslav Kondrat'ev, "Ochen' nadeius'," *IK*, No. 1 (1989), 54.
17 Muratov, "Neizvestnoe kino," 34.
18 From the film soundtrack, reported in Muratov, "Neizvestnoe kino," 25.
19 From the film soundtrack, *ibid*.
20 See Stites, "Soviet Popular Culture in the Gorbachev Era," 6.
21 Aleksandr Pozdniakov, "Nevskaia volna protiv damby zastoiia," *SE*, No. 12 (1989), 21.
22 Reported in Pozdniakov, "Nevskaia volna protiv damby zastoiia," 20. On Soviet rock in general, see A. Troitskii, *Back in the USSR: The True Story of Rock in Russia* (Boston: Faber & Faber, 1987).
23 Muratov, "Neizvestnoe kino," 34.
24 See V. Shmyrov, "Dusha sfinksa," *Ekran* (1989), 118–22.
25 From Latin, "plumbum" (lead). One of the characters in the film makes a joke, connecting Plyumbum to Stalin, whose name was derived from the Russian word "stal'" (steel).
26 *SE*, No. 24 (1987), 17. Several articles on the film, in *Ekran* (1989), 124–34.
27 Stites, "Soviet Popular Culture in the Gorbachev Era," 8.
28 Valentina Lakhtionova, "Bez illiuzii," *SE*, No. 14 (1987), 18.
29 *Little Doll* had a difficult release. See chapter 2.
30 Forrest S. Ciesol, "Kazakhstan Wave," *Sight and Sound*, vol. 59, (Winter 1989/90), 56. See also, Rebecca A. Morrison, "Kazakhfilm Studio: From the Doldrums to Prominence in the Era of Glasnost," MS, Georgetown University (1990).
31 Quite unexpectedly and unprecedentedly, because of his age and relative inexperience (he was still a student at VGIK), Nugmanov was elected the head of the creative association "Alem," and the First Secretary of the Kazakh Filmmakers Union (April 1989). Beside giving an impetus to production, he immediately started renovation projects: revamping of the Union's headquarters and construction of a new building at Kazakhfilm. See Ciesol, "Kazakhstan Wave," 58.
32 Forrest Ciesol's Film Notes in *Preview* (American Film Institute, January 1991), 13.
33 Viktor Tsoy won Best Actor category for *The Needle*, in the *Sovetskii ekran* poll. But Tsoy was no actor. He was an extraordinary interpreter of his own "image." For a profile of Viktor Tsoy, his musical career that started ten years ago in Leningrad, his personality that closely resembles the

hero's in *The Needle*, his "image" that became the real Tsoy in life as well as on stage and screen, see Artem Troitskii, "Otvergaia soblazny," *SE*, No. 8 (1990), 15.

34 Sergei Sholokhov, "Igla v stogu sena," *SE*, No. 9 (1989), 7.

35 For an extensive discussion of neo-romanticism, see Sholokhov, "Igla v stogu sena," 6–7.

36 Anna Kagarlitskaia, "My vse – Orfei," *SE*, No. 14 (1987), 21.

37 Avdot'ia Smirnova, "Assa ye-ye," *SE*, No. 7 (1988), 12. Film director, Evgeny Kondratev, an exponent of parallel cinema (see chapter 8), made a short in 1984, called *Assa*. Kotyolnikov belongs to that same movement. Solovev was in touch with the Leningrad underground, and his film is full of quotations from the counterculture.

38 Quotes in E. Tirdatova, "*Assa*, gran' vekov ili nabor fenichek?," *SE*, No. 12 (1988), 4–5.

39 Andrei Shemiakin, quoted in Tirdatova, "*Assa*, gran' vekov ili nabor fenichek?" 5.

40 Quoted in A. Danilina, "Starik Kozlodoev i kapitan Afrika," *SE*, No. 9 (1987), 13. In the director's view, these artists represent a link with the historical avant-garde of the 1920s. Several exponents of the "red wave" appeared in *Assa*. Among them, the Leningrad artist and theoretician, Timur Novikov, and the Moscow artist, Sergei Shutov. Well-known art objects also played a role, like the *Iron Book* (early 1980s), by Leningrad artist Vadim Ovchinnikov, considered an heir to the Futurists. And to force the cultural connection a bit, Viktor Tsoy's handsome Asian features remind us of the mystical expectations of the early avant-garde for the new coming of the Scythians, the Eastern horde bound to destroy an agonizing civilization.

41 All quotes are in Eldar Askerov, "Pochemu zabuksoval eksperiment?," *SE*, No. 4 (1988), 22. See also, S. Solov'ev and D. Dondurei, "'Assu v massy, massy v kassu . . . ili, Igrovoe prostranstvo parallel'noi real'nosti," *IK*, No. 10 (1988), 6–19; *IK*, No. 6 (1988), 51–58; *IK*, No. 8 (1988), 46–52; A. Mitta, "Kukushonok v gnezde," *SK*, (January 9, 1988), 3.

42 Quoted in A. Lipkov, "Vtoraia chast' zaboinoi trilogii," *SE*, No. 17 (1989), 18.

43 Quoted in Lipkov, "Vtoraia chast' zaboinoi trilogii," 19. The trilogy's name may be a coy reference to Vertov's film *Three Songs of Lenin* (1934). About independent distribution of *Black Rose*, see chapter 3.

44 From a conversation with Savva Kulish (Moscow, July 1989).

45 "Vera" in Russian means "faith." The authors underlined the double meaning in the title by avoiding calling the film "Verochka," the usual diminutive for the name.

46 It also found a market abroad, including the United States, which is very rare for Soviet films. Moreover, *Little Vera* won the FIPRESCI Prize at the Venice Festival, the Special Jury Prize at the Montreal Festival, and the Golden Hugo at the Chicago Festival, among others.

47 For a discussion of the new realistic style, see Herbert Eagle, "The Index-icality of *Little Vera* and the End of Socialist Realism," in Kepley ed. *Wide Angle*, vol. 12, No. 4 (1990), 26–37.

48 For details about the creation of Pichul's independent production coopera-tive Podarok, and the financing deal for the film, see chapter 3.

49 From an interview with Aurelien Ferenczi, in a film brochure released at Cannes Film Festival, 1990.

50 All quotes are from the Cannes Film Festival brochure.

51 Mikhalkovich, "Sumbur vmesto kino?" 11.

52 *ibid.*

53 The script is by Riazanov and Braginskii, based on their play, "Amoral'naia istoriia."

54 The Directorate of Leisure Time reminds us of another agency's pre-posterous name: The Institute for the Protection of Animals Against the Environment, in the film *Garage*. As for "Leonid," the viewer would have no trouble guessing whom the name alludes to – certainly not Leonid Filatov, the talented actor in the leading role.

55 Ryazanov's attention to realistic details is one of the strengths of the film. The sequence involving the avant-garde play – Gogol's *Inspector General* – takes place at the Club of the Medical Workers, at Nikitskikh Vorot. In the early 1980s, the Club hosted the Theater Studio of Mark Razovsky, which specialized in avant-garde staging of classics, and was constantly harassed by the authorities.

56 See *SE*, No. 8 (1989), 4–7.

57 See a survey of critical opinions and viewers' comments, edited by Viktor Matizen, "Ekskursiia po museiu smyslov," *SE*, No. 10 (1988), 18–19.

58 Mark Zak, "Infarkt kak sotsial'naia kategoriia, ili k voprosu o zrelishch-nom kino," *Ekran* (1989), 106–11.

59 A. Egorov, "Dve versii o *Che Pe*," *SE*, No. 2 (1990), 14; Mikhail Gurevich, "Strasti po sekretariu," *SE*, No. 10 (1989), 5. *Sovetskii ekran* chose *Che Pe* as the Film of the Month, "for an insightful and powerful look at those representatives of the ideological front, who, under the cover of the Kom-somol banner, have until now recklessly and not unsuccessfully fought against you and us." (No. 9, (1989), 2).

60 Viacheslav Shmyrov, "Nam li boiat'sia kommertsializatsii?," *SE*, No. 18 (1989), 10.

61 The Russian inscription reads: "Utoli moia [sic] pechali." This Old Church Slavonic grammar construction has been retained in the film's title, attract-ing attention to the icon's "alienation" in the contemporary world.

62 See chapter 2 about the film's difficulties with censorship. In Orthodox practice, icons must be covered during sexual intercourse.

63 M. Levitin, "Argumenty i fakty," *SE*, No. 11 (1989), 23. A similar opinion is voiced by Aleksandr Kiselev, "Slepoi parikmakher," *SF* (R), No. 7 (1990), 11 and 28–29.

64 Levitin, *ibid.*

65 Talankin made his debut with the delightful film *A Summer To Remember* (1960), co-directed with Georgi Danelia.

66 See the following caustic reviews: Boris Berman, "Zamorochki v stile rok," *SE*, No. 11 (1989), 18; and Mikhail Gurevich, "Strasti po sekretariu," *SE*, No. 10 (1989), 5.

67 Interview with Vincent Amiel and Eric Derobert, *Positif* (December 1986), 37.

68 Also, older viewers cannot fail to make associations with the stormy political history of Shostakovich's opera of this name, later renamed *Katerina Izmailova*.

69 See chapter 2.

70 "*Astenicheskii sindrom* Kiry Muratovoi," *SE*, No. 3 (1990), 10–11.

71 Boris Vladimirskii, "Ne teriaite otchaianiia," *Zerkalo* (June 1990), 4.

72 *Repentance* and *Commissar* had a modest circulation. *Little Vera* reached the mass audience, but was not a box-office hit. A few other features had occasional runs.

73 Interview with Teimuraz Ponarin, "Raskvitat'sia s epokhoi," *SE*, No. 13 (1990), 19.

74 *ibid*.

75 This is a rendition of Lungin's comments in his interview. *ibid*.

76 See chapter 4.

77 *Capucines* was seen by 50.6 million viewers, in fifteen months. Precise data for *Kings of Crime* are not available, due to its independent distribution, but sources put it at 70 million (see discussion below). *Intergirl* is above the 50 million mark. *Little Vera* has also been a blockbuster in 1988, with almost 54.9 million viewers, in twelve months. Its melodrama features have been noted above, but its superior artistic level warrants its placement in a different category. See, "Anketa kinokritikov," *IK*, No. 6 (1990), 40–41.

78 Here and below, quotations are from the script in *IK*, No. 7 (1986), 137–74.

79 For a more detailed discussion, see Anna Lawton, "'Lumière' and Darkness: The Moral Question in the Russian and Soviet Cinema," *Jahrbücher für Geschichte Osteuropas*, vol. 38, (1990), 244–54.

80 *SE*, No. 10 (1988), 2–5.

81 See chapter 3.

82 Aleksei Erokhin, "Zavtra byl shliager," *SE*, No. 3 (1989), 10; "Moscow Gorki Studio Leads the Way," *Variety* (July 5–11, 1989), 91.

83 "Sopernichat' na ravnykh," *SE*, No. 2 (1990), 6.

84 A trend common in American cinema that first appeared in the films of Sam Peckinpah and evolved in various forms, up to the most recent manifestations in David Lynch's pictures and others, such as *Miller's Crossing*, and more blatantly *Dick Tracy*.

85 The film is based on a novella by Vladimir Kunin, and is a co-production of Mosfilm and Filmstallet AB, Sweden. The input of Western technology gave the film a sleek look. This, together with the fact that Part II was shot

on location, in Sweden, rather than in the "phony West" of the Baltic, contributed to the film's success.

86 "Poor Lisa" is a novella by Nikolay Karamzin, published in 1792, now a classic of Russian Sentimentalism. The publication of "Poor Lisa" started the spread of narrative genres among the general public.

87 As Elena Stishova noted: "Cinderella used to be at the factory, now Cinderella is on the sidewalk." Quoted in Viktor Gul'chenko, "Stokgol'm slezam ne verit," *IK*, No. 1 (1990), 62.

88 *ibid.*

89 *Chapayev* (1934), by the Brothers Vasil'ev. *Jolly Fellows* (*Veselye rebiata*, 1934), *Circus* (*Tsirk*, 1936), *Volga–Volga* (1938), by Grigorii Alexandrov.

8 Peering into the future

1 The term was first used by literary theoretician, Mikhail Bakhtin, who applied it to the grotesque prose of Nikolay Gogol and the polyphonic novels of Dostoevsky. See Mikhail Bakhtin, *Problems of Dostoevsky's Poetics* (Ann Arbor: Ardis, 1973) (original, 1929); Mikhail Bakhtin, *Rabelais and His World* (Cambridge, MA: Harvard University Press, 1968) (original, 1965).

2 Sovexportfilm Catalog, *Molodoe sovetskoe kino* (1987).

3 O. Nenasheva, "Fontan," *SE*, No. 17 (1988), 10; T. Khlopliankina, "Anek-dot?", *SE*, No. 4 (1989), 18–19; A. Timofeevskii, "It Would Have Been Funny . . . " *SF* (E), No. 4 (1989), 8–9; B. Berman, "Fontan," *NF*, No. 4 (1989), 9–10.

4 *Fountain* won the first prize, the Golden Duke, at the first Odessa Festival of Popular Genres (1988). It then collected some thirteen awards at home and abroad. It has been bought by twenty countries and shown on television in Europe and Japan.

5 On utopia in Russian–Soviet culture, see Richard Stites, *Revolutionary Dreams* (New York/Oxford: Oxford University Press, 1989).

6 *Sideburns* was awarded the Fipresci prize at the San Sebastian Film Festival (September 1990).

7 From an oral interview with Yuri Mamin (New Orleans, October 25, 1990). The story was confirmed by Soviet scholars, and as late as December 1990 there had been no change. See, Anna Lawton, "Sideburns Bushy O'Seas But Clipped in USSR," *Variety* (December 17, 1990), 38.

8 About *Zero City*, see P. Cherniaev, "Gorod Zero," *SE*, No. 22 (1988), 12–13; A. Shemiakin, "Po tu storonu zdravogo smysla," *SE*, No. 16 (1989), 14–15; B. Berman, "Zero City," *SF*, No. 5 (1989), 22–24. Viewers' opinions (mainly negative) in "Igra pustogo i porozhnego," *SE*, No. 9 (1990), 5.

9 About *It*, see Natal'ia Lagina, "Ono," *SE*, No. 6 (1989), 8–10; Vitalii Kniazev, "It," *SF* (E), No. 5 (1989), 10–12.

10 Some of the war movies of 1985 are: *Victory* (*Pobeda*), by Evgeny Matveev; *The Shore* (*Bereg*), by Alexander Alov (who recently died) and Vladimir Naumov; *The Battle for Moscow* (*Bitva za Moskvu*), by Yuri Ozerov, who also directed the 1972 epos *Liberation* (*Osvobozhdenie*).

11 *IK*, No. 12 (1985), 38. See also, E. Gromov, "Nabat Khatyn," *Ekran*, (1987), 91–95; Ales Adamovich, "Uiti iz bezdny . . . " *Ekran*, (1989), 24–30.

12 All quotes are from the brochure, *"Posetitel' muzeia,"* released by Soiuzinformkino, 1989.

13 Interview with Sokurov in *SE*, No. 19 (1988), 5.

14 Natal'ia Rtishcheva, "Gospozha Bovari na konechnoi ostanovke," *SE*, No. 11 (1990), 18.

15 S. Dobrotvorskii, in *Parallel'noe kino v SSSR* (Moscow: Sine-Fantom, 1989), 4.

16 Gleb Aleinikov, in *Parallel'noe kino*, 2.

17 Aleinikov. *ibid*.

18 *Parallel'noe kino*, 15.

19 G. Aleinikov, "Blesk i nishcheta industrii parallel'nykh grez," *IB*, No. 3–4 (1989), 36.

20 Sergei Dobrotvorsky, "The Most Avant-Garde of All the Parallel Ones," *The New Orleans Review*, vol. 17, (1990), 84–85. "Sots-art" is commonly used to refer to the art of Socialist Realism.

21 S. Dobrotvorskii, "Evgenii Iufit," *SF* (R), No. 7 (1990), 26.

22 Iurii Aleinikov, in *Parallel'noe kino*, 6.

23 Dobrotvorsky, "The Most Avant-Garde of All the Parallel Ones."

24 Dobrotvorskii, "Evgenii Iufit," 27. The others are the Aleinikov Brothers, with *Someone Was Here* (see below). A similar case was *Angel Day* (see chapter 7).

25 *Assa* was quoted in Sergei Solov'ev's own film. See chapter 7.

26 *Parallel'noe kino*, 28.

27 Alexander Kiselyov, "From Euclid to Lobachevsky," *SF* (E), No. 7 (1989), 27–29.

28 Ekaterina Degot', in *Parallel'noe kino*, 18.

29 Aleinikov, "Blesk i nishcheta industrii parallel'nykh grez."

30 Kiselyov, "From Euclid to Lobachevsky," 29.

Bibliography

Alova, L. "Zarubezhnaia pechat' o tvorchestve Tarkovskogo," in *Khudozhestvennyi mir sovremennogo fil'ma*, 27–48. ed., A. A. Volkov *et al.*

Amengual, B. "Andrei Tarkovski après sept films," in *Andrei Tarkovsky. Etudes Cinématographiques*, 157–78. ed., M. Estève

Animatsionnoe kino mezhdu s'ezdami, Moscow, Soiuz kinematografistov SSSR, 1990

Anninskii, L. "Popytka ochishcheniia?" *Iskusstvo kino*, No. 1 (1989), 24–33

Bakhtin, M. *Problems of Dostoevsky's Poetics*, Ann Arbor, Ardis, 1973/original, 1929

Rabelais and His World, Cambridge, MA, Harvard University Press, 1968/ original, 1965

Batkin, L. "Ne boias' svoego golosa," *Iskusstvo kino*, No. 11 (1988), 77–101

Bleiman, M. *O Kino – Svidetel'skie pokazaniia, 1924–1971*, Moscow, Iskusstvo, 1973

Bogomolov, Iu. *Andrei Mikhalkov-Konchalovskii. Tvorcheskii portret*, Moscow, Soiuzinformkino, 1990

"Po motivam istorii sovetskogo kino," *Iskusstvo kino*, No. 8 (1989), 56–67

Bordwell, D. "The Idea of Montage in Soviet Art and Film," *Cinema Journal*, vol. 11, No. 2 (1972), 9–17

Burbank, J. and Rosenberg, W. G., (eds.) *Perestroika and Soviet Culture, Michigan Quarterly Review* (Fall 1989)

Cahiers du cinéma. Edition spéciale (January 1990)

Carynnyk, M., (ed., tr.) *Alexander Dovzhenko: The Poet as Filmmaker*, Cambridge, MA, MIT Press, 1973

Chernenko, M. *Sergei Paradzhanov. Tvorcheskii portret*, Moscow, Soiuzinformkino, 1989

Chernykh, V. "Mozhno-to mozhno, no tol'ko nel'zia . . . " *Iskusstvo kino*, No. 1 (1989), 91–92

Chiesa, G. and Medved'ev, R. *La rivoluzione di Gorbačëv*, Milan, Garzanti, 1989

Christie, I. "The Cinema," in *Culture and the Media in the USSR Today*, eds., J. Graffy and G. A. Hosking. New York, St. Martin's Press, 1990

Ciesol, F. "Kazakhstan Wave," *Sight and Sound*, vol. 59, No. 1 (Winter 1989/90), 56–58

Cohen, L. *The Cultural–Political Traditions and Developments of the Soviet Cinema 1917–1972*, New York, Arno Press, 1973

Condee, N. and Padunov, V. "The Frontiers of Soviet Culture: Reaching the Limits?" *The Harriman Institute Forum*, vol. 1, No. 5 (March 1988), 1–8

Demin, V. "Strel'ba po sletevshim misheniam," *Iskusstvo kino*, No. 9 (1989), 5–8

Dobrotvorsky, S. "The Most Avant-Garde of All Parallel Ones," *New Orleans Review*, vol. 17, No. 1 (1990), 84–87

Doder, D. *Shadows and Whispers*, New York, Random House, 1986

Dolmatovskaya, G. and Shilova, I. *Who's Who in the Soviet Cinema*, Moscow, Progress, 1979

Dondurei, D. "Novaia Model' kino: Trudnosti perekhodnogo perioda," *Kinovedcheskie zapiski*, No. 3 (1989), 3–13

Drobashenko *et al.* (eds.) *Sovetskoe kino. 70-ye gody*, Moscow, Iskusstvo, 1984

Drozdova, M. "Dendi perioda postpank, ili 'Proshchai Amerikas, o . . . '''' *Iskusstvo kino*, No. 3 (1989), 75–78

Dubrovin, A. G. *et al.* (eds.) *Kino i vremia*, Vypusk 3, Moscow, Iskusstvo, 1980 "Ne povodia itogov," *Iskusstvo kino*, No. 8 (1989), 31–54

Dunlop, J. "Soviet Cultural Politics," *Problems of Communism* (November–December 1987), 34–56

Dymshits, N. *et al.* (eds.) *Besedy na vtorom etazhe*, Moscow, VNIIK, 1989

Dymshits, N., Troshin, A. *et al.* (eds.) *Iz proshlogo v budushchee: Proverka na dorogakh*, Moscow, VNIIK, 1990

Eagle, H. "The Indexicality of *Little Vera* and the End of Socialist Realism," in *Wide Angle*, 26–37. ed., V. Kepley

Edelhajt, B. "Entretien avec Andrei Tarkovski," *Cahiers du Cinema*, No. 392 (February 1987), 37–41

Egorov, E. and Davydova, L. "Novaia kinomodel', v chem sut'?" *Ekonomicheskaia gazeta*, No. 17 (1988), 24

Eisenstein, S. *Selected Works in English: Writings 1922–34*, ed., tr., R. Taylor. Bloomington, IN, Indiana University Press, 1987

Eklof, B. *Soviet Briefing*, Boulder, San Francisco, London, Westview Press, 1989

Estève, M. (ed.) *Andrei Tarkovsky. Etudes Cinématographiques*, No. 135–38. Paris, Minard, 1983

Ferro, M. (ed.) *Film et Histoire*, Paris: Editions de l'Ecoles des Hautes Etudes en Sciences Sociales, 1984

Film URSS '70: Materiali critici e informativi, Venice, Italy, Marsilio Editori, 1980. vol. 1

Film URSS '70: La critica sovietica, Venice, Italy, Marsilio Editori, 1980. vol. 2

Film URSS: Il cinema delle repubbliche asiatiche sovietiche, Venice, Italy, Marsilio Editori, 1986. vol. 3

Film URSS: Il cinema delle repubbliche transcaucasiche sovietiche, Venice, Italy, Marsilio Editori, 1986. vol. 4

Fomin, V. (ed.) *Kinopanorama: sbornik statei*, Moscow, Iskusstvo, 1977 (ed.) *Zhanry kino*, Moscow, Iskusstvo, 1979

Gerstenkorn, J. and Strudel, S. "La quête et la foi, ou le dernier souffle de l'ésprit," ed., M. Estève. *Andrei Tarkovsky. Etudes Cinematographiques*, No. 135–38. Paris, Minard, 1983, 75–104

Golovskoy, V. *Behind the Soviet Screen*, Ann Arbor, MI, Ardis, 1986

Govorukhin, S. "Zametki retrograda," *Ekran* (1989), 134–41

Grashchenkova, I. N. *Sovetskaia kinorezhissura*, Moscow, Znanie, 1982

Gul'chenko, V. "Stokgol'm slezam ne verit," *Iskusstvo kino*, No. 1 (1990), 62–68

Gusev, V. "Priroda videoizobrazheniia i neigrovoe kino," *Iskusstvo kino*, No. 8 (1988), 91–102

Horton, A. "Nothing Worth Living For. Soviet Youth and the Documentary Movement," in *Wide Angle*, 38–46. ed., V. Kepley

Iampol'skii, M. "Kino bez kino," *Iskusstvo kino*, No. 6 (1988), 88

Igrovoe kino mezhdu s'ezdami, Moscow, Soiuz kinematografistov SSSR, 1990

Iurenev, R. *et al.* (eds.) *Grani rezhisserskogo mastertva*, Moscow, VNIIK, 1987

Kratkaia istoriia sovetskogo kino, Moscow, Biuro propagandy sovetskogo kinoiskusstva, 1979

Iutkevich *et al.* (eds.) *Kino, entsiklopedicheskii slovar'*, Moscow, Sovetskaia entsiklopediia, 1986

Kepley Jr., V. *In the Service of the State: The Cinema of Alexander Dovzhenko*, Madison, WI, University of Wisconsin Press, 1986

(ed.) *Wide Angle. Contemporary Soviet Cinema*, vol. 12, No. 4 (1990)

Kino i zritel', Vypusk 1 and 2. Moscow, Soiuzinformkino, 1987

Kino mezhdu s'ezdami (Shirokim vzgliadom), Moscow, Soiuz kinematografistov SSSR, 1990

Klimontovich, N. "Liubov' pod berezami," *Iskusstvo kino*, No. 6 (1988), 78–87

Kondrat'ev, V. "Ochen' nadeius'," *Iskusstvo kino*, No. 1 (1989), 52–55

Kovalov, O. and Plakhov, A. "Golos pokoleniia," *Iskusstvo kino*, No. 8 (1987), 61–72

Krasnova, G. B. *et al.* (eds.) *Fil'my molodykh sovetskikh kinematografistov (80-ye gody)*, Moscow, VNIIK, 1986

Lawton, A. *Cinema and the Russian Avant-Garde: Aesthetics and Politics*, Occasional Paper of the Kennan Institute, No. 213 (1986)

"'Lumière' and Darkness: The Moral Question in the Russian and Soviet Cinema," *Jahrbücher für Geschichte Osteuropas*, vol. 38, No. 2 (1990), 244–54

(ed.) *The Red Screen: Politics, Society, Art in Soviet Cinema*, London, Routledge, 1992

"Soviet Cinema Four Years Later," in *Wide Angle*, vol. 12, No. 4 (1990), 8–25. ed., V. Kepley

"Toward a New Openness in Soviet Cinema, 1976–1987," *Post New Wave Cinema in the Soviet Union and Western Europe*. ed., D. Goulding. Bloomington, IN, Indiana University Press, 1989

Leszcylowski, M. "A Year With Andrei," *Sight and Sound*, vol. 56, No. 4 (Fall 1987), 282–84

Levaco, R., (ed., tr.) *Kuleshov on Film*, Berkeley/Los Angeles, University of California Press, 1974

Leyda, J. *Kino: A History of the Russian and Soviet Film*, Princeton, NJ, Princeton University Press, 1983

Liehm, A. J. and Liehm, M. *The Most Important Art: Soviet and East European Film After 1945*, Berkeley/Los Angeles, University of California Press, 1980

Lifshits, G. M. *et al.* (eds.) *Sotsial'naia zhizn' fil'ma. Problemy funktsionirovaniia repertuara*, Moscow, VNIIK, 1983

et al. (eds.) *Sotsial'no-esteticheskie kharakteristiki fil'ma i prognozirovanie zritel'skoi poseshchaemosti*, Moscow, VNIIK, 1984

Lipkov, A. "Proverka na dorogakh," *Novyi mir*, No. 2 (1987), 202–25

Mamatova, L. *et al.* (eds.) Aktual'nye problemy sovetskogo kino nachala 80-kh godov, Moscow, VNIIK, 1983

"Nakanune obnovleniia," *Ekran* (1988), 20–30

Menashe, L. "Glasnost in Soviet Cinema," *Cineaste*, vol. 16, No. 1–2 (1987–88), 28–33

Michelson, A. (ed.) *Kino-Eye, The Writings of Dziga Vertov*, Berkeley/Los Angeles, University of California Press, 1984

Mickiewicz, E. *Split Signals: Television and Politics in the Soviet Union*, New York/Oxford, Oxford University Press, 1988

Molodoe sovetskoe kino, Sovexportfilm Catalog (1987)

Muratov, S. "Neizvestnoe kino," *Iskusstvo kino*, No. 12 (1988), 22–39

"Nashe kino segodnia: Vzgliad iz-za granits," (Kruglyi stol). *Kinovedcheskie zapiski*, No. 4 (1989), 4–21

Navailh, F. "La commissaire de Berditchev," *Pardès*, No. 8 (1988), 229–34

Neigrovoe kino mezhdu s'ezdami, Moscow, Soiuz kinematografistov SSSR, 1990

Nove, A. *Glasnost' in Action. Cultural Renaissance in Russia*, Boston/London, Unwin Hyman, 1989

O situatsii v kinematografii i sovershenstvovanii organizatsii kinodela, Moscow, Goskino, 1990

Pankin, B. *Demanding Literature*, Moscow, Raduga Publishers, 1984 (two chapters on cinema)

Parallel'noe kino v SSSR, Moscow, Sine-Fantom, 1989

Passek, J-L. (ed.) *Le cinéma russe et soviétique*, Paris: Equerre, Centre George Pompidou, 1981

Petric, V. *Constructivism in Film*, Cambridge/New York, Cambridge University Press, 1988

Plakhov, A. "Ne bukva, a sut'!" *Ekran* (1987), 39–44

"Pokushenie na mif," *Iskusstvo kino*, No. 8 (1988), 35–38

Pogozheva, L. *Iz dnevnika kinokritika*, Moscow, Iskusstvo, 1978

Quart, B. "Between Materialism and Mysticism: The Films of Larisa Shepitko," *Cineaste*, vol. 16, No. 3 (1988), 4–11

Riordan, J. (ed.) *Soviet Youth Culture*, Bloomington, IN, Indiana University Press, 1989

Salinskii, D. "Rezhisser i mif," *Iskusstvo kino*, No. 12 (1988), 79–91

Savitskii, N. *Razgovor nachistotu. O fil'makh Vadima Abdrashitova i Aleksandra Mindadze*, Moscow, Soiuz kinematografistov SSSR, 1986

Sepman, I. V. *Nravstvennaia problematika kinematografa 70-kh godov*, Leningrad, LGITMiK, 1983

Shepotinnik, P. "With Perestroika, Without Tarkovsky," *New Orleans Review*, vol. 17, No. 1 (1990), 79–83

Shlapentokh, V. *Public and Private Life of the Soviet People*, New York/Oxford, Oxford University Press, 1989

Shmyrov, V. "Dusha sfinksa," *Ekran* (1989), 118–22

Solov'ev, S. and Dondurei, D. "'Assu' v massy, massy v kassu . . . ili, Igrovoe prostranstvo parallel'noi real'nosti," *Iskusstvo kino*, No. 10 (1988), 6–19

"Soviet Cinema: Into the 90s," *Sight & Sound*, vol. 58, No. 2 (Spring 1989), 80–85

Starr, S. *Red and Hot. The Fate of Jazz in the Soviet Union*, New York, Oxford University Press, 1983

Stishova, E. "Blizkoe proshloe (Moi drug Ivan Lapshin)," *Ekran* (1987), 107–12

"Lavry i ternii," *Ekran* (1989), 31–36

"Strasti po 'Komissaru," *Iskusstvo kino*, No. 1 (1989), 110–21. Translated in *Wide Angle*, ed. V. Kepley

Stites, R. *Revolutionary Dreams*, New York/Oxford, Oxford University Press, 1989

Soviet Popular Culture: Entertainment and Society in Russia Since 1900, Cambridge, Cambridge University Press, 1992

"Soviet Popular Culture in the Gorbachev Era," *The Harriman Institute Forum*, vol. 2, No. 3 (March 1989), 1–8

The Women's Liberation Movement in Russia, Princeton, NJ, Princeton University Press, 1978

Tarkovskii, A. *Sculpting in Time*, New York, Alfred A. Knopf, 1987

Taylor, R. "Boris Shumyatsky and the Soviet Cinema in the 1930s: Ideology as Mass Entertainment," *HJFRT*, vol. 1, No. 1 (1986)

Taylor, R. and Christie, I. (eds.) *The Film Factory*, Cambridge, MA, Harvard University Press, 1988

Tiurin, Iu. "Istoricheskii fil'm Andreia Tarkovskogo," in *Khudozhestvennyi mir sovremennogo fil'ma*, 5–27, ed. A. A. Volkov *et al.*

Kinematograf Vasiliia Shukshina, Moscow, Iskusstvo, 1984

"Tri goda spustia," *Iskusstvo kino*, No. 5 (1989), 14–21. No. 7 (1989), 29–33. No. 9 (1989), 17–21

Troitskii, A. *Back in the USSR: The True Story of Rock in Russia*, Boston, Faber & Faber, 1987

Troshin, A. S. *et al.* (eds.) *Prikliuchencheskii fil'm. Puti i poiski*, Moscow, VNIIK, 1980

Tsivian, Iu. *et al.* (eds.) *Silent Witnesses. Russian Films 1908–1919*, London, British Film Institute, 1989

Turovskaia, M. *Pamiati tekushchego mgnoveniia*, Moscow, Sovetskii pisatel', 1987

Varshavskii, I. *Esli fil'm talantliv*, Moscow, Iskusstvo, 1984

Vil'chek, V. M. *et al.* Fil'm v kino i na televidenii, Moscow, VNIIK, 1987
Volkov, A. A. *et al.* Khudozhestvennyi mir sovremennogo fil'ma, Moscow, VNIIK/Goskino SSSR, 1987
Vorontsov, Iu. *The Phenomenon of the Soviet Cinema*, Moscow, Progress Publishers, 1980
Vronskaya, J. *Young Soviet Filmmakers*, London, George Allen and Unwin Ltd., 1972
Woll, J. "Glasnost and Soviet Culture," *Problems of Communism* (November–December 1989), 40–50
Youngblood, D. *Soviet Cinema in the Silent Era, 1918–35*, Ann Arbor, MI, UMI Research Press, 1985
Zak, M. "Infarkt kak sotsial'naia kategoriia, ili k voprosu o zrelishchnom kino," *Ekran* (1989), 106–11
   Rodoslovnaia fil'ma, Moscow, Soiuz kinematografistov SSSR, 1987
Zhabskii, M. I. *et al.* (eds.) *Metodologiia i metodika sotsiologicheskogo issledovaniia kinoauditorii*, Moscow, VNIIK, 1987
Zhdan, V. N., (ed.) *Kinematograf segodnia*, Moscow, Iskusstvo, 1983
Zlotnik, O. Ia., (ed.) *Kinematograf molodykh*, Moscow, Iskusstvo, 1979
Zorkaia, N. "Dorogoi, kotoraya vedet k Khramu," *Iskusstvo kino*, No. 5 (1987), 33–53
   The Illustrated History of Soviet Cinema, New York, Hippocrene Books, 1989
   "Nostal'giia Andreia Tarkovskogo," *Sputnik kinofestivalia*, No. 1 (May 19, 1987)
   Portrety, Moscow, Iskusstvo, 1966
   "Zametki k portretu Andreia Tarkovskogo," in *Kinopanorama*, 143–65, ed., V. Fomin

Journals, newspapers, reports

Argumenty i fakty
Bianco e nero
Cahiers du cinéma
Christian Science Monitor
Cineaste
Cinema journal
Cinématographe
Current Digest of the Soviet Press
Dom kino
Dumaite o reklame
Ekonomicheskaia gazeta
Ekran
Ekran i stsena (*LG* supplement)
FBIS Daily Report – Soviet Union
Film Comment
Film Criticism
Film Studies Annual

Historical Journal of Film, Radio and Television
Informatsionnyi biulleten' Soiuza Kinematografistov SSSR
Iskusstvo kino
Izvestiia
Jahrbücher für Geschichte Osteuropas
Jump Cut
Kadr
Katalog fil'mov
Kennan Institute Reports (KIAR Reports)
Kino i literatura
Kinokalendar'
Kinopublitsistika i sovremennost'
Kinostsenarii
Kinovedcheskie zapiski
Kommunist
Komsomol'skaia pravda
Krasnaia zvezda
Literaturnaia gazeta
Los Angeles Times
Mneniia
Moscow News
Moskovskie novosti
New Orleans Review
New York Times
Novoe russkoe slovo
Novye fil'my
Novyi mir
Ogonek
Positif
Pravda
Preview
Problems of Communism
Radio Liberty Research Report
Sight & Sound
SKIF (Sputnik kinofestivalia)
Sovetskaia kul'tura
Sovetskaia Rossiia
Sovetskii ekran
Sovetskii fil'm
Soviet and East European Performance
Soviet Film
Soviet Observer
Sputnik kinozritelia
Tekhnika kino i televideniia
Time
Trud

Variety
Vestnik kinorynka
Washington Post
Wide Angle
World & I
Zerkalo

Filmography

Adonis XIV (*Adonis XIV*; Sadykov, 1977/rel. 1986) see ch. 5
Adventures of a Dentist (*Pokhozhdeniia zubnogo vracha*; Klimov, 1965) see ch. 2
Adventures of Tom Sawyer (*Prikliucheniia Toma Soiera*; Govorukhin, 1981) see ch. 7 note 9
Afonia (*Afoniia*; Daneliia, 1975) see ch. 1
Against the Current (*Protiv techeniia*; Delov, 1988) see ch. 7
Alexander Nevsky (*Aleksandr Nevskii*; Eisenstein, 1938) see ch. 8
Allies (*I nechego bol'she*; Sokurov, rel. 1987) see ch. 5
Alto Sonata (*Al'tovaia sonata*; Sokurov, 1987) see ch. 5
Among the Grey Stones (*Sredi serykh kamnei*; Muratova [Ivan Sidorov], 1983) see ch. 5
And the Past Seems But a Dream (*A proshloe kazhetsia snom*; Miroshnichenko, 1987) see ch. 6
And What About You Guys? (*A u vas vo dvore?*; Kuz'mina, 1987) see ch. 7
And What If . . . (*A chto esli . . .* Lebedev, 1988) see ch. 7
Andrei Rublev (*Tarkovskii, 1965*) see ch. 1
Angel (*Angel*; Smirnov, 1967/rel. 1987. See, *Beginning of an Unknown Era*) see ch. 5
Angel Day (*Den' angela*; Sel'ianov and Makarov, 1988) see ch. 7, ch. 8 note 24
Are You Going to the Ball? (*Vy poedete na bal?*; Khvorova, 1987) see ch. 7
Arsonists (*Podzhigateli*; Surin, 1989) see ch. 7
Ascent (*Voskhozhdenie*; Shepitko, 1977) see ch. 1, ch. 5
Assa (*Assa*; Kondrat'ev, 1984) see ch. 7 note 37, ch. 8
Assa (*Assa*; Solov'ev, 1988) see ch. 3, ch. 7
Assuage My Sorrow (*Utoli moia pechali*; Prokhorov and Aleksandrov, 1989) see ch. 2, ch. 7
Asthenic Syndrome (*Astenicheskii sindrom*; Muratova, 1990) see ch. 2, ch. 5, ch. 7
Asya's Happiness (see, *Story of Asya Klyachina*) see ch. 5
At Home Among Strangers, A Stranger At Home (*Svoi sredi chuzhikh, chuzhoi sredi svoikh*; Mikhalkov, 1975) see ch. 1
Autumn (*Osen'*; Smirnov, 1975/rel. 1987) see ch. 5 note 20
Autumn, Chertanovo . . . (*Osen', Chertanovo . . .* Talankin, 1988) see ch. 7
Autumn Marathon (*Osennii marafon*; Daneliia, 1980) see ch. 1
Balcony (*Balkon*; Sadykov, 1989) see ch. 7

Ballad of a Soldier (*Ballada o soldate*; G. Chukhrai, 1959) see ch. 1 note 24, ch. 3 note 20

BAM Zone: Permanent Residents (*Zona BAM, postoiannye zhiteli*; Pavlov, 1987) see ch. 7

Battle for Moscow (*Bitva za Moskvu*; Ozerov, 1985) see ch. 8 note 10

Battleship Potemkin (*Bronenosets Potemkin*; Eisenstein, 1925) see ch. 6

Begin From the Beginning (*Nachni snachala*; Stefanovich, 1986) see ch. 1 note

Beginning (*Nachalo*; Peleshian, 1967) see ch. 5

Beginning of an Unknown Era (*Nachalo nevedomogo veka*; Smirnov and Shepitko, 1967/rel. 1987) see ch. 3, ch. 5

Believe It Or Not (*Nebyval'shchitsa*; Ovcharov, 1983) see ch. 8

Belorussia Station (*Belorusski vokzal*; Smirnov, 1972) see ch. 1, ch. 5 note 20

Beware of Automobiles (*Beregis' avtomobilia*; Riazanov, 1965) see ch. 1

Bezhin Meadow (*Bezhin Lug*; Eisenstein, 1935) see Introduction

Black Rose Is a Symbol of Sorrow, Red Rose Is the Symbol of Love (*Chernaia roza – emblema pechali, krasnaia roza – emblema liubvi*; Solov'ev; 1989) see ch. 3, ch. 6

Black Square (*Chernyi kvadrat*; Pasternak, 1988) see ch. 6

The Blonde Around the Corner (*Blondinka za uglom*; Bortko, 1984) see ch. 1

Blue Mountains, or An Improbable Story (*Golubye Gory, ili nepravdopodobnaia istoriia*; E. Shengelaia, 1985) see ch. 1

Bonus (*Premiia*; Mikaelian, 1975) see ch. 1

Brief Encounters (*Korotkie vstrechi*; Muratova, 1967) see ch. 5

Burglar (*Vzlomshchik*; Ogorodnikov, 1987) see ch. 7

Cage For Canaries (*Kletka dlia kanareek*; P. Chukhrai, 1984) see ch. 1 note 44

Cancan in Englischen Garten (*Kankan v Angliiskom Parke*; Pidpalyi, 1985) see ch. 1

Change of Fortune (*Peremen' uchasti*; Muratova, 1987) see ch. 5, ch. 7

Chapayev (*Chapaev*; "Brothers" Vasil'ev, 1934) see ch. 7

Che Pe (see *Extraordinary Occurrence at Local Headquarters*)

Chernobyl: Chronicle of Difficult Weeks (*Chernobyl'; khronika trudnykh nedel'*; Shevchenko, 1988) see ch. 7

Circus (*Tsirk*; Aleksandrov, 1936) see ch. 7

Clear Sky (*Chistoe nebo*; G. Chukhrai, 1961) see ch. 1 note 24, ch. 3 note 20

Cold Summer of '53 (*Kholodnoe leto piatdesiat' tret'ego*; Proshkin, 1988) see ch. 3, ch. 4, ch. 6

Colors of the Pomegranate (*Tsvety granata*; Paradzhanov, 1968) see ch. 1

Come and See (*Idi i smotri*; Klimov, 1985) see ch. 2, ch. 8

Commissar (*Komissar*; Askol'dov, 1967) see ch. 3, ch. 5

Commotion (*Perepolokh*; Gogoberidze, 1977) see ch. 1

Confession. Chronicle of Alienation (*Ispoved'. Khronika otchuzhdeniia*; Gavrilov, 1988) see ch. 7

Contraband (*Kontrabanda*; Govorukhin, 1975) see ch. 7 note 9

Cranes Are Flying (*Letaiut zhuravli*; Kalatozov, 1957) see ch. 1 note 24

Crew (*Ekipazh*; Mitta, 1979) see ch. 1 note 47

Cruel Male Disease (*Zhestokaia bolezn' muzhchin*; Brothers Aleinikov, 1987) see ch. 8

Dark Nights in Sochi (*V gorode Sochi chernye nochi*; Pichul, 1989) see ch. 3, ch. 7

Day Is Longer Than the Night (*Den' dlinnee nochi*; Gogoberidze, 1984) see ch. 1

Daydreams (*Grezy*; Kondrat'ev, 1988) see ch. 8

Days of the Eclipse (*Dni zatmeniia*; Sokurov, 1988) see ch. 8

Dear, Dearest, Beloved (*Milyi, dorogoi, liubimyi, edinstvennyi* . . . Asanova, 1984) see ch. 1

Dear Elena Sergeyevna (*Doragaia Elena Sergeevna*; Riazanov, 1988) see ch. 7

Debut (*Nachalo*; Panfilov, 1970) see ch. 1

Defense Counsel Sedov (*Zashchitnik Sedov*; Tsimbal, 1989) see ch. 6

Dialogues (*Dialogi*; Obukhovich, 1987) see ch. 7

Don't Get Mad! (*Ne goriui!*; Daneliia, 1969) see ch. 3

Don't Get Married, Girls (*Ne khodite devki zamuzh*; E. Gerasimov, 1985) see ch. 1

Doping for the Angels (*Doping dlia angelov*; Popkov, 1990) see ch. 3

Early On Sunday (*V voskresen'ie utrom*; Mamedov, 1987) see ch. 7

Elegy (*Elegiia*; Sokurov, rel. 1987) see ch. 5

End of the Film (*Konets fil'ma*; Brothers Aleinikov, 1988) see ch. 8

Eugene Onegin (*Evgenii Onegin*; Tikhomirov, 1959) see ch. 5

European Story (*Evropeiskaia istoriia*; Gost'ev, 1984) see ch. 1

Evening Sacrifice (*Vecherniaia zhertva*; Sokurov, rel. 1987) see ch. 5

Extraordinary Occurrence at Local Headquarters (*Chrezvychainoe proiskhozhdenie raionnogo masshtaba*; Snezhkin, 1989) see ch. 7

Faith and Truth (*Vera i pravda*; Smirnov, 1979) see ch. 5 note 20

Fall of Berlin (*Padenie Berlina*; M. Chiaureli, 1950) see ch. 6

Fall of Otrar (*Gibel' Otrara*; Amirkurov, 1990) see ch. 7

Farewell (*Proshchan'e*; Klimov, 1982) see ch. 1, ch. 2 note 5

Fate of A Man (*Sud'ba cheloveka*; Bondarchuk, 1959) see ch. 1 note 24

Feast of Balthazar, or A Night With Stalin (*Pir Valtazara, ili noch' so Stalinym*; Kara, 1990) see ch. 3, ch. 6

Final Verdict (*Vysshii sud*; Frank, 1987) see ch. 7

Fire in Nature (*Ogon' v prirode*; Kondrat'ev, 1988) see ch. 8

Five Evenings (*Piat' vecherov*; Mikhalkov, 1979) see ch. 1

Flight 222 (*Reis 222*; Mikaelian, 1985) see ch. 1

Forgotten Melody for Flute (*Zabytaia melodiia dlia fleita*; Riazanov, 1988) see ch. 3, ch. 7

Forty First (*Sorok pervyi*; G. Chukhrai, 1957) see ch. 5 note 9

Fountain (*Fontan*; Mamin, 1988) see ch. 8

Freeze, Die, Resurrect (*Zamri, umri, voskresni*; Kanevskii, 1989) see ch. 6

Fox Hunt (*Okhota na lis*; Abdrashitov and Mindadze, 1980) see ch. 1

From the Life of Vacationers (*Iz zhizni otdykhaiushchikh*; Gubenko, 1981) see ch. 2 note 10

Garage (*Garazh*; Riazanov, 1980) see ch. 1

Getting to Know the Wide World (*Poznavaia belyi svet*; Muratova, 1979) see ch. 5

Happiness (*Schast'e*; Medvedkin, 1935) see ch. 5, ch. 8

Have Mercy and Forgive (*Pomilui i prosti*; Muratov, 1988) see ch. 7

Heat (*Znoi*; Shepitko, 1964) see ch. 5 note 23

Homecoming (*Vozvrashchenie*; Chubakova, 1987) see ch. 7

Homeland of Electricity (*Rodina elektrichestva*; Shepitko, 1967/rel. 1987. See *Beginning of an Unknown Era*) see ch. 5

Husband and Daughter of Tamara Alexandrovna (*Muzh i doch' Tamary Aleksandrovny*; Narutskaia, 1989) see ch. 7

I Came to Talk (*Prishla i govoriu*; Ardashnikov, 1985) see ch. 1

I Forgot, the Idiot . . . (*Ia zabyl, debil* . . . Kondrat'ev, Part I, 1986/Part II, 1987) see ch. 8

I Served In Stalin's Guard (*Ia sluzhil v okhrane Stalina*; Aranovich, 1989) see ch. 6

I Start Dreaming of You (*Ia nachnu vas mechtat'*; G. Chukhrai, 1985) see ch. 3

If Your Home Is Dear to You (*Esli dorog tebe tvoi dom*; Ordynskii, 1967) see ch. 3

In Broad Daylight (*Sred' bela dnia*; Gurianov, 1984) see ch. 1 note 44

Intergirl (*Interdevochka*; Todorovskii, 1989) see ch. 4, ch. 7

Irony of Fate, or Have a Good Sauna (*Ironiia sud'by, ili s legkim parom*; Riazanov, 1975) see ch. 1

Is It Easy To Be Young? (*Legko li byt' molodym?*; Podnieks, 1986) see ch. 7

Is Stalin With Us? (*Stalin s nami?*; Shakhverdiev, 1989) see ch. 6

It (*Ono*; Ovcharov, 1989) see ch. 8

Ivan's Childhood (see *My Name Is Ivan*)

Ivan the Terrible (*Ivan groznyi*; Eisenstein, 1944–1946) see Introduction

Ivan Vasilevich Changes Profession (*Ivan Vasilevich meniaet professiiu*; Gaidai, 1973) see ch. 3

Jazzman (*My iz dzhaza*; Shakhnazarov, 1983) see ch. 1

Jolly Fellows (*Veselye rebiata*; Aleksandrov, 1934) see ch. 7

Kinfolk (*Rodnia*; Mikhalkov, 1982) see ch. 1

Kings of Crime (*Vory v zakone*; Kara, 1988) see ch. 3, ch. 7

Knights of the Skies (*Rytsari podnebes'ia*; Iufit, 1989) see ch. 8

Kuban Cossacks (*Kubanskie kozaki*; Pyr'ev, 1950) see ch. 5

Lady Macbeth of the Mtsensk District (*Ledi Makbet Mtsenskogo uezda*; Balaian, 1989) see ch. 7

Larisa (*Larisa*; Klimov, 1980) see ch. 2

Last Stop (*Konechnaia ostanovka*; Aprymov, 1989) see ch. 7

Lefty (*Levsha*; Ovcharov, 1987) see ch. 8

Legend of the Suram Fortress (*Legenda o Suramskoi kreposti*; Paradzhanov, 1984/ rel. 1986) see ch. 1

Lena's Men (*Leniny muzhchiny*; Kondrat'ev, 1989) see ch. 8

Lenin in Paris (*Lenin v Parizhe*; Iutkevich, 1981) see ch. 1

Letters of a Dead Man (*Pis'ma mertvogo cheloveka*; Lopushanskii, 1986) see ch. 8

Liberation (*Osvobozhdenie*; Ozerov, 1972) see ch. 8 note 10

Lieutenant Kizhe (*Poruchik Kizhe*; Feinzimmer, 1934) see ch. 5

Life and Adventures of Robinson Crusoe (*Zhizn' i udivitel'nye prikliucheniia Robinzona Kruzo*; Govorukhin, 1973) see ch. 7 note 9

Life Is Beautiful (*Zhizn' prekrasna*; G. Chukhrai, 1980) see ch. 3

Life, Tears, and Love (*I zhizn', i slezy, i liubov'*; Gubenko, 1984) see ch. 2 note 10

Limit (*Granitsa*; Skabard, 1988) see ch. 7

Little Doll (*Kukolka*; Friedberg, 1989) see ch. 2, ch. 7
Little Fish in Love (*Vliublennaia rybka*; Karpikov, 1989) see ch. 7
Little Vera (*Malen'kaia Vera*; Pichul, 1988) see ch. 3, ch. 4, ch. 7
Logger (*Lesorub*; Iufit, 1985) see ch. 8
Look Back (*Oglianis'*; Manasarova, 1984) see ch. 1
Lost Bus (*Brodiachii avtobus*; Kheifits, 1990) see ch. 3
Lovers' Romance (*Roman o vliublennykh*; Konchalovskii, 1974) see ch. 5 note 17
Loyal Friends (*Vernye druz'ia*; Kolatozov, 1954) see ch. 5
Madness (*Bezumie*; Kiisk, 1969/rel. 1986) see ch. 5
Man from Boulevard des Capucines (*Chelovek s Bul'vara Kaputsinov*; Surikova, 1987) see ch. 4, ch. 7
Man's Lonely Voice (*Odinokii golos cheloveka*; Sokurov, 1978/rel. 1987) see ch. 5
Maria (*Leto Marii Voinovoi*; Sokurov, 1988) see ch. 5
Marshal Blücher (*Marshal Bliukher*; Eisner, 1988) see ch. 6
Marshal Rokossovsky, Life and Time (*Marshal Rokossovskii, zhizn' i vremia*; Golovnia, 1988) see ch. 6
May I Die, Oh Lord . . . (*Pust' ia umru, Gospodi . . .* Grigor'ev, 1988) see ch. 7
May I Have the Floor (*Proshu slovo*; Panfilov, 1977) see ch. 1
Member of the Government (*Chlen pravitel'stva*; Zarkhi and Kheifits, 1940) see ch. 1 note 14
Memory (*Pamiat'*; G. Chukhrai, 1971) see ch. 3
Messenger (*Kur'er*; Shakhnazarov, 1987) see ch. 4, ch. 7
Mimino (*Mimino*; Daneliia, 1977) see ch. 1
Mirror (*Zerkalo*; Tarkovski, 1975) see ch. 1
Mirror for the Hero (*Zerkalo dlia geroia*; Khotinenko, 1988) see ch. 6
Mochebuitsy-trupolovy; Mertvyi, 1988 see ch. 8
More Light (*Bol'she sveta*; Babak, 1988) see ch. 6
Moscow Does Not Believe in Tears (*Moskva slezam ne verit*; Men'shov, 1980) see ch. 1
Moscow Elegy (*Moskovskaia elegiia*; Sokurov, 1987) see ch. 5
Mournful Indifference (*Skorbnoe bezchuvstvo*; Sokurov, 1987) see ch. 8
My Friend Ivan Lapshin (*Moi drug Ivan Lapshin*; German, 1983/rel. 1985) see ch. 1, ch. 6
My Name is Harlequin (*Menia zovut Arlekino*; Rybarev, 1988) see ch. 7
My Name Is Ivan (*Ivanovo detstvo*; Tarkovsky, 1962) see ch. 1 note 24
Name Day (*Den' angela*; Govorukhin, 1969) see ch. 7 note 9
Necrorealism of Yufit (*Nekrorealizm Iufita*; Kondrat'ev, 1985) see ch. 8
Needle (*Igla*; Nugmanov, 1989) see ch. 7
Neptune Festival (*Prazdnik Neptuna*; Mamin, 1986) see ch. 8
Nest of Gentry (*Dvorianskoe gnezdo*; Konchalovskii, 1969) see ch. 5 note 17
No Ford in the Fire (*V ogne broda net*; Panfilov, 1968) see ch. 1
Non-professionals (*Neprofessionaly*; Bodrov, 1987) see ch. 7
Nostalghia (*Nostalgiia*; Tarkovskii, 1983) see ch. 1, ch. 5
Office Romance (*Sluzhebnyi romans*; Riazanov, 1978) see ch. 1
On the Eve of Ivan Kupala (*Vecher na kanune Ivana Kupaly*; Ilen'ko, 1969) see ch. 1
Once Upon a Time There Was an Old Man and an Old Woman (*Zhili-byli starik so starukhoi*; G. Chukhrai, 1965) see ch. 3

Scenes at a Fountain (*Stseny u fontana*; Gonopolskii, 1986) see ch. 7
School Waltz (*Shkol'nyi val's*; Liubimov, 1979) see ch. 1
Seasons (*Vremena goda*; Peleshian, 1975) see ch. 5
S.E.R., Freedom Is Paradise (*S.E.R., Svoboda – Eto Rai*; Bodrov, 1989) see ch. 7
Servant (*Sluga*; Abrashitov and Mindadze, 1989) see ch. 6
Shadows of Our Forgotten Ancestors (*Teni zabytykh predkov*; Paradzhanov, 1965)
    see ch. 1
Shooting Party (*Moi laskovyi i nezhnii zver'*; Loteanu, 1979) see ch. 1 note 21
Shop Crumbs (*Pechki-lavochki*; Shukshin, 1973) see ch. 1
Shore (*Bereg*; Alov and Naumov, 1985) see ch. 8 note 10
Siberiade (*Sibiriada*; Konchalovskii, 1979) see ch. 1, ch. 5 note 17
Sideburns (*Bakenbardy*; Mamin, 1990) see ch. 8
Sincerely Yours . . . (*Iskrenne vash . . .*; Surikova, 1985) see ch. 1
Sky of Our Childhood (*Nebo nashego detstva*; Okeev, 1967/rel. 1986) see ch. 5
Slave of Love (*Raba liubvi*; Mikhalkov, 1976) see ch. 1
Snow Leopard (*Potomok belogo barsa*; Okeev, 1985) see ch. 5
Soldier Came Back From the Front (*Prishel soldat s fronta*; Gubenko, 1972) see ch. 2
    note 10, ch. 3
Solovki Power (*Solovetskaia vlast'*; Goldovskaia, 1988) see ch. 4, ch. 6
Some Days in the Life of I. I. Oblomov (*Neskol'ko dnei iz zhizni I. I. Oblomova*;
    Mikhalkov, 1980) see ch. 1
Some Interviews on Personal Matters (*Neskol'ko interv'iu po lichnym voprosam*;
    Gogoberidze, 1979) see ch. 1
Someone Was Here . . . (*Zdes' kto-to byl . . .*; Brothers Aleinikov, 1989) see ch. 8
Soviet Elegy (*Sovetskaia elegiia*; Sokurov, 1990) see ch. 5
Speech for the Defense (*Slovo dlia zashchity*; Abrashitov and Mindadze, 1977)
    see ch. 1
Sport, Sport, Sport (*Sport, sport, sport*; Klimov, 1971) see ch. 2
Spring (*Vesna*; Iufit, 1987) see ch. 8
Stalker (Tarkovskii, 1980) see ch. 1
Stern Youth (*Strogii iunosha*; Room, 1936) see ch. 5
Story of Asya Klyachina Who Loved But Did Not Get Married (*Istoriia Asi Klyachinoi
    kotoraia liubila da ne vyshla zamuzh*; Konchalovskii, 1967) see ch. 5
Story of Marshal Konev (*Povest' o Marshale Koneve*; Danilov, 1988) see ch. 6
Story of a Story (*Istoriia odnoi istorii*; Sadykov, 1988) see ch. 7
Strange People (*Strannye liudi*; Shukshin, 1970) see ch. 1
Strange Woman (*Strannaia zhenshchina*; Raizman, 1978) see ch. 1
Stretcher-bearers Werewolves (*Sanitary-oborotni*; Iufit, 1985) see ch. 8
Strike (*Stachka*; Eisenstein, 1924) see ch. 5
Success (*Uspekh*; Khudiakov, 1984) see ch. 1
Suicide Boars (*Vepri suitsida*; Iufit, 1988) see ch. 8
Summer to Remember (*Serezha*; Daneliia and Talankin, 1960) see ch. 1
Sweet Woman (*Sladkaia zhenshchina*; Fetin, 1977) see ch. 1
Swimmer (*Plovets*; Kvirikadze, 1981/rel. 1988) see ch. 5
Tailor (*Portnoi*; Mirzoian, 1988) see ch. 6
TASS Is Authorized to Announce (*TASS upolnomochen zaiavit'*; Fokin, 1984) see
    ch. 1

Taxi Blues (*Taksi-bliuz*; Lungin, 1990) see ch. 7
Temple (*Khram*; D'iakonov, 1987) see ch. 7
Ten Little Negroes (*Desiat' negritiat*; Govorukhin, 1988) see ch. 7 note 9
Theater in the Time of Perestroika and Glasnost (*Teatr vremen perestroiki i glasnosti*;
    Ruderman, 1988) see ch. 2, ch. 3
Theater Square (*Teatral'naia ploshchad'*; Arutunian, 1988) see ch. 7
Theme (*Tema*; Panfilov, 1979/rel. 1986) see ch. 1
This Is How We Live (*Tak i zhivem*; Oseledchik, 1987) see ch. 7
This Is No Way To Live (*Tak zhit' nel'zia*; Govorukhin, 1990) see ch. 7
Three (*Troe*; Baranov and Kilibaev, 1988) see ch. 7
Three Songs of Lenin (*Tri Pesni o Lenine*; Vertov, 1934) see ch. 7 note 43
Time of Desires (*Vremia zhelanii*; Raizman, 1984) see ch. 1
To Kill the Dragon (*Ubit' drakona*; Zakharov, 1988) see ch. 6
Tomorrow Is a Holiday (*Zavtra prazdnik*; Bukovskii, 1987) see ch. 7
Tomorrow There Was War (*Zavtra byla voina*; Kara, 1987) see ch. 6
Tough Kids (*Patsany*; Asanova, 1983) see ch. 1
Tractors (*Traktora*; Brothers Aleinikov, 1987) see ch. 8
Tragedy in the Rock Style (*Tragediia v stile rok*; Kulish, 1989) see ch. 2, ch. 7
Train Station for Two (*Voksal dlia dvoikh*; Riazanov, 1983) see ch. 1
Train Stopped (*Ostanovilsia poezd*; Abdrashitov and Mindadze, 1982) see ch. 1,
    ch. 6
Tree of Desire (*Drevo zhelaniia*; Abuladze, 1978) see ch. 1, ch. 6
Trial (*Protsess*; Beliaev, 1988, Part I and II) see ch. 6
Trial on the Road (*Proverka na dorogakh*; German, 1971/rel. 1986) see ch. 1
Turning Point (*Povorot*; Abdrashitov and Mindadze, 1979) see ch. 1
Twenty Days Without War (*Dvadtsat' dnei bez voiny*; German, 1976) see ch. 1
Two Arrows (*Dve strely*; Surikova, 1989) see ch. 7
Two Versions of One Accident (*Dve versii odnogo stolknoveniia*; Novak, 1985) see
    ch. 1
Typist (*Mashinistka*; Brothers Aleinikov, 1988) see ch. 8
Uncle Vania (*Diadia Vania*; Konchalovskii, 1971) see ch. 5 note 17
Unfinished Piece for a Player Piano (*Neokonchennaia p'esa dlia mekhanicheskogo
    pianino*; Mikhalkov 1977) see ch. 1
Unmarked Freight (*Gruz bez markirovki*; Popkov, 1985) see ch. 1
Vertical (*Vertikal'*; Govorukhin, 1967) see ch. 7 note 9
Victory (*Pobeda*; Matveev, 1985) see ch. 8 note 10
Visitor to a Museum (*Posetitel' muzeia*; Lopushanskii, 1989) see ch. 8
Volga-Volga (*Volga-Volga*; Aleksandrov, 1938) see ch. 7
Vow (*Kliatva*; M. Chiaurieli, 1946) see ch. 6
Waiting for Love (*Liubimaia zhenshchina mekhanika Gavrilova*; Todorovskii, 1983)
    see ch. 1
War and Peace (*Voina i mir*; Bondarchuk, 1966) see ch. 3
Wartime Romance (*Voenno-polevoi roman*; Todorovskii, 1984) see ch. 1
We (*My*; Peleshian, 1969) see ch. 5
We Accuse (*My obviniaem*; Levchuk, 1985) see ch. 1
Welcome, Unauthorized Persons Not Allowed (*Dobro pozhalovat', postoronnim
    vkhod zepreshchen*; Klimov, 1964) see ch. 2 note 5

White Bird with a Black Mark (*Belaia Ptitsa s chernoi otmetinoi*; Ilen'ko, 1972) see ch. 1

White Explosion (*Belyi vzryv*; Govorukhin, 1970) see ch. 7 note 9

White Pigeon (*Chuzhaia belaia i riaboi*; Solov'ev, 1987) see ch. 7

White Ship (*Belyi parakhod*; Shamshiev, 1977) see ch. 1

White Sun of the Desert (*Beloe solntse pustyni*; Motyl', 1970) see ch. 3

Wife Has Left (*Zhena ushla*; Asanova, 1980) see ch. 1

Wife of the Kerosine Seller (*Zhena kerosinshchika*; Kaidanovskii, 1989) see ch. 6

Wind of Hope (*Veter nadezhdy*; Govorukhin, 1978) see ch. 7 note 9

Wings (*Kryl'ia*; Shepitko, 1966) see ch. 5 note 23

Winter Evening in Gagry (*Zimnii vecher v Gagrakh*; Shakhnazarov, 1985) see ch. 1

Without a Dowry (*Bezpridannitsa*; Protazanov, 1936) see ch. 1 note 38

Without Witnesses (*Bez svidetelei*; Mikhalkov, 1983) see ch. 1

Wolf Cub Among People (*Volochok sredi liudei*; Temenov, 1989) see ch. 7

Wood-Goblin (*Leshii*; Kustov, 1987) see ch. 6

Woodpeckers Don't Get Headaches (*Ne bolit golova u diatla*; Asanova, 1975) see ch. 1

Ya-ha (*Ia-khkha*; Nugmanov, 1986) see ch. 7

You And I (*Ty i ia*; Shepitko, 1971) see ch. 5 note 23

Your Contemporary (*Vash sovremennik*; Raizman, 1967) see ch. 1 note 8

Young Wife (*Molodaia zhena*; Menaker, 1979) see ch. 1

Zero City (*Gorod Zero*; Shakhnazarov, 1989) see ch. 8

Index